A Heart to Belong

A SEQUEL TO HeartBridge

ISBN 978-1-885270-92-4

Layout and cover design: Lydia Zook
Front cover train photo: © Benjamin Beachy

Printed in the USA

For more information about Christian Aid Ministries, see page 285

Published by:
TGS International
P.O. Box 355
Berlin, Ohio 44610 USA
Phone: 330·893·4828
Fax: 330·893·2305
www.tgsinternational.com

3823

Johnny Miller

A Heart to Belong

A SEQUEL TO HeartBridge

Joys and Sorrows at
Nathaniel
Christian
Orphanage
in Romania

Dedication

I dedicate this book to those sponsors who so faithfully sacrificed in order to provide a Christian upbringing for the Nathaniel children. They gave their finances, but even more importantly, they gave their hearts through love, visits, and prayers. Heaven alone shall reveal the results of their selfless giving.

—Johnny Miller

ACKNOWLEDGMENT

I want to acknowledge the sustaining grace of our loving God in the ongoing account of our second and third years of caring for the precious Nathaniel Christian Orphanage children. I also wish to acknowledge the dedicated souls who have made Christian Aid Ministries a channel through which God's love flows to bless the lives of many.

CONTENTS

Nathaniel Christian

Boys' and girls' dorm
(boys' dorm after 1997)

bakery

electrical house

Johnny's house

church house

gym and school
(girls' dorm after 1997)

chicken and horse barn

Alvin Stoltzfus's house

greenhouse
(added in 1998)

Orphanage Compound

wood shop and
machinery storage

school house
(built in 1998)

dairy barn

feed mill

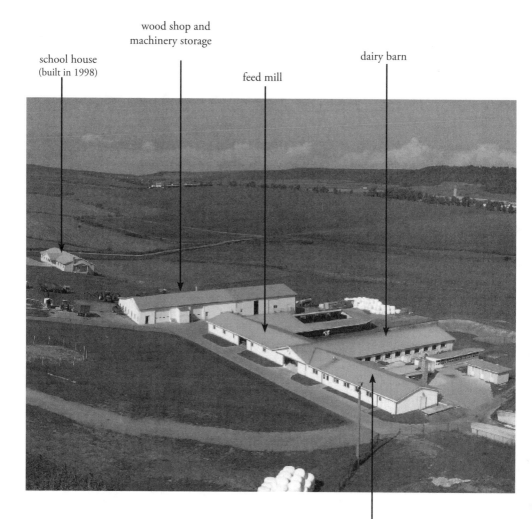

milk processing plant

Chapter 1

Visitations

Frigid gusts of wind whipped tears from our eyes and stung our unprotected faces. We huddled together on the hard-packed snow before a group of forty men. They stood facing us with their backs to the wall of the large concrete building that was their home. We were warmly dressed in heavy overcoats, while they wore thin, drab-brown uniforms.

A group of concerned Christian brethren from Suceava* had organized this visit to the large prison of Botoşani. It was Christmas time, and we desired to share our joy and eternal hope with the many prisoners housed here. Pain and suffering lined the faces of these desperate men. As we sang "Angels We Have Heard on High," our hymn of joy was flung mockingly back at us by the high, concrete, barbed-wire-crowned wall which formed their horizon. "O Little Town of Bethlehem" made no perceivable impression on those solid cement walls or on the hardened faces of the men before us.

Cold was already creeping into my shoes. My heavy winter coat was not adequate for these conditions. I was shivering by the time we ceased singing and the evangelist, Petrică Huţuţui, began his sermon. Patiently the men in brown stood in the cold listening to this message of hope. But was there hope for them?

My thoughts wandered as I forced myself to think of something other than the cold. In my mind I saw a thin arm raised in our Wednesday evening service and heard a girl's sweet voice saying, "Please pray for

*See Glossary on pages 277-280 for pronunciation of Romanian words.

my father, that he might be saved." Elena's younger sisters and her brother had also often raised a hand and said, "Pray for my daddy, that he will repent." And now I stood in the very prison where he had begun serving his eighteen-year sentence for the brutal murder of their mother. Was he here? Would I get to meet him? I wondered how he would respond if I told him of his dear children living at our orphanage. Would it touch his hard heart to know how completely they had forgiven him? Maybe I could also tell him about their unceasing prayers imploring God to bring repentance to his heart. The horror of the murder they had witnessed was so indelibly etched upon their souls that, except for the grace of God, it would scar their lives forever.

The evangelist concluded his message and closed with an invitation to the prisoners to open their hearts to Christ and experience His cleansing power. Several brethren from our group carried large sacks under the scrutiny of the prison guards. A sergeant barked an order and the men in brown stood stiffly at attention. Another order was given and the prisoners began filing past. Each was handed a packet containing fruit, homemade cookies, and a pair of warm gloves. As they reached out to receive their gifts, I noticed a flicker of warmth momentarily lighten their stoic countenances. Yes, even the hardest of hearts can be touched by human compassion.

Following several more groups of men, sessions of singing in the snow, messages preached into the frigid winds, and packets given into rough, hurried hands, we were ready to leave. However, my mission had not been completed. I knew the prison officials respected our evangelist, so I took him aside. "In the Nathaniel Orphanage are four children by the family name of Bițica," I explained. "Their father was incarcerated here. His children love him. They have forgiven him and pray continually for him. Would you ask the captain if Mr. Bițica is still here?"

"I will," replied our evangelist, and he strode confidently in the direction of the office. I waited, hardly daring to hope. When he returned, he told me, "Mr. Bițica began serving his sentence here five years ago. Then he was transferred to a prison in București, and from there to yet another facility. Either they don't know his whereabouts, or they don't want to disclose any more information. I'm sorry," he concluded, "but that is all I could find out."

"Would you do me another favor?" I asked.

"If I can," he responded warmly.

"Since you visit various prisons, would you be willing to help me find the Bițica children's father? He needs to know that his children love him, have forgiven him, and are praying for him. They are old enough now to write to him. It could be a healing experience for both the children and their father if we could only learn of his whereabouts."

"I will certainly try, and if I learn anything further, I will let you know," he promised.

My wife Ruth and I had been asked by Christian Aid Ministries (CAM) to become "Mom and Dad" to their orphanage children in Romania. The Nathaniel Christian Orphanage had been established near the city of Suceava in 1992 and had enjoyed two directors, each serving several years prior to our coming. Leaving our Ohio home in January 1997, we arrived with our three youngest children: nineteen-year-old Ida Jane, armed with her cheerful disposition; twelve-year-old Franklin with his compassionate, sensitive nature; and ten-year-old Caroline with her loyal heart. Each contributed to create a warm and loving atmosphere for our extended orphanage family.

During our first year we learned to know the personalities of each of our orphanage children. We learned about their bruised hearts, their hidden fears, and God's wonderful grace. Our hearts overflowed with love for these dear children, and we enjoyed working with our dedicated staff as well.*

---

* Introductions into the personalities of the Nathaniel Orphanage children and those life-changing, first-year experiences are recorded in our first book, *HeartBridge*.

Now that first year with its rainbow of experiences was drawing to a close. It was Christmas Eve, and I smiled as I reflected on the differences between Romanian Christmas celebrations and what I had been used to in America. I shook my head and stifled a yawn as I recalled the seven groups of carolers who had come to our door during the past three nights. Most were youth choirs from neighboring churches, but one was our Romanian farm director with his accordion, his wife, and their two dark-eyed children.

Just as we were preparing for bed, we heard a knock on our door and opened to find yet another group of carolers. Their cheery faces and harmonious singing touched our hearts. We invited them into our warm house for pastries and fruit juice. Romanians far and wide make sure they have goodies on hand for carolers. It is the host's way of saying, "I am so pleased that you honored me with your caroling!"

More singing aroused us from our slumbers just after midnight. We quickly dressed and hurried to the door. The youth choir from the Pentecostal church filled our porch and spilled onto our walkway and lawn, their eyes sparkling and their rosy faces smiling. We stood at the open door drinking it all in. How they sang! By the time their fifth carol had ushered in the wise men, our bare toes were numb. I welcomed the guests into our home while Ruth scurried about setting out her goodies.

Our carolers left and we went back to our interrupted slumbers. It seemed like only minutes later when my wife's startled voice awakened me out of a deep sleep. "Johnny, what's that?" she demanded, sitting up and listening.

"Why, it sounds like angels."

"It's another group of carolers! Come on!" she urged. She was already up and dressing.

I rubbed my tired eyes and tried to focus on the luminous dial of my alarm clock as I dressed. I rubbed and peered again. It was 4:20 a.m.! I joined my wife as we rushed to welcome the Baptist youth choir. Their breath hung in the crisp night air as they raised their voices in sweet harmony to the miracle of His coming. Such gorgeous singing! We welcomed them into the warmth of our home and shared the waiting snacks as we chatted. Soon they left and we headed back to our much-needed rest.

"Surely there won't be any more carolers tonight," Ruth said. But she climbed into bed fully clothed, just in case.

Soon we were blissfully sleeping once more.

Somewhere in the distance a persistent bell was ringing. I fumbled for the alarm clock before I heard my wife say, "Aren't you going to answer that phone?"

"Phone? What?" I asked in confusion. "Oh!" I jumped out of bed and stumbled through the darkness into the kitchen and hurriedly lifted the receiver.

"Hello?" I said in a thick, sleep-laden voice. I waited, but the only sound was that of static and the high-pitched hum of current passing through the wires. Then, from across the thousands of miles, all the way from Costa Rica, came the shout of our oldest daughter, Vicki. "Hello, Dad! Merry Christmas and a happy New Year!"

"Well, thanks!" I shouted back, hardly knowing what else to say. I shook my head in an effort to clear my foggy brain. I could feel my heart pounding.

"What are you doing for Christmas with the orphanage children?" she asked. "Are you planning anything special with Ida, Franklin, and Caroline? What did you get for Mom? Is it snowing there? Dad," she rushed on, "you don't seem too talkative. What time is it there, anyway?"

"Well," I said, stifling a yawn, "it's not quite six o'clock, and we had three groups of carolers during the night."

"Oh, Dad!" came Vicki's chuckle. "I forgot about the time change between us, and I didn't know about the carolers. I'm sorry I woke you! I have been trying all day to get a call through to you, but I wasn't able to until just now. I won't keep you long; I just want to talk a little. It makes you seem so much closer if we can just talk a little bit, especially at this time of year."

We exchanged tidbits of family news, and then she said, "Bye, Dad. Give Mom a big Christmas hug for me!"

"Goodbye," I replied. "Have a wonderful Christmas, and thanks for calling!"

I hung up and stood there a moment savoring Vicki's call. She and her husband Nathan Yoder lived with their two children in Costa Rica where they assisted the mission churches Nate's father had helped establish when Nate was just a boy. Vicki had called just to stay in touch, and I was blessed.

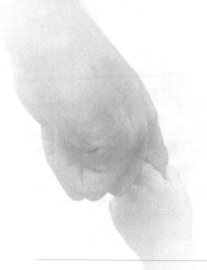

Chapter 2

The Gift

Christmas Day dawned blustery and cold. Snow lay everywhere. I got dressed sleepily and made my way to the office, where I sat at my desk remembering the many enjoyable Christmases at home with our family in America.

Later that day, the tantalizing aroma of a Christmas feast wafted down the orphanage hallway. It wasn't ham or turkey as it would have been back home. Instead, I recognized the aroma of those savory cabbage rolls for which Romanian cooks are famous. The hamburger-rice-vegetable filling is seasoned with locally grown spices and hand rolled in specially selected, pickled cabbage leaves. The *sarmale*, as they are called, are then baked to perfection and served with a liberal portion of thick sour cream. Romanians so love *sarmale* that it is unthinkable to have a special event, such as a wedding or a funeral, without them. Our head cook Roza had agreed to make this special treat for our orphanage family's Christmas celebration.

"Come, Tata Johnny," called Elena Biţica, motioning with both hands. "Mama Ruth said you should come and get the children to the table. The *sarmale* are almost ready. Yum!" She smacked her lips and rolled her eyes. Then she dashed off toward the dining room.

How did she turn out to be so sweet? I wondered as I recalled the horrible tragedy of her past. I rose and followed her.

The hallway was lined with energetic children whose talk was filled with Christmas excitement. As I passed by on the way to the dining room, little Davucu reached out and tugged at my hand. I glanced down at him, and he flashed me his own special smile. Liviu, the new boy, also clasped my hand as I passed by. These children craved a parent's love and attention, but most had been abandoned by their parents. I glanced back at the wiggling line of girls and boys and was once more reminded that behind every one of those excited, smiling faces was a tragic story. Alcohol abuse figured into more than half of their family histories. They had suffered much pain and heartache.

I retrieved the bell from the kitchen cupboard and stood expectantly, waiting for the children to become quiet. However, animated conversations flowed up and down the line as our twenty-nine girls and twenty-six boys shared their excitement. I waited, knowing that sooner or later they would notice and become quiet. Several of the older girls saw me waiting and loudly whispered *shhhh!* This signal was repeated farther down the line. I smiled appreciatively at the children and rang the bell.

"Children," I reminded them, "I expect you to file through quietly and orderly. Remember to walk single file, as always."

All went well until the boys' half of the line reached me. "Come on, fellows," I said as I smiled at the Gheorgheş brothers, Iosif and Daniel. They walked down the hall side by side, talking loudly together like long-lost friends. "Can't you even keep a straight line on Christmas Day?" I teased.

"Oops," said Iosif, "I forgot." He ducked back to his place in the line. Iosif and Daniel were from a family of ten children. Their father had developed severe mental difficulties. That, coupled with heavy drinking, caused most of their children to be placed into orphanages. Four of the Gheorgheş children had become a part of our Nathaniel family. I was happy whenever their godly grandparents visited because of the positive influence they had on these children.

Finally, each of the children was standing in his own place beside one of the six loaded dining room tables. Most Romanian Christians consider it irreverent to pray while seated, so we always stood for our mealtime prayers. I rang the bell for silence, but what was one little bell's *ding* among so many children with endless wonderful things to talk about? It was all pleasant talk, like a big, happy family, but somehow we needed to bring a bit of order to all of these good family feelings. Mama Ruth, as the children called my wife, had taken her place at the opposite end of the table from where I stood. Again I rang the bell and announced, "We will have prayer and begin eating as soon as you children are finished talking."

A hush finally settled over the dining room, and we bowed our heads for prayer. A Christmas prayer was offered, thanking God for the gift of His Son as well as for the blessings He had so wonderfully provided for each one of us. As soon as the "amen" sounded, the dining room erupted once again with the children all talking at once. The noise level was nearly deafening, and I glanced imploringly at my wife.

She smiled at me from her end of the table but shook her head "no" and mouthed the words, "It's Christmas."

Each dining room table had a colorful bowl filled with a delicious salad of grated red beets mixed with homegrown horseradish. But the children were not nearly as crazy about this dish as they were for the *sarmale*. Large platters of *sarmale* were being disposed of at an unbelievable rate. Several of the boys appeared to be racing to see who could consume the most. Near the end of the meal I overheard chubby little Gheorghe grunt that he had consumed nine.

Fruit and dessert completed our Christmas dinner, and I dismissed the children one table at a time with instructions to meet in the orphanage living room in half an hour.

The children were so excited they just couldn't wait thirty minutes. They assembled immediately—and noisily—in our big living room. As soon as the dining room was cleared and the dishes washed, I hushed them and announced, "Children, we will sing Christmas carols until Ionică comes, and then we will pass out the gifts."

Ionică Bădiliță had worked tirelessly with government officials to obtain authorization to open this orphanage and had served as the Romanian director from the onset. We would wait to pass out the gifts until his arrival.

At this point the tantis* took over and led the children in singing until the room echoed with the joy of their childish voices. But even during their heartfelt singing, eyes continually strayed to the far corner of the living room where a large pile of colorfully wrapped packages lay begging to be opened.

Tina's eyes wandered from the pile of gifts to the window. Suddenly she clapped her hands and announced, "He is come! Nenea* Ionică is come!"

Moments later Ionică's tall figure strode into the living room. I rose to meet him and welcomed him warmly. "The children have been waiting impatiently for you, since I told them we would not pass out the gifts until you arrive. Would you offer the prayer before we begin passing them out?"

"Sure," he said, and he motioned for the children to stand. Ionică paused and allowed his gaze to rest momentarily on one child's face, then another, and another. As he did so, a respectful hush spread over the entire group. When all was quiet, he bowed his head and prayed a prayer of blessing upon the children, the orphanage, and its workers.

"Now children," he instructed, "you bigger ones sit on the couches and chairs around the room, and you smaller ones may sit on the floor in front of them so all can see. When I call your name, come get your gift and take it back to your seat, but do not open it. After everyone has received his gift, I will tell you when to open them. Is that clear? Do you all understand?"

"Yes, yes, we understand," came a chorus of responses.

Ionică picked up the first gift from the pile and read the name in a mock, official-sounding voice. "Mr. Silviu," he said and handed the

* *Tanti* and *Nenea* are Romanian titles of respect meaning aunt and uncle. Every younger person must use these terms when addressing someone older than himself.

gift to me while he turned to pick up the next one. Silviu faltered for a moment and, pointing to himself, asked, "Me?"

"Yes, you," I said, waving the gift in his direction. Scrambling to his feet, Silviu darted forward. His eyes met mine as he shook my hand, received his gift, and said, "Thank you."

"Parnica Neli," boomed Ionică's voice as he thrust the next gift into my hand, reminding me again that I was living in a foreign country where family names are always mentioned before the given name in an official setting. Neli moved across the room. Her sober countenance melted into a self-conscious grin as she neared me. She received her gift and turned to go, faltered a moment, and bit her lip. Her dark eyes sought mine for a split second as she softly whispered, "Thank you."

"Mocanu Elisabeta," Ionică called out next, and I watched as Beti walked gracefully toward me. She seemed to float as she made her way around the seated children. A huge smile lit her face. "Thanks!" she said matter-of-factly as she clasped my hand, gave it a smart shake, and received her gift.

Next it was "Sandu Iliuţă." I watched as the neat, trim little fellow came forward with quick, sure movements. "Thank you!" he said as he took his gift and returned to his seat.

And so it went, name after name and child after child, until finally the last gift had been given. Ionică looked to see that every child had a gift and then commanded, "Please listen." The children momentarily stopped probing with their fingers and shaking their packages trying to figure out what was inside. "We will let the youngest class of girls open their gifts first," he explained, "and then the next oldest class, and then the next, until all the classes have opened their gifts. Does everyone understand?" Heads nodded soberly, and the older children smiled in resignation.

"Okay, you smaller girls move out here into the middle of the room." A group of ten little girls scurried to the center of the room with their precious gifts and looked up at Ionică expectantly. With a fatherly grin, he nodded toward them and said, "You may begin!"

Some of the girls, even in this moment of heightened excitement, maintained their feminine composure and carefully loosened the Scotch tape from their packages. Others tore the wrapping off without regard for the beautiful paper. Gasps of surprise arose as they lifted their gifts from the wrappings—darling, cuddly dolls with combable hair!

Mihaela and Vasilica delightedly examine their new dolls.

I had my camera ready to capture this moment, but I hadn't anticipated the older girls' level of interest. They immediately surrounded their little sisters. "Do their eyes close when you lay them down? Do they cry when you squeeze them?" they wanted to know. By the time I finally maneuvered about to get my photo, the new mothers and their dolls were already bonding.

"Nenea Ionică, please let us open our gifts too. Please!" begged Davucu.

"Bring your gifts over here where you have a bit more room," instructed Ionică. "Are you ready?" he asked when the boys were situated.

"Yes!" they chorused in unison.

"Then go!" he said, enjoying himself immensely.

The boys tore into their colorful wrapping paper as if it were a race. Costică suddenly let out a whoop and held aloft a toy John Deere tractor for all to admire. Each of the young boys had received a tractor and an implement that could be hitched to it. There were wagons, discs, planters, and balers. They spun the tires, turned the tractors' steering wheels with their fingers, and showed one another how marvelously everything worked.

It was soon time for the older classes to open their gifts. They went at it with a bit more reserve. "Thank you! Thank you!" the older children said as they held aloft their new Romanian Bibles and admired their soft leather bindings. The orphanage had supplied Bibles, but those had been hardback, thick, and somewhat cumbersome. These were beautiful, pliable, and their very own Bibles to keep.

I looked about at the children. The smaller boys had begun their farming operation amidst the mounds of crumpled wrapping paper. The little girls stood together in groups of twos and threes, holding their dolls and extolling their attributes, as new mothers are wont to do the world over. All of them seemed most pleased with their gifts, though I did notice several of the middle-aged boys reverently holding their Bibles while glancing longingly at the John Deere toys.

Mama Ruth and I walked down the long hallway to the kitchen where Roza determined to stuff us with Romanian Christmas pastries, and I had to admit they did go well with generous mugs of rich, Romanian coffee.

"Tata Johnny." Ten-year-old Ovidiu appeared suddenly at my side. "My brother and sister came to see me, and they want to meet you too."

He led me to the living room, where I welcomed his visitors. Ovidiu, who was usually sober, just couldn't stop smiling. These were the first visitors he had received in the six months since he had come to live with us. His older brother talked nonstop, but Ovidiu's seventeen-year-old sister Ileana was overcome with emotion. I welcomed them and got them situated in a corner of the big living room where they could talk in spite of all the activity going on about them. To my surprise, when I checked on them ten minutes later, Ileana was still crying.

"Ovidiu, what's wrong?" I asked. "Why is your sister crying?"

"She is crying because someone told her I was dead and that if she came, she would only find my body. She was so scared, and now that she sees me alive, she just can't stop crying." He smiled, glad that she cared.

"Well, you tell her you have been very much alive and that there doesn't seem to be anything wrong with you," I said with a grin. I felt sorry for her, knowing how vicious village gossip could be.

Later we sat together and talked. "I can hardly believe how much Ovidiu has grown!" his sister exclaimed. "I am happy he is already attending school and adjusting well."

My heart went out to her and the boys. Through no fault of their own, their family had been pulled apart by harsh circumstances following the deaths of their mother and father, who had both been heavy drinkers. I could see she really cared for her little brother and that Ovidiu was close to her as well.

That evening, a little before it was time to take his brother and sister to the train station, Ovidiu came into my office.

"Tata Johnny," he said, "my brother has become a *pocăit* (a repentant one, a believer), and he would really like to have a study Bible. Could you give him one?"

"I don't have one here, but I'll see if I can get a study Bible through our Gospel literature department. They're closed tonight, but we can send one along with the evangelist next time he goes to Vaslui."

Before leaving, we loaded Ovidiu's brother's bags with Christmas food from our kitchen and medicines from our supply room to share with their neighbors. Ovidiu rode along to the train station with us. His brother and sister hugged and kissed him repeatedly before boarding the train for the seven-hour trip back to their village in Vaslui.

As we drove back to the orphanage, Ovidiu was quiet. He was thinking—thinking of all God had blessed him with this Christmas. Yes, he had enjoyed the *sarmale* feast with its rich sour cream, the tangy red beets, the pastries, and the fruit. Never in all his life had he experienced anything like the gifts. He was thrilled with his Bible. But the gift he treasured above all else was the visit from his brother and sister. They loved him, and they were family.

Chapter 3

The New Year

Mihaela stood in front of my desk as Lavinia flopped into a chair. I was pleased to see that the skin above Lavinia's lip was almost healed. She had a nervous habit of licking it excessively, and it had been chapped and raw for weeks. Ruth had made a pact with her that when she overcame this habit to the point that it healed, we would cook a special supper at our house to celebrate and allow Lavinia to invite her closest friends.

"Is it true, Tata Johnny, that Ovidiu doesn't have a sponsor to pay for him to stay here anymore?" asked Lavinia.

"What makes you say that?" I asked in surprise. I had only received that fax from the home office the day before, and I hadn't spoken about it to anyone.

"Well, I, uh, I saw a paper lying on your desk yesterday, and that's what it said," she replied nervously.

"But that was in English, and you can't read English!" I exclaimed.

"Well, I guess I can a little," replied Lavinia with a self-conscious grin.

"And now he doesn't have a sponsor," added eight-year-old Mihaela. Her sober eyes registered grave concern.

"That's true," I responded, making a mental note to take more care with my English paperwork. "First Ovidiu's mother died when he was six years old. Then just three months later his father died. CAM found a sponsor to support him so that he could come here to live with us. And now circumstances are such that his sponsor can no longer continue sending support."

"I feel so sorry for him," said Mihaela in her low, sober voice. I glanced in her direction and noticed that her lips were pursed, her forehead furrowed, and her eyes very sad. *These children really feel for one another, and that is so good,* I thought to myself.

"Tata Johnny," Costică blurted as he rushed into my office, "Ovidiu doesn't have a sponsor anymore. He's going to have to leave the orphanage, isn't he?"

"Where's he going to go?" asked Lavinia, leaning her elbows on my desk. Her father had also died, and she knew from experience the need for a sponsor. It meant more than merely meeting a financial need. A sponsor also brought a sense of security and belonging.

Iliuță shares the joy of a sponsor letter from the States.

Sponsors occasionally wrote to their child, and every child hoped his sponsor would someday come visit him in Romania.

"Wait a minute. Who is talking about Ovidiu having to leave?" I asked.

"Well . . . all of the boys are saying he's going to have to leave the orphanage because he doesn't have a sponsor," sputtered Costică.

"You children have a problem," I said, looking from one to the other. "You hear something and you let your imaginations run wild. You worry and talk about things you do not understand. Listen, Christian Aid Ministries is not about to send Ovidiu away just because he doesn't have a sponsor. They will find someone else to sponsor him."

"Really?" Costică looked relieved. "You mean he can stay?" he asked as he edged toward the door.

"Of course he is staying, and don't let anyone tell you differently."

"How long will it take them to find another sponsor?" asked Lavinia, blinking nervously as she did when something really bothered her.

"I really don't know," I answered, "but God has always met this need. From the day you arrived at the Nathaniel Orphanage, God has supplied all your needs, hasn't He?" I asked.

"Yes, I guess He has," she answered thoughtfully.

Within minutes Gigi and Costică reappeared at my office door with a worried and frightened Ovidiu in tow. "Tell him, Tata Johnny. You tell him," said Costică.

"He can stay, can't he?" chimed in Gigi.

I looked down into nine-year-old Ovidiu's freckled face. His dark eyes told me he was feeling very frightened and alone in the world. I reached out my hand and rested it lightly on his shoulder. "Ovidiu," I said convincingly, "it's true that your sponsor won't be able to continue paying for you to stay here, and right now you do not have anyone sponsoring you. But you can keep right on living here as usual, and CAM will pay for all your needs until they find someone else to become your sponsor." His black eyes stared back at me as though not quite sure he could trust me.

"You just go right on sitting at your place at the table, sleeping in your own bed, and going to school like you have been doing, and I'll tell you just as soon as CAM finds you a new sponsor. Okay?" He nodded soberly, but did not return my smile.

"See?" said Lavinia, turning to Ovidiu reassuringly. "You will soon have another sponsor like the rest of us. Don't worry."

"It's going to be all right. Tata Johnny isn't going to let them push you out," Mihaela said, her expression loaded with compassion.

"Come on," said Gigi, "let's go feed the rabbits!"

I watched as the three boys entered the coatroom across the hall, pulled on their coats, caps, and gloves, and headed out the door toward the little animal barn. I made a mental note to walk down later to see how Ovidiu was doing.

"Someday when we get big we'll leave the orphanage, won't we?" asked Lavinia thoughtfully.

"Yes. But by that time you will be big enough to have a job, and you won't need a sponsor anymore," I explained.

An hour later I donned my winter garb and strolled down to the little barn. Our white mare, Stela, and her darker colt, Steluța, stood side by side in their stall contentedly pulling little tufts of hay from the rack. Several older boys were putting the finishing touches on a new rabbit hutch. I counted and there were no less than eight rabbit hutches, most of them fully occupied.

"Whose are these black and white ones?" I asked as the curious rabbits nipped at my fingers through the wire netting.

"Those are mine," spoke up Daniel as he strode over to the hutch. "You want to hold one?"

"Sure," I said, moving aside for him to open the hutch door. Deftly he reached in, caught the mother rabbit, and handed her to me. "How many rabbits do you have?" I asked Daniel.

"I have eight right now, but I think the one you are holding is going to have little ones in about a week. Then I'll have lots more," he beamed.

"Daniel, just what are you going to do with all these rabbits? Are you going to butcher them so Roza can fix them for a Sunday dinner at the orphanage?" I asked as I winked at the older boys.

"Never!" he said. "I'll just raise them to sell."

"Who owns all those other rabbits?" I asked, peering into the other hutches. Nicu grinned shyly as he walked over, laid his hand on a low hutch, and announced, "These three are mine."

Daniel said, "Those four belong to my brother Iosif, and that pair is Pavel's."

"How many are there altogether?" I asked, stroking the long, silky ears of Daniel's black and white doe.

"Twenty-seven, counting all the little ones in the tall hutch along the wall," said Daniel with a smile.

"What do you feed them?" I asked.

"Alvin lets us get a little hay and cow feed from the big barn. Rabbits really don't eat very much," Daniel explained.

During the whole conversation I was keeping an eye on Ovidiu. He was skillfully helping Ionuț stretch the wire mesh over the front of a new hutch. Working with the other boys and their animals seemed to have had a settling effect on Ovidiu, I was pleased to see. I placed Daniel's rabbit back into her pen and walked over to inspect Nicu's new hutch.

Satisfied that all was well with Ovidiu, I headed toward my office to complete the year-end report for CAM. As I approached, I heard a familiar voice from Vali's office. I entered and found the evangelist who had preached for us in the Botoşani prison. Had he remembered my request to help locate the father of our four Bițica children?

"Brother Johnny," he said soberly, "I have talked to officials in the prisons wherever I have ministered, but I have not found one bit of information concerning Mr. Bițica's whereabouts. I'm afraid they just are not giving information. I am truly sorry, but I've done everything I could. I shall continue to check and will certainly pass along any information that might be helpful."

"Thank you so much," I said. "I wish that somehow Mr. Bițica could hear about his children."

"Well, God certainly knows where he is, so let's continue to pray that God will help us find him," said the evangelist.

In writing my report to CAM summarizing our first year of work, I was amazed at all that the Lord had taught us through our experiences.

Several of the older children had been given the opportunity to earn a small wage feeding and tending the chickens in their movable cages. Our records showed that we had been able to hatch, raise, butcher, and freeze nearly four hundred broilers with the help of many willing hands.

We also were able to process and can three hundred pounds of cherries and freeze four hundred pounds of strawberries. Our half-acre garden had provided abundantly. With the help of the orphanage children, we had pared, peeled, snapped, shelled, frozen, and canned throughout the summer months, and now we were enjoying the fruits of our labors. The children had worked right beside us in all these projects. Through it, they were learning to work, and we were learning to know the heart of each child.

The large heads of cabbage harvested from our garden had been grated and mixed with just enough chopped carrots to add color. Peppercorns were added for flavor. This mixture was then stuffed into twenty-gallon plastic drums, saturated with salt brine, and buried deep in the garden to season. We had exhumed these drums just before serious winter weather set in and stored them in our sizable root cellar. They supplied our orphanage with winter salad that was quite delicious when rinsed and lightly dressed with olive oil. Although this was a new dish for us, we soon learned to like it.

Another food we found fascinating was *slănină*, or lightly smoked bacon side. Quarter-inch strips of fat with hardly any meat showing are cut into one-inch lengths and eaten nearly raw with a clove of garlic and a dash of mustard.

Roza had taken it upon herself to orient us to the rich cultural practices of Romania, specifically the food.

"Here, Tata Johnny," she said as I strolled into the kitchen, "I have some fresh *slănină* for you." She held the plate toward me.

"That's okay, Roza," I graciously declined. "I don't care for any just now. Thanks anyway."

"Oh, you just don't like Romanian food," she said with one hand on her hip, the other still offering the *slănină*.

"I love Romanian food, but you don't understand," I responded. "This food isn't good for my heart."

"Pshaw," Roza snorted with a toss of her head. "Our people have eaten this for hundreds of years, and it has never hurt them. You just don't like it." She placed the saucer back on the countertop with an offended air.

"Roza," I said, "that's not true. Listen, your people eat *slănină*, which is raw fat. Then they go out on the hillside with a hand scythe and cut hay from early morning until nightfall. This burns up the fat they have eaten, and it doesn't clog their arteries. But if I eat it and sit at my desk day after day punching computer keys, this stuff will give me a heart attack!"

"Humph," replied Roza, quite unconvinced. She turned back to her cooking.

Yes, on the surface I could see Roza was razzing me a bit, but underneath, I also saw she had deeper feelings about the issue.

A week later I passed through the kitchen and saw another plate with several pieces of *slănină* and peeled garlic sitting conspicuously on the counter, prepared as a treat for anyone passing through. On impulse, and just to show my dedication, I walked over to the drawer, got a fork, and stabbed a garlic clove and a *slănină* strip. Then, watching out of the corner of my eye to make sure Roza wasn't missing this, I deftly slid the entire arrangement into my mouth and, steeling my senses, chomped down. I was pleasantly surprised to find that the slippery fat and garlic combination wasn't all that bad.

Roza was ecstatic. "Oh, Tata Johnny, you ate *slănină!* And do you like it?" she asked.

"Hmmm, I guess it's all right," I said as I stabbed another piece for effect.

The next day Roza gleefully told my wife, "Mama Ruth, I saw Tata Johnny eating *slănină,* and I didn't even tell him to. I think he will like Romania very much!"

Another cultural practice which surprised us was New Year's celebration. The explosive pops of firecrackers were heard continuously for several days prior to New Year's Day. Groups of non-Christian youth roamed the streets, beating on washtubs or drums, lighting firecrackers, drinking, and singing coarse ballads. These revelers are called *maskcats,* meaning "the masked ones." Some dressed in all manner of furs and feathers representing various animals and birds, while others masqueraded as famous historical figures. Some were dressed as American Indians, others as knights in cardboard and tinfoil armor. A costume that especially caught my attention was a tall, slim youth wearing a black swallowtail suit and a tall, black stovepipe hat—Abe Lincoln!

But I was about to discover what it was like to try to tuck fifty-five children into their beds at 9:30 on such a night.

"Tata Johnny, what is Nenea Bill doing in America right now?" asked nine-year-old Bogdan as Ruth and I made our nightly rounds tucking in the children. We had started an hour late, but they coveted these moments and dreamed up ways to coerce us into remaining with them just a little longer.

"Is it night where he is?" came little Silviu's voice from the next bed. Bill, the orphanage's former director, was still alive in these children's hearts. I was working my way toward the door, remembering six more rooms of boys waiting with questions of their own.

"Okay, I've got to go now," I told Bogdan and Silviu, and I gave them each a squeeze and bid them goodnight.

I entered the next room where I found Leon and Gheorghe sitting on their haunches on top of their dresser. Their heads and shoulders were protruding through the open window, their eyes gazing in the direction of Suceava. The cold winter wind was swirling the curtains about them.

"What do you boys think you're doing?" I asked. "Get back in here right now. It is far too cold for this. Close that window!"

"Oh, Tata Johnny, we were just watching the fireworks in Suceava," said Gheorghe disappointedly.

Leon pulled his head back inside the room and exclaimed, "They zoom up into the sky and *pow*, they sparkle real nice!" Leon stood on the dresser, mimicking the fireworks with his hands.

"Hey, come on now, it's time you boys were in bed." I held up my arms and Leon vaulted into them. Gheorghe jumped to the floor with a resounding *thump* and dove into his bed with a giggle. I boosted Leon onto his upper bunk and told him goodnight. I warned them both not to get out of bed again.

In the next room I found Manu and Iliuță standing at an open window. They, too, were gazing in the direction of Suceava.

"What's up, fellows?" I asked.

"We were just watching the fireworks," said Iliuță.

"Well, it is way past your bedtime, and if you boys get sick from hanging out the window, Sora Viorica is going to be very upset with me. So come on, shut the window and climb into your warm beds. Hurry. And please be quiet so you do not disturb those who are nearly asleep."

Manu sat on the edge of his bed. I could see that he wasn't ready to go to sleep, though it was more than an hour past his normal bedtime. "Tata Johnny," he said with a mischievous grin on his face, "I thought you were the orphanage director. Why are you afraid of Sora Viorica?"

"I am the director, but I respect Sora Viorica very much, and she is a good nurse. She has the responsibility to keep us all well. We should all do our part," I explained.

"I know," replied Manu as he slid under the covers. "Goodnight, Tata Johnny," he called as I snapped off the light.

"Goodnight," I echoed as I headed for the next room.

Over in the girls' dorm, Ruth entered another room to tell its little pajama-clad occupants goodnight. "Mama Ruth, how long will Nenea Willis be gone?" eight-year-old Larisa asked as Mama Ruth leaned over to hug her.

Two days earlier, Ruth had been part of a large group gathered at the train station to bid the Bontragers farewell. She recalled the fear they had experienced when they learned of Willis's severe heart attack and his need to return to America for treatment. She had been moved by the group singing Pastor Willis's favorite song "Alive, Alive, Alive Forevermore" as the train began to roll down the tracks.

"I'm not sure," Ruth responded thoughtfully. "That depends on how much damage his heart attack has caused and what the doctors will have to do to fix it. It is possible that he will have an operation on his heart. If they do surgery, it could be a number of months before he will be able to return."

"I'm really going to miss him," chimed in eight-year-old Vasilica, who shared Willis's birthday.

"I'll pray that God will make him better so he can come back soon," said Vasilica wistfully.

"Would you like to pray together now?" asked Ruth.

"Yes, let's," chorused several girls.

They knelt at the bedside on either side of Mama Ruth. Her heart was touched as she heard each of them pray that God would heal their pastor and bring him back soon. When they got up from their knees, Mama Ruth gave them each a special hug before tucking them into their beds. Oh, how she loved these girls! She savored these precious moments with them.

On the boy's side I entered yet another room. "Marinel!" I exclaimed in surprise as I glanced about. "Where is Andi? And where is Marius?"

"Oh," he answered sleepily, "they're with the others watching the fireworks from the landing."

I lost no time in getting to the landing on the outside staircase where I discovered six little shavers shivering in their pajamas as they scanned the southwestern skies in hopes of yet another burst of fireworks.

"Boys!" I exclaimed.

"One more, Tata Johnny, just one more!" pleaded Costică. "Then we will go in."

"Do you all promise?" I asked.

"Yes, yes," they murmured. I stood with them and watched. A long minute passed, and the cold was starting to get to me. Just as I turned to go, several voices said at once, "There it is! Look!"

Sure enough, the sky over Suceava thundered as a brilliant star-

The boys crowd onto the landing outside their dorm.

burst of green, blue, red, and yellow cascaded earthward in a spec-
tacular display. As the last falling light faded from sight, I ordered the
boys back to their beds. Several reminded me that this was vacation
and it was not important to be in bed quite so early. I didn't argue,
but tucked a boy in here, another there, and snapped off the lights,
wishing them all a good night and a happy New Year. I wondered if
Ruth was about finished tucking the girls into their beds.

Things were quiet as I entered the last room. "Tata Johnny, come
here," said Daniel. "Let me see your watch." I pushed back my sleeve,
and in the darkness his little fingers felt for the tiny button. "There,"
he said as he pushed it, illuminating the face. "See, it's after midnight, and that means it is now the year 1998, doesn't it? And it's the
New Year where Nenea Bill is too, isn't it?" he asked.

"Well, no, Daniel, but in seven more hours it will be the New Year
there too," I answered.

"But why?" asked Daniel. "What's the difference?"

At that moment I heard the rhythmic pounding of drums as a
group of *maskcats* turned up our street and marched toward the orphanage, singing coarsely as they came. Loud thumps resounded
throughout the boys' dorm as boys leaped from their bunks. The
sound of running feet accompanied the swish of opening windows.
With Daniel right at my heels, I hurried to the side of the boys' dorm
that faced the road. Nenea Bill and time zones were momentarily
forgotten. I could hear commotion coming from the girls' dorm and
knew Mama Ruth was faring no better. I could hardly find a window
with enough free space for me to look out. But when I did, I saw five
young men marching up our street, croaking out a ballad. One was
beating a sizable drum and another was beating a club against the
lid of a five-gallon bucket. As they passed under the streetlight and
their outlandish garb became visible, the children began laughing,
pointing, and exclaiming to one another. Soon the *maskcats* passed
the orphanage and I began closing the windows, but within several

minutes the youth returned, passing by in the opposite direction and producing another mass stampede and more opened windows.

The children were excited, and I could well understand why. But I also realized it would take at least another half hour to get them settled down for the night. I sighed and started making rounds, tucking little boys back into their beds again, some for the third time.

Later that night Ruth and I compared notes. We had to chuckle at how absolutely powerless we were to prevent the children from tumbling out of their beds to witness the events ushering in the New Year.

Chapter 4

Enriched

Our faithful Tanti Larisa and her husband were expecting their first child. Thursday would be her last day of work. She was going to become a full-time mom as soon as their child was born.

On Friday evening our staff and children gathered in the gym where a special supper was being served in Larisa's honor. We would all miss her. The children made her promise to bring the baby for a visit as soon as it was old enough.

The cooks outdid themselves with a splendid supper. Afterward, Larisa and her husband Mihai opened their gifts, and the class of orphanage children she had cared for during the past several years sang a special song for her.

Since Tanti Larisa was not moving to faraway America but would live close by in Suceava, her farewell supper was different from other partings. The children were happy for Larisa, her husband, and their coming baby. A group of little boys gathered around Nenea Geo, a childcare worker, who held them spellbound with stories. Older boys engaged Mihai in conversation, while the girls gathered about their favorite tantis.

I retired early from the celebration and sat at my desk reminiscing. It was difficult to grasp all the changes God had brought into our lives since our move to Romania. A new world of human experience had opened to us through ministering to these children. As I recounted the many experiences that had enriched our lives, I remembered Laura.

It had been after supper a few months before when Ionică had walked down from the orphanage to where a number of us were working in the garden. It was late summer, and the garden had certainly needed our attention. I had weeded my way to the end of one of the long rows when Ionică indicated that he wished to speak with me.

"Yes?" I asked as I stepped to the edge of the garden to hear what was on his mind.

"I just had a long talk with Laura," he explained, his face beaming, "and I wanted to tell you that she has invited Jesus Christ into her heart."

"Wonderful!" I responded. "This is just wonderful! And when did this happen?"

"This evening she wanted to talk with me, and in the course of our conversation she told me of her experience with the Lord. We prayed together. I wanted to share this good news with you," he said.

"Oh, thank you!" I had been impressed with eleven-year-old Laura's serious concern about spiritual issues. Thanking Ionică again, I turned back to the garden where Ruth was hoeing. I couldn't wait to tell her!

That evening we rejoiced together. God was answering prayers, and the Biblical truths being taught were taking effect. Praise the Lord!

In the weeks that had followed, several others had thrilled us with their decisions to become followers of Christ. Yes, they were young and immature, yet we were overjoyed to observe their attitudes and actions becoming more and more Christ-like. They had come at various times and told us of their desire to repent and give their hearts to Jesus.

It blessed us to witness these newborn babes in Christ as they knelt beside their bunk beds to pray or lay on their beds to read their Bibles. They felt a need for personal time with God in spite of the fact that they had just finished participating in group devotions.

Several of the American sisters were knotting comforters in the home of Alvin Stoltzfus. His wife, Lil, had invited these ladies, along with the older orphanage girls, to help. Mihaela Sveduneac had joined them from her home in Suceava. She was seventeen years old and had suffered the trauma of a broken home. Her grandparents and mother were devout Christians, and she, too, had opened her heart to the Lord. Mihaela was being instructed at the Nathaniel Christian Church in preparation for baptism. She was thrilled at the prospect of sharing this time in work and fellowship with the orphanage girls and staff.

Interesting conversations flowed freely about the quilt frames where the ladies worked. Mihaela was the only one present who was fluent in both languages. At times she was asked to interpret. As the afternoon progressed, the conversation turned more serious.

"I have a question," said Laura. "Why do some sisters put up their hair and cover it with a veiling while others leave their hair hanging? And some sisters wear the veiling wherever they go while others wear it only for church services. Why?"

The orphanage girls who were gathered around the quilt frame immediately offered their varied opinions. Laura turned to Mihaela and

Mihaela Sveduneac and Loredana knot a comforter.

asked, "Mihaela, why do you wear the veiling all the time instead of just for church services, as I see other Romanian sisters doing?"

"Well," said Mihaela as she tightened the knot she was tying, "I have studied 1 Corinthians 11, and from that I believe the Lord doesn't want me to display my long hair publicly. I believe He is honored when I put my hair up in such a way that I can properly cover it with a veiling wherever I go, and not just for church services. I want to honor God's Word always and be ready to speak about the Lord or pray to the Lord at any time."

"Then why do we orphanage girls wear our veils only for church? And why do we have our hair hanging?" Laura asked with a sincere thirst for a deeper understanding. "You know," she continued, "I have given my heart to the Lord Jesus, and I would like to have my head covered. I also want to put up my hair as you do."

Mihaela responded, "If that is what you feel in your heart, then why don't you? I believe this is what the Bible teaches us to do."

Lil was reminded of her own daughter, Rose, who at a tender age felt moved to wear the Christian woman's covering. Mihaela interpreted this account to the others as Lil explained how Rose chose to follow the Word of God and her own tender conscience in this matter, and how God had blessed her in doing so. Although not all who were working on the comforters that afternoon agreed on how this Bible truth should be carried out, all were moved by this discussion.

One morning soon afterward I noticed that Laura and several other Nathaniel girls had chosen to wear their veils to the breakfast table. This seemed most appropriate for them, especially as Nenea Geo led our morning devotions. He read a portion of Scripture and gave examples about how important it is to follow the Bible above all else.

Not all of our workers saw the veiling issue alike. Brother Ionică brought a challenge to us in our monthly staff meeting. He explained that the Bible is very clear that when a woman prays, she is to have her head covered. He reminded us that these children pray many times throughout the day. "Be very careful," he cautioned, "that you never discourage one of these little ones from doing what they feel God is telling them to do. It is a serious thing," he continued, "to confuse a child's heart or do anything that would turn their feet from the pathway of God."

<hr />

"Tata Johnny," said Laura as she looked through my office doorway, "may I come in?"

"Certainly," I responded.

"Tata Johnny, I have some things I really would like to talk over with you when you have time. But I know you are busy, and—"

"Hey," I interrupted, "I'm not that busy. I certainly have time to hear what you have to tell me. Go ahead, I'm listening." I pushed back from my desk and gave her my full attention.

"It's too hard for me to express this in English, and I want to bring Caroline to interpret for me. Is that all right?" she asked.

"Sure, if that is easier for you," I responded.

"Good, I'll go see if she can come now," she said as she turned to leave.

Laura soon returned with my daughter Caroline. "As you know, Tata Johnny," she began as Caroline interpreted, "I have opened my heart to the Lord Jesus, and I really want to live as a Christian."

"Yes, and I'm so happy for you," I said.

"I want to tell you about my early life and the things that have happened," Laura continued. "I lived in the village of Vicov, and there were two small houses in one courtyard. My grandparents lived in the one house, and my family lived in the other one. My mother had gone to the field to work and left me, my twin sister Loredana, and my younger sister Ionela alone in the house. Loredana and I were three years old at that time, and Ionela was only two.

"I'm not sure how the fire began, but I always liked to play with a light switch and turned it off and on over and over again. Perhaps it was that, or it might have been something with the heating stove which was burning at that time. Suddenly we noticed the house was filling with smoke. I wanted to run outside and find Mama, but the smoke was thick and the crackling fire was between me and the door. We couldn't leave. Instead, we ran into the bedroom and shut the door, but soon the smoke grew thick in the bedroom as well. We were so afraid that we began to scream and cry out for our mother to come get us. By now all three of us were crying hard. Smoke was burning our eyes. We were choking and could hardly breathe. We crawled under the bed, hoping the smoke couldn't find us there, but it did. We ran into the washroom and I slammed the door to keep out the fire and smoke.

"Our neighbors saw smoke pouring from our house and ran to help. It was terrible! Mother rushed in from the field and joined our neighbors in trying to save us. A neighbor man fought his way through the heat and the smoke. He heard our screams and followed them. Finally he found us. He bundled us into a large blanket and carried us out through the burning house to safety. We were almost unconscious from the smoke. Our hair was singed, and our skin was blistered in several places. It hurt terribly, but God spared our lives.

"When our father came home from his job on the railroad that evening, he was shocked to find out his home had burned down. The house was totally destroyed, and we moved in with our grandparents until another house could be built.

"Then when I was six, an even worse thing happened. My mother and father separated and Mother left us. We couldn't understand what was happening, and we didn't see her for a long time. Months passed, and she finally returned, planning to take us to live with her. Our father was away working at his job, but our grandfather and two uncles had been drinking heavily and became very angry. They attacked my mother and beat her severely, and they wouldn't quit . . ."

Laura's chin quivered and her eyes filled with tears as the brutal scene flashed back into her mind.

"I saw what was happening and ran to the neighbors for help. As I ran, I heard my mother screaming for mercy. I felt in my heart that they were planning to kill her. I was desperate! I knew I needed God's help, and I began to pray. The only prayer I knew at that time was the prayer my grandmother had taught me, and I prayed earnestly, 'Our Father, which art in heaven, hallowed be thy name . . .' Simple as it was, I believe God heard my prayer and the cry of my heart, because neighbors quickly assembled in our courtyard and broke up the fight. To this day I believe they saved my mother's life.

"Soon after this incident our mother left us for good. This was the most difficult time in my life." Laura's face registered deep suffering. Her voice shook and tears trickled down her cheeks.

"What happened next?" I gently prompted.

Wiping away the tears, Laura continued, "We moved eight miles away to the village of Straja to live with my mother's mother. She was kind to us, and we dearly loved our grandmother. After living with her for nearly a year, we were brought here to live at the Nathaniel Orphanage."

Her head was bowed, her voice soft, and I waited, feeling that there must be more.

She took a deep breath and continued. "A couple of weeks ago a brother spoke in our church from Psalm 23. He explained our need to follow the Shepherd. These thoughts impressed me.

"Then in our Sunday school, Nathan Bange read from 1 Corinthians 13 about the love of God. He explained how His love works in our lives. These truths sank deep into my heart, and I have thought about them many times since.

"You preached a message, and at the very end you talked directly to us children. You said that up until now we may have felt that all was well between us and God. You went on to explain that there will come a time when this will change and we will begin to realize that not all is well. You told us that when this happens we should listen to the voice of the Holy Spirit. You explained that it won't be a voice we can hear with our ears, but He will speak to us in our thoughts and in our hearts. You warned us to not ignore that voice, but respond to the Holy Spirit and follow what He is telling us to do.

"That evening I went to bed with those thoughts rolling about in my mind. I couldn't sleep, so I began reading my Bible. I felt the Holy Spirit speaking to my heart. I began battling with the devil and I prayed. This was when I committed my life to follow the Lord Jesus with my whole heart."

I sensed the depth of Laura's sincerity, and my heart was touched by it. I had so many things I wanted to say to her. Where should I begin?

"First of all," I warned, "the devil is not going to give up just because you have given your heart to the Lord. He has a plan to destroy your faith and ultimately take you to hell. However, the Holy Spirit also has a plan, and that is to see you through—all the way to heaven. The devil will try to discourage you and tempt you to do wrong. If, however, you are willing to follow the Lord, He will help you overcome these temptations."

Laura listened attentively. "And now," I suggested, "why don't we conclude this time of sharing with prayer."

There in my small office Laura, Caroline, and I stood in reverence before God, and as we prayed, the sweetness of that spiritual incense reached all the way to our Father in heaven.

Later Caroline and Laura sought each other out and held a prayer vigil of their own. Caroline shared with us that through these experiences God showed her the need for rededicating her own life to the Lord. These deeply moving times of prayer and sharing drew Caroline and Laura close in a special bond of friendship.

Yes, God had indeed enriched our lives. With hope and assurance I looked into the future, awed by what God was doing in our midst.

Chapter 5

The Seed

Ten-year-old Ionela was at it again. "Tata Johnny," she pleaded, "please may I go help with the seed packing? Please? They need workers."

Our farm director, Alvin Stoltzfus, had inherited the mammoth job of organizing and distributing garden seeds in villages throughout northeastern Romania. Right now he was overseeing a group who was packaging seeds in our large farm shop. "Please?" Ionela begged again when she saw that I was considering her request.

"Is all your homework done?" I asked.

She hesitated a moment before answering. "Well, yes. All but one little page of math, and I can easily do that after supper."

"I'll tell you what," I said. "You run quickly and complete that math; then come back and I'll go along to ask Alvin if you may help. Is that a deal?"

"It's a deal!" she said, jumping to her feet and hurrying to her room.

"Tata Johnny," asked Costică a few minutes later as he entered my office. "What are you planning to do with the greenhouse the boys have been talking about? Are you going to paint it green?"

"No," I responded with a chuckle, "we're not going to paint it, but I think you'll love it. The plants that will grow in it will be green long after the frost kills all the plants in the garden."

"See, I told you," said Iliuță, who had entered my office behind his younger brother.

"It will have a framework of metal piping," I continued, "and that will be covered with two layers of plastic. A fan will maintain a slight air pressure between those layers, forming an insulating barrier to help keep our plants warm. It will also have a heater to keep the plants from freezing when the weather becomes really cold. I'm looking forward to you boys helping me grow our own vegetables and flowers this year."

"You mean like we did last year in Styrofoam cups in the bakery garage?" asked Costică.

"Exactly," I answered. "Wouldn't you like to help? We will begin planting in the bakery garage and then transfer them to the new greenhouse as soon as it is ready."

"Well, it might be fun to help," replied Costică, though he didn't sound too convinced.

"Are you going to build it behind the church where the men dug all those holes?" asked Iliuţă.

"Yes. A man who has experience with these types of buildings is coming from America shortly after the greenhouse arrives to show us how to construct it. Hopefully by the first of March we will be ready to begin."

"Come on, Costică, let's go watch the men," said Iliuţă as he started for the door.

Twenty minutes later Ionela had finished her math. As she and I entered the farm shop, we looked about in amazement. A beehive of activity buzzed all about us. Long rows of tables were lined with workers measuring out seeds into thousands of waiting envelopes, which were then sealed and sorted into large bins. Other workers were busily selecting one envelope from each bin and placing them as sets in plastic bags to be sealed for distribution.

"There he is! Come on!" begged Ionela as she tugged at my hand. "See?" she pointed.

There was Alvin, circulating among the workers. He was double-checking labeled packets and refilling empty seed containers. While we watched, he ordered a heavy bin filled with packets to be dragged aside and an empty one put in its place.

Leaving Ionela, I approached Alvin and explained my request. He replied that they had a deadline to meet with distribution meetings planned in numerous villages and he could not have children upsetting the procedure.

"I'll tell you what," said Alvin. "I need someone to sweep up the spilled seeds around the packaging tables. I'll have my daughter Rose watch out for her."

"Fine," I replied and made my way back to where Ionela was waiting hopefully. I explained what Alvin had said and told her to ask Rose for instructions.

"Thanks!" she said and rushed off to find Rose.

It was interesting to watch sixty people working together so harmoniously for the benefit of others. I took a stroll among them, fascinated by their commitment. Many poor families in remote villages were going to be blessed by these packets containing twelve kinds of certified vegetable seeds. At the very end of the line I saw a young lady placing a Gospel pamphlet into each bag before sealing it. *How wonderful to place spiritual seed in the packets along with the physical seeds,* I thought. *May God bless them both with much increase!*

I noticed Franklin was dragging bins into position and opening gunnysacks of seed as needed. I watched enviously as he spoke Romanian freely with the youth who were measuring seeds into the envelopes and packing the envelopes into bags. He had learned so much during our first year in Romania without even trying. I, on the other hand, had attended language classes and was still struggling just to make myself understood. Often when I spoke to a group of Romanians, one of them would guess at what I was trying to say and translate it into good Romanian for the rest to understand. It was rather embarrassing.

Several ladies began singing a hymn, and soon the sixty-voice seed chorus was in full swing. The workers were from a Pentecostal church several villages to the north.

I reached for the doorknob. Although my fingers itched to help with the seed packaging program, I knew I was needed at the orphanage. I glanced back over the crowd of workers and saw Ionela pull her head out from under a table where she had been sweeping. *I like her spirit!* I thought as I closed the door behind me.

I heard a flutter of wings when I entered the orphanage and instinctively jerked the door shut behind me and locked it. "Oh, Tata Johnny," wailed Florica, looking self-consciously down at me from where she was standing on a chair. "I was letting Papagal perch on my finger in his cage. I was talking to him when he just flew right out the door before I could even close it. And now I can't catch him. He's so bad!"

I glanced up at the bright blue and white parakeet side-stepping back and forth on the curtain rod. "Florica, Florica, what am I ever going to do with you?" I asked. "I have told you often that you are never to take Papagal out of his cage unless I give you permission. Suppose he had flown out the door just now. We would have lost him, and he would have frozen to death!"

"But I didn't take him out of his cage. Honest! I was just letting him sit on my finger in the cage while I talked to him, and he just flew out. It wasn't my fault," she said with a careless toss of her head.

"Well," I tried to reason, "you opened the cage door. Who else would be responsible?"

Her only response was a shrug.

"Florica, you should never, never open Papagal's cage door unless you have direct permission from me," I repeated.

After chasing our wayward Papagal from curtain rod to bookcase and back again, we were finally able to tire him out enough to catch him. He screeched his protest and bit furiously. Florica retrieved a pair of scissors from my desk drawer, and with her help I carefully trimmed the primary feathers of his right wing to keep him from flying so effortlessly.

"Tata Johnny, quick, come to the farm!" called Iliuță.

"Why? What's happening down at the farm?" I asked.

"A big, long truck is here, and Steve is unloading large bundles of shiny pipe and great big boxes and huge fans!" he exclaimed, his eyes gleaming with excitement.

"Well, it sounds like our greenhouse has finally arrived."

"Oh, goody!" said Iliuță. "Can I help build it?"

"Yes, when the time comes and you are free from school."

By this time I had donned my coat and was following an enthusiastic Iliuță toward the farm. Steve Stoltzfus, our single worker from Pennsylvania, was operating the forklift and had already unloaded most of the greenhouse. I was thrilled at the prospect of starting plants for our own garden and raising flowers to fill the spacious flower beds around the orphanage. I was sure this would spark interest among the children.

That afternoon Ruth informed me that we were having visitors at our house for supper. "Could you please be on time?" she pleaded.

I left Nenea Daniel in charge of the orphanage supper and went down to our little gray house. We washed up and waited for our visitors to arrive.

"How did you like the seed packing?" I asked our son Franklin.

"Good!" he replied with enthusiasm. "It's hard work, but we had lots of fun too."

"What fun were you having?" I asked, immediately interested.

"Well, it's fun to sing with the workers," began Franklin. "Then, too, I was working and talking with the Romanian youth when a group of American visitors showed up. After watching us work for a while, a grandma among the visitors must have overheard me speaking in English to Alvin. She was impressed and asked me where I had learned to speak such good English. I realized that she had mistaken me for a Romanian because I had been speaking Romanian most of the time, so I thought I would just help her along a little bit."

"What do you mean, help her along?" I asked.

"Well, I just turned and spoke to her in broken English," he said, laughing. "I told her, 'I stody Englesh at the schule.' When she said, 'But your accent sounds nearly American,' I said, 'Tank you very much!' "

Franklin and I were still chuckling when there was a knock at the door, and I rose to welcome our visitors. As I shook hands and took their coats, I heard a noise behind me and turned just in time to see Franklin vanish up the staircase toward his room.

Later that evening at the supper table when I introduced Franklin as our son, a perplexed look crossed one older lady's face. Franklin smiled. "Yes," he said in perfect English. "Yes, I believe we met when you were watching the seed packing."

"But," stammered our confused visitor, "I thought . . ."

"I'm sorry," apologized Franklin, "I was just having a bit of fun."

The prank proved to be a wonderful ice-breaker, and we thoroughly enjoyed the evening with our visitors.

———————————————

There was excitement in the air. Streams of villagers had been pouring through the orphanage gate long before the seed meeting was scheduled to begin. The farm shop had been cleared to make room for the slide presentation. Silvia Tărniceriu was on hand to translate and help with the slide narration. There were only seats for half of the people who came, and many who had walked a considerable distance had to stand for the two-hour presentation.

Finally the moment arrived, and slides of beautiful farmland both in America and Romania appeared on the screen. An impressive slide was shown of one of our top-quality cows with the proper amount of feed she received daily. In front of her were fifty liters of milk—the amount she produced daily.

Another slide showed a father working closely with his young sons on their farm. Still another showed a barn raising where a hundred Amish men were working together to bless the life of a brother. Silvia's lilting voice urged the audience to consider the blessing of helping one another rather than taking from each other. "It is futile," she said, "to lament that which you do not have. Rather be thankful and put to good use that which God has given you."

Next, a slide showing the four destitute Biţica children filled the screen. They were thin and underfed, and their faces reflected the horror of losing their mother to a brutal murder.

"You well remember this incident, I am sure," said Silvia, "because it happened in the nearby village of Mitoc. I see that some of you are from Mitoc. This father and mother should have been spending their money on proper food, good books, and a nice home for their children. Instead they spent their money on alcohol. And what were the results?" she asked. "I'll tell you what the results were."

Every eye was glued to Silvia's face as she continued. "Daddy came home in a terrible frame of mind. He was very angry and had been drinking. He tied up his wife and beat her mercilessly. She screamed and screamed for help, but nobody came because the neighbors were all afraid. The children were frightened and climbed up on the ledge behind the stove. From there they pleaded with their father to stop hurting their mother, but he wouldn't listen. He told his children that if they wouldn't be quiet, he would kill them all, and he continued to beat his wife cruelly. Then in the wee hours of the morning he sent one of the small children to bring the butcher knife from the kitchen, and with that knife in his hand he murdered the mother of these dear children before their very eyes."

I heard sobbing and tore my eyes from Silvia's face to glance around the audience. Many were wiping tears from their eyes, and several grown men were openly weeping.

"Yes," Silvia continued, "what have these innocent children suffered because of alcohol? Mamas, daddies, listen to me. Take a good look at this picture and think about it the next time you are tempted to buy another bottle. Use what God has given you to bless the lives of your children and not to harm them."

The picture changed and four beautiful, healthy children appeared on the screen. "Look what love has accomplished," Silvia urged her audience. "These are the same children. You can hardly recognize them! Look at the smiles on their faces. Look at the sparkle in their eyes. See how happy and alive they are? This picture was taken just six months after these children came to live in the Nathaniel Christian Orphanage. Here they have experienced the love of God. They go to church. They pray. And, my dear friends, what do you suppose they pray for? Are they praying that they will get rich?"

Silvia stepped in front of a group of children and spoke to them. "Perhaps you think they have been praying for a new bicycle. No, they are not praying for anything for themselves. Instead these children have been praying that their father will repent. As you know, he was taken to prison, where he is serving an eighteen-year sentence. But, my dear friends, these children have completely forgiven their father for what he has done. They love him, and again and again I hear these children praying for their daddy, because they want God to forgive him too. Isn't that beautiful? Isn't that wonderful?" Silvia asked.

Although I had heard the Bițica story numerous times, I still found myself brushing tears from my eyes right along with the rest of the listeners.

"Now children," said Silvia, "do you know the Lord's Prayer?" Here and there heads nodded. "You do? Good! Can we say it together, just the children?" A chorus of childish voices followed Silvia as she slowly led them. "Our Father which art in heaven, Hallowed be thy name.

Thy kingdom come. Thy will be done in earth, as it is in heaven. Give us this day our daily bread. And forgive us our debts, as we forgive our debtors. And lead us not into temptation, but deliver us from evil: for thine is the kingdom, and the power, and the glory, forever. Amen."

"Parents," said Silvia as she looked over the audience, "you know this prayer too, don't you? When we pray 'Our Father,' we are acknowledging that we have only one Father, and if we have one Father, that means we are brothers. And why should brothers hurt each other or take advantage of one another? Notice also that this prayer says God will forgive us only as we forgive others. Think of what these four children have forgiven. Some of you have been holding family grudges for many years, and you still have them. Can a person ever truly be happy if he is bearing a grudge in his heart? You need to take an example from these children, and then you can be happy as they are."

Here and there in the audience I saw nods of agreement. Silvia not only spoke their language; she spoke their hearts.

The picture changed, showing unsanitary conditions in a poor village. Silvia began explaining the virtues of sanitation and how flies spread disease. She gave simple, inexpensive solutions for making even the most primitive situations healthier.

Soon the program ended and a group of orphanage children entered the shop. Silvia announced that these children had all suffered from their home situations, but they were thankful to God for all He had given them, and they were going to sing several songs. As the orphanage children found their places up front and began to sing, Alvin and his helpers opened their gunny sacks filled with family seed packets. It was touching to see recipients turn their seed packets over and over in their hands, marveling at all they contained. In their hands they held seeds to be planted in their gardens, but in their hearts the spiritual seed had already been planted. Would they cultivate it and allow it to grow?

During the next month, Alvin took the seed meetings to over thirty villages, and Silvia communicated godly principles to her people. Numerous others assisted them in controlling the crowds and distributing the seed packets, and thousands of people were blessed.

Chapter 6

Lost and Found

Brother Paul Yoder from Berlin, Ohio, arrived and immediately began erecting the greenhouse, though the ground was still covered with snow. The older orphanage children had been interested in watching plants grow. In the bakery garage, lush young tomato, cabbage, cucumber, and flower plants were pushing their way up through soil the children had helped sift. Homemade flats and Styrofoam cups were bursting with life from seeds their little fingers had pushed into the soft soil. Now their interest was readily transferred to building the greenhouse. Each afternoon right after school the older children walked to the site behind the church to watch. Our handyman, Steve Stoltzfus, engineered the water and electrical work. It was exciting to watch the greenhouse skeleton steadily taking shape.

We constantly watched for opportunities to develop the orphanage children's individual abilities. These opportunities set the Nathaniel Christian Orphanage apart from the state-run orphanages. We were blessed with a farm where boys took turns helping with the milking, feeding calves, and doing other chores. Some were assigned to feed the horses and clean their stalls. During the summer months several of the more dependable children were responsible to move the broiler pens to fresh grass several times a week as well as feed and water the chickens twice daily.

The season's first batch of broiler eggs had been placed into our incubators. Twelve-year-old Loredana had proven herself trustworthy

during the past sea-
son and was given
sole responsibility
for rolling the eggs
three times a day.
Each egg had been
marked on one side
to insure that none
would be missed
and all would be
turned uniformly.
It was a blessing to
see how seriously
Loredana took this
responsibility.

Andi helps with the milking.

Having a farm also offered opportunities for hobbies like raising
dogs, rabbits, and pigeons. These activities taught personal responsibility and work ethics. In addition to these healthy activities, we
had loving, godly workers who really cared for the children's spiritual
well-being. They played with them, worked with them, sang with
them, and prayed with them.

Ida Jane saw that Loredana had a gift for drawing and began devel-
oping that aptitude. Loredana was a ready student and soon produced
some rather striking pencil drawings. It was interesting to observe the
themes Loredana chose for her pictures. One was a sad little girl with
a dirty face and a big pair of boots. The caption read, "Everyone is
important in God's sight."

"Marinel," I called as he passed my office, "would you go tell Ovidiu I want to see him when he finishes his homework? Tell him I will
be here in my office."

"Sure, Tata Johnny, I'll tell him," responded Marinel as he dashed up the stairs toward the boys' dorm. In a short time not only Ovidiu arrived, but Marinel and Marius as well.

"Tata Johnny, why do you want to talk with Ovidiu?" Marius asked.

"What did he do bad?" asked Marinel, nervously pulling at his bottom lip.

"Why, he hasn't done anything wrong," I responded. "I simply wanted to tell him some good news."

"I know, I know! Ovidiu has a new sponsor!" blurted out Marinel.

"Really, Tata Johnny?" asked Marius, grinning. "Did he get a new sponsor?"

I looked at Ovidiu, who had been silent through all these speculations. His face was sober, and my heart went out to him. "Ovidiu," I said, "God has provided you with a new sponsor. I know this man, because when I was a missionary in Belize many years ago, he was a youth there. Now he is married and has a family of his own. In fact, I wouldn't be surprised if he would have children about your age. And God has moved his heart to become your sponsor. See, here is the fax that just came in from CAM's Ohio office," I said as I traced the name with my finger. "Ben and Lois Friesen," I read for him.

Ovidiu stared at the names.

"Where do they live?" asked Marius.

"They live in Pennsylvania," I responded.

"Are they going to come visit him?" asked Marinel. But he didn't wait for an answer.

"Hey, Nenea Geo, Nenea Geo!" shouted Marinel as he scrambled to his feet and rushed out into the hall to intercept our childcare worker who happened to be passing at that moment. "Ovidiu has a new sponsor! His other sponsor stopped, and he already has a new one!"

"It is truly wonderful how God provides for all of us," Nenea Geo said.

"Ovidiu, I really don't know if your new sponsor is coming to visit or not, but I'm sure they would love to meet you," I said. "Maybe they will send you a picture of their family to put in your photo album."

I sincerely wished Ben and Lois could have seen the contented smile that spread over Ovidiu's face as he turned to go. Now he belonged again!

A photo album had been created for each child in our orphanage, and dedicated workers regularly added pictures that would become important to the children later in life. The children had their pictures taken when they first came to the Nathaniel Christian Orphanage. Other photos included the children with their own birthday cakes, or when they received a special award at school. Poems, cards, and letters were also included. We photographed family members who came to visit, and photos of each child's sponsor were especially prized.

These children would eventually grow into young adults and leave the orphanage to begin life on their own. We wanted these albums to preserve the good memories of their childhood. The albums had two special places. One was at the very top of the bookcase in the big living room, and the other was in the heart of every child. Often a child would ask for his album and sit reviewing it alone, lost in thought. At other times they would ask to share an album with a visitor. They would sit and discuss page after page, sharing incidents from their lives.

Nicu Cotleţ, a CAM-assisted evangelist, had an idea. God was moving him to begin working in yet another unchurched village. Alvin had been giving his slide presentation and passing out seed packets in numerous villages. Nicu wondered if CAM would consent to give such a presentation in the village where he intended to work. This could soften the people and get a Gospel pamphlet into nearly every home. Then he would follow up a week later by going door to door inviting the people to attend a preaching service. Nicu was excited about this prospect and was thrilled to learn that his targeted village had been placed on the list for a seed meeting.

Finally the day arrived. Nicu stood among the villagers and for the first time heard the principles explained as the slides were shown. He was deeply moved as Alvin and Silvia gave the account of the Bițica children. He heard the Biblical precept that it is more blessed to give than to receive interwoven throughout the presentation. Then Silvia gave the analogy of pulling the weeds from our hearts so that God's love can grow there. Nicu's heart rejoiced.

The seed meeting was a success, and people drifted toward their homes, carrying their precious seed packets and Gospel pamphlets. Nicu could hardly wait until he could return and speak personally to these villagers. But he had promised to drive three hours south to Bacău the next day and participate in a prison ministry with another evangelist. The work in this village would have to wait until the following week. Until then, he would pray.

Many thoughts tumbled about in Nicu's mind as he traveled toward the prison. He relived the message of CAM's slide presentation. He thought about the village and the spiritual darkness that existed among its people. He thought about the glorious Gospel bringing light into that darkness. But as he entered the prison and looked into the faces of its hardened inmates, his heart was filled with compassion for them also. They needed to hear God's message of love, forgiveness, and deliverance.

Nicu stood before a group of sixty men and began preaching the Word of God. His deep bass voice resounded from the bare concrete walls that surrounded them. His eyes moved from face to face, and he wondered what lay behind each mask. Here and there men bowed their heads, unable or unwilling to meet his gaze. But there were others whose eyes never left his face. These seemed to be drinking in the message he was sharing. One face in particular was beaming with interest.

Near the end of his message, Nicu felt the Holy Spirit nudging him to speak on the healing power of forgiveness. As he did so, he thought of the beautiful example of those four children from the Nathaniel Orphanage. He told of their tragedy and of the sweetness they had experienced through forgiving their father. Then he urged his audience to forgive others who had hurt them.

"You must forgive your family members who have turned their backs on you since you've been imprisoned. But above all else," he begged them, "seek forgiveness for your own sins by coming to God in repentance."

When the invitation was given, four inmates came forward to repent and seek cleansing and forgiveness. The joy in Nicu's heart was but a reflection of the rejoicing that was going on in heaven.

Shortly after the service ended, most of the men shuffled back toward their cells; however, several approached Nicu to thank him for coming. The man with the beaming face also came. He had a burden on his heart that he wanted to share. His heart had been touched by the story of the four children who had forgiven their father for murdering their mother. "I, too, murdered my wife," said the inmate as he lowered his eyes in shame. Then he lifted his gaze and with a clear countenance declared, "I came to the Lord in repentance, and God has graciously washed my sins away! The Lord Jesus has come into my heart and made me a new man. But," continued the man, "I have a big problem. I have eight children, and I have no idea what has happened to them. Could you help me locate them? In the five years that I have been imprisoned, I have not received so much as one phone call or even a postcard. Please help me find my children," he pleaded as tears filled his eyes.

Brother Nicu tore a small piece of paper out of his notebook and asked the man to write down his name and address. The guard was becoming impatient and shouted once more for the inmates to hurry. The man quickly scrawled his name and address on the scrap of paper, shook hands with Nicu, and hurried toward the waiting guard.

On Sunday Nicu attended a church dedication in a remote village in Suceava County, where two years earlier seed meetings had been held and Gospel literature distributed along with the seed packets. Evangelists had followed up with preaching, and a number of people had repented and come to know the Lord. These believers had worked hard to build a church, which had been completed recently, and many had come for its dedication. What a change had come to his country in the nine short years since the fall of communism! Nicu was now able to openly preach in most villages and even in prisons. Many churches had been built, and here he was, observing the dedication of yet another one. His heart was full. God certainly had been good to them!

The moderator was making closing remarks when Nicu heard his name. "I'd like to ask Brother Nicu Cotleț to come forward and bring a greeting to the church and then lead us in closing prayer."

Nicu dutifully rose and made his way toward the front of the church. As he cast about in his mind what he should say, he was reminded of his promise to help that Christian prisoner find his lost children. He turned to face the audience and encouraged them to serve God with their lives. Then he asked them to pray for the man he had met in prison. "This man," he explained, "killed his wife, but has repented and wants to find his eight children." With that, Nicu led the audience in a closing prayer, and the service was ended.

Nicu was speaking with several brethren when a woman made her way up the crowded aisle. It was Silvia, who had assisted with the village seed meetings.

"Brother Nicu," she asked, "what is the name of the man you met in prison?"

"Sister Silvia, I am sorry, but I have it written on a piece of paper at home, and I didn't think to bring it with me. And right now I can't recall the man's name."

"What if he is the father of the Bițica children? Wouldn't that be something? Wouldn't that be a miracle!" she declared.

"But," replied Nicu, "this man has eight children, and there are only four Bițica children."

"Oh, yes," said Silvia. "I guess you are right. But anyway, call me when you get home. I want the man's name, okay?"

"Sure," said Nicu, turning to speak to another brother who had been waiting patiently.

That afternoon Silvia had just finished writing a letter when the phone rang. She picked it up.

"Nicu here," came the deep voice from the other end of the line.

"Do you have the man's name whom you met in prison yesterday?" asked Silvia, her pen poised to write.

"The man's name is Bițica," Nicu said. "Nelu Bițica."

"Nelu Bițica!" shouted Silvia into the receiver. "That's him, Nicu! That's got to be the father of the Bițica children in our orphanage. I'm sure of it! He has the same family name as they do, and he said that he had murdered his wife, right? Brother Nicu, it has to be their father! And you said that he is a believer, right? Oh, praise the Lord! Praise the Lord!"

"Wait a minute," cautioned Nicu. "This man told me he has eight children, but there are only four Bițica children."

"Nicu, listen," said Silvia. "Didn't you tell me he was from Suceava County, and that he had been in prison five years? And he murdered his wife, and his family name is Bițica. It has to be the same man! Perhaps there are other children in this family who were sent elsewhere. I don't know. But I am sure this is the father of the four children in our orphanage. I'm going over to the orphanage right now to ask Elena for more details. Thanks Nicu! God bless you! Goodbye."

With that, Silvia threw on her jacket and hurried the short distance to the orphanage, where she sought out Elena and began asking questions about her family and her earliest recollections of other children who might have also been in her family. Silvia was surprised to learn that she had an infant brother named Nicolae who had been with them at the time of their mother's death. Also, Elena vaguely recalled a boy and a girl who had visited their home at Christmas long ago, but she wasn't sure if these were her siblings or not. Silvia verified the date of Elena's mother's death, and it matched the information she had gotten from Nicu. More and more of the pieces of the puzzle were falling into place.

Late that afternoon the telephone rang at the little gray house, and I answered it.

"Hello, Tata Johnny?" said Silvia. "I have just learned that the Bițica's father has been found in a prison in Bacău. And Johnny," she continued, her voice trembling with excitement, "he has repented and is living for the Lord! Can you believe it? Those many prayers of his children have been answered!"

"Silvia, how do you know all this?" I asked.

Silvia quickly filled me in about Nicu Cotleț attending a seed meeting and seeing slides of the children. She informed me of Nicu's meeting with Mr. Bițica in prison, although at the time Nicu hadn't known who he was. Then she told me about the other Bițica siblings.

"Silvia," I interrupted, "does Elena know about all this?"

"Yes she does, and she is simply overjoyed!"

"Do you think it will be possible to take the children to visit him?" I inquired.

"I hope so, and I want to go along," she answered.

"Thank you so much, Silvia, for informing me about all this. I want to run up to the orphanage right away and talk with Elena. If you learn anything more, be sure to let me know."

"Sure thing," she replied. "Let's keep in touch. Bye."

I hung up the phone and told Ruth the wonderful news. Then I grabbed my camera and headed for the orphanage. Most of the children were in their Sunday afternoon quiet time and were sleeping or quietly reading on their bunks as I slipped through the girl's dorm to Elena's room. I found her lying on her top bunk, staring at the ceiling.

"Elena," I called softly.

"Tata Johnny!" she responded in surprise as she rolled over to face me. "They have found my dad, and guess what. He has repented! He is a believer! Oh, I am so happy! Really, he is born again. Isn't it just so wonderful? Oooh, I can't wait to see him! Just think, Tata Johnny, it has been five years! Why, that's nearly half of my life! You'll come along when we go visit him, won't you?" she asked.

"I sure would love to go with you to visit your father," I said. "This will really be exciting!"

"Yes," responded Elena, "but I think I am a little bit scared too."

In the days that followed, the wonderful news traveled throughout the community and all the way to America. Nelu, the lost father, had been found!

Chapter 7

The Meeting

I entered the neatly kept courtyard through the green garden gate. "Come on, boys," I urged Gheorghe, Costel, Marian, and Costică who were hanging back just a bit. I had invited these boys to go with me to visit a handicapped neighbor, Dumitru. The door to the small cottage opened before I could knock. Dumitru's sister Maria offered me her hand and bid us enter.

"Take your shoes off here," I instructed the boys.

"That's not necessary," protested Maria. "Please enter."

We were standing in the small cubicle that served as the vestibule and storage area for the house. To the left was a kitchen equipped with a wood-burning cookstove and a couch which opened into a bed. From the kitchen doorway an elderly woman greeted us graciously. She appeared to be in her upper seventies, and it was obvious that her life had not been an easy one. I knew from previous visits that she was Dumitru's mother and had been a widow for many years. Placing our shoes neatly along the wall, we accepted the invitation to enter the only other room in the house.

Dumitru was lying in his bed but raised his hand in welcome, and a big smile creased his face. He was genuinely happy to see us. I grasped his hand and bent to greet him with the kiss of charity. Immediately his questions were about my health, my wife, and my children. "And the orphanage?" he continued. "Are these the boys from the orphanage?"

"Well," I replied with a chuckle, "these certainly aren't all of them, but yes, these are some of the boys from the orphanage. I was passing by and thought I'd stop in for a visit. Only Gheorghe has visited you before."

Dumitru placed his hand behind his head and raised it slightly off the pillow so he could see Gheorghe better. "Ah, yes," he said. "I believe this young man was here with Brother Ionică a month or so ago."

Gheorghe grinned self-consciously at being singled out.

"Now you boys are going to sing for me, aren't you?" Dumitru asked. "Sure you will," he encouraged them.

Costel and Costică shrugged, but Marian and Gheorghe nodded in agreement. Soon our voices blended together in that wonderful hymn of adoration, "How Great Thou Art!" Dumitru couldn't help but sing along with us.

"Boys, do you know how great our God really is?" Dumitru asked. "God looked down in His love and allowed an accident to happen to me, and after I couldn't walk anymore or even get out of bed, He reached down with His great mercy and saved me from my ungodly life. Isn't that wonderful? If He hadn't allowed this accident, I believe I would still be lost and headed for hell. Yes, He is great, and God has been so good to me.

"What are you boys going to be when you get big?" asked Dumitru, looking from one young visitor to the next. "Here," he instructed, "step over this way so I can see your faces. That's better. Now what do you want to be when you get big?" he asked again.

"I don't know what I want to be," answered Costel, shuffling a bit. "Maybe a farmer."

"I think I want to drive a tractor," Gheorghe said.

"I want to drive a big truck," Costică said.

"And you?" asked Dumitru, pointing his only arm toward Marian.

"I think I'd like to work in a woodshop," he responded.

"Now, boys," said Dumitru. "In all of your work, and whatever you do in life, be sure you follow Jesus. You see," he continued, "that is what really makes life worth living. What would my life be worth if I didn't have Jesus living in my heart?"

The boys opened up and began talking to Dumitru about school, the farm, their pets, and their hobbies. Then Costică asked, "What's that?" and pointed to a twenty-inch disc near the head of Dumitru's bed.

"Come up here and I'll show you," Dumitru invited.

Costică moved up to the head of the bed and looked at the opposite side of the disc.

"Now what do you see?" Dumitru asked.

"Why, it's a big mirror!" Costică answered in surprise. The other boys crowded up to the head of the bed.

"And what do you boys see?" asked Dumitru.

"I see the road with big trucks and cars," responded Costică as he squinted into the mirror.

"Yes, and there goes a tractor too," added Gheorghe, pointing at the mirror.

"So, which one of you boys is smart enough to figure out how I use this mirror?" asked Dumitru.

"I think I know," volunteered Marian. "When you are lying in bed, you can look into this mirror and see who is passing along on the road."

"You're right," smiled Dumitru. "But did you notice," he nodded toward the mirror, "that it's not flat like other mirrors? It's convex. This allows me to see a much larger area than normal. I can see the villagers as they walk up and down the village street past my house, and I wave to them as they go by. Sometimes I can see the big blue van from your orphanage drive past on the national highway. I know you can't see me, but it warms my heart just to know that some of God's servants are passing by."

"Dumitru," I said as I drew close to his bed, "we need to be going, but we would like to pray with you before we go."

"Please do," he invited.

We gathered close about his bed and prayed, thanking God for this opportunity to be together and receive spiritual encouragement.

One by one we bid Dumitru goodbye and prepared to leave. As we exited the vestibule, Maria stood just outside the door. She thanked us for coming and said, "It means so much to Dumitru when brothers come to visit him. You have been an encouragement to him today."

"No, Maria," I protested, "it is always I who receive encouragement whenever I visit your brother."

Maria said goodbye, smiled, and reached out to shake my hand. I read surprise and gratitude in her eyes as she felt the rolled-up bill pressed into her palm. "This is something God wants you to have," I explained. Tears threatened to overflow as she tried to thank me. I turned quickly and joined the boys in the waiting van.

We drove farther along the narrow village street, and I found a place to turn around. Then we headed back past Dumitru's house. I drove slowly as the boys crowded to the windows. "I saw him! I saw him!" shouted Costică. "I saw him waving to me in his mirror!"

The boys were quiet for several minutes and then Costel asked, "Tata Johnny, what kind of accident did he have?" The boys leaned forward.

"Well," I began, "some years before Dumitru became a believer, he was coming home on a train one afternoon and had to change trains at one of the stations. There he met up with an old friend. His friend was so happy to see him that he offered to buy him a drink. At first Dumitru protested. He didn't want anything to drink. But his friend insisted—one drink just for old time's sake, and they went into the bar together. One drink led to another and then another. By the time Dumitru's train was ready to leave, he was no longer steady on his feet. He staggered out to the train just as it began to pull out of the station. Dumitru thought he could jump onto the moving train, but he missed his step and was flung under the wheels. His right arm was severed at the shoulder, and both of his legs were rendered useless."

"Do you mean," interrupted Costel, "that he can use only one arm and nothing else?"

"That's right," I explained. "In that one moment Dumitru became totally dependent upon others for the rest of his life. That was twenty-seven years ago."

There was a gasp from the boys.

"Maria and his mother have been at his bedside constantly throughout all those years. They have bathed him, changed him, and fed him. He can do nothing for himself. Instead of getting married, Maria has dedicated herself to caring for her brother. Through all these hardships she has never complained or become bitter. And as you could see for yourselves, Dumitru is happy in the Lord and is a challenge to all who visit him. Ionică told me once that Dumitru knows the Bible so well that many people have come to him with their questions. He is able to point out in the Bible where to find the answers they are seeking."

As we neared the orphanage, Marian said, "I'm glad you took us to see Dumitru. The next time you visit him, I want to go along."

"Me too," chorused the others.

Early Saturday morning Alvin, Lil, Silvia, my wife, and I packed into the big Suburban, along with the four very excited Bițica children. We hoped and prayed that today, after five long years of separation, they would finally be able to see their father. We didn't know if they would be allowed to speak directly with him or not. However, we encouraged them to bring their personal photo albums to show their father, just in case.

Evangelist Nicu Cotleț had worked with the prison officials to arrange for a possible meeting. However, since we were not sure the meeting would be permitted, we thought it best not to notify Mr. Bițica that four of his children had been found and would be coming to visit.

Silvia sat in the back of the Suburban and talked to the children as we traveled.

"What is it going to be like to see your daddy again?" she asked. The children mostly shrugged and said little. She knew their emotions were confused, so she tried to prepare them. The last time they had seen their father, his hands had been bloody and their mother dead. Now, five years later, they were to meet him, and though they had been told that he had repented, their little hearts were still plagued with unanswered questions.

"Vasilica," probed Silvia, "what are you going to tell your daddy if you get to speak with him today?"

A slow smile spread over eight-year-old Vasilica's features. "Tanti Silvia," she answered, "I am going to hug him and tell him that I love him and have forgiven him and that Jesus loves him and has forgiven him too."

Tears stung Silvia's eyes. The Lord looked down from heaven and smiled. "Except ye be converted, and become as little children, ye shall not enter into the kingdom of heaven."

After driving nearly three hours, we arrived at the prison gates where we met Nicu Cotleț. It was not at all what we had envisioned. It turned out to be a prison hospital where inmates from various penitentiaries were sent when they contracted a serious disease while serving their sentences. We were informed that Nelu Bițica had been diagnosed with tuberculosis and transferred to this hospital prison for treatment.

Papers and passports were carried to and fro as we waited outside the locked prison gate. Finally the gate was opened and we were asked to park inside the prison enclosure near the office. A guard then ushered us into the commandant's spacious office, where we were welcomed and shown to a couch and chairs on the far side of the room. The commandant was a large man of military bearing and wore the regulation blue uniform of a prison official. He sat behind his massive desk, completing some paperwork as we entered. An attendant stood at attention near the door as we talked, watched, and waited. The commandant caught the attendant's eye and gave a slight nod, and the attendant immediately left the office. The commandant ordered glasses of orange drink served to the children, who seemed tense. He tried to thaw the apprehensive atmosphere while the minutes ticked slowly by.

The door opened. A trim, dark prisoner hesitantly entered, wearing a prisoner's uniform of olive green with bright blue stripes sewn to its sides. He glanced nervously toward us before focusing his full attention on the large man seated behind the massive desk. A hush filled the room.

No one spoke. Again the prisoner glanced at us, then back at the commandant. Suddenly the prisoner's head snapped in our direction and he stared hard and long. Recognition dawned as he mentally added the changes of the missing years. Then his features melted as he doubled over and buried his face in his hands. His wail rent the stillness of that room and pierced our hearts. He wept there alone in the middle of that great room, his shoulders heaving as sobs wracked his body.

I glanced down at Elena, his oldest. "Go," I said. "Go meet your father."

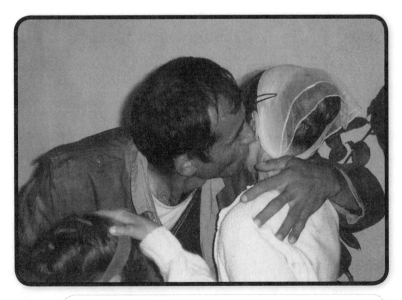

Elena meets her dad in prison for the first time.

Slowly, as though in a daze, Elena walked to where her father stood sobbing uncontrollably. Nelu Biţica sensed her presence and straightened. He threw his arms about his daughter and crushed her to his chest as though he had done it many times in his dreams. Then, cupping his rough hands about her tender face, he kissed her over and over again until her face was wet with his kisses and with their mingled tears. Looking deeply into her eyes, he cried, "Elena! Oh, Elena!" as tears coursed down his cheeks. Then he crushed her to him again.

Silvia urged the rest of the children to go to their father, and they stood beside Elena. Vasilica threw her arms about her father's neck and buried her face in his shoulder. Clinging to him, she whispered into his ear. Nelu Biţica cupped her tear-stained face in his hands and kissed her again and again. "Vasilica! My little Vasilica!" he said as if he couldn't believe his own eyes.

Ştefania had been only two years old when this tragedy had occurred. Her memories were vague. Was this man really her father? Would he remember her? She stood lost in a world of swirling action and sweeping emotions. But her father hadn't forgotten. He opened his arms for her to come and hugged her over and over. He kissed her fondly, smoothed back the hair from her forehead, and cried, "My baby! Oh, my baby Ştefania!"

Ten-year-old Marian stood there quietly, taking it all in. Then his father turned to him. "Oh, Marian," he groaned. "My son!" And he hugged him for a long moment and kissed him, first on one cheek and then on the other, while his tears flowed afresh.

I had to get pictures of this reunion! Blinking the tears from my eyes, I readied my camera as I moved close to the commandant's desk. With my eyes riveted on the scene before me, I asked the commandant if I could possibly take photos, but he didn't respond. I repeated my request, knowing that I didn't dare take photos without explicit permission. "Sir, may I please take photos?" I repeated in desperation. When he still made no response, I tore my gaze from the scene and looked directly at the commandant. Despite his military bearing, the commandant was having a hard time of it. He swallowed hard and looked at me through tear-filled eyes and nodded his assent.

The children stood close beside their father as the rest of us blew our noses and wiped our eyes. The commandant stood and ordered the attendant to allow Mr. Biţica and his children to spend time together in the courtyard instead of in the normal wire-meshed, guarded visiting cubicles. We were ushered into the mess hall where coarse food was being served. There we met and spoke with numerous inmates while the Biţica family became reacquainted. The other inmates seemed to know Mr. Biţica's history. They seemed to respect him and appeared genuinely happy that we had brought his children to visit him.

The children couldn't get done telling their father all about life at the orphanage. They showed him their album pictures of the orphanage, their friends, their sponsors, the cows, horses, chickens, sheep, rabbits, pigeons, and even Papagal. They talked about the Nathaniel Church and the people who worshiped there. Elena, Vasilica, and Marian told him how they loved to sing in the Little Choir and sang "Jesus Loves Me" to their father, first in Romanian and then in English. They quoted poems they had learned in school and told him of many important incidents in their lives.

Nelu Biţica took it all in like a starving man while he feasted his eyes hungrily upon the little family nestled about him on the lush grass of the prison courtyard. Tomorrow they would be gone and he would be alone once more. Thirteen more long, weary years. But his newfound life in Christ would supply him with the grace he needed to meet those years, one day at a time.

Nicu Cotleţ announced that we had permission to conduct a short program for the inmates. We gathered with seventy prisoners in a large room readied for that purpose and began singing. We quickly discovered that seventy untrained, gruff, all-male voices singing unfamiliar hymns in unison left much to be desired. Silvia suggested that the Biţica children sing, but they were reluctant to do so until Silvia offered to stand with them and help get them started. The message of God's love, sung by the tender, angelic voices of these innocent children, and the knowledge of the tragedy that had shattered their lives touched that roomful of hardened prisoners, and they began to weep. Seeing and hearing these precious children awakened suppressed longings in their own souls to be with their families again. They saw forgiveness written in the hearts of this little group singing before them, and it crushed them with a longing to have that kind of forgiveness from their own children, whom they, too, had deeply wronged. The sound of grown men sobbing, mingled with the children's innocent singing, was almost more than we could bear.

At the end of the service we urged the men to write their families and ask them to forgive them for the wrongs they had committed and try to reconnect broken family ties.

Then it was time to leave. We gathered to tell Nelu Biţica goodbye. His children stood close beside him, reluctant to leave. Prison officials watched with open interest from a respectful distance. Several spoke with the children. I embraced Brother Nelu and said, "I realize that you will not be able to care for your children personally. But I want to assure you that, as director of the Nathaniel Christian Orphanage, I will, by God's grace, do my utmost to care for them in your absence, even as I would care for my own."

Nelu kissed me on both cheeks and said with a noticeable catch in his voice, "Thank you, and may God richly reward you for helping my children!"

Our emotions had climbed to such heights and we had so much to think upon that our homeward journey was filled with long stretches of complete silence. Finally, Silvia began asking the children about their day. "So, Vasilica, what did you say to your father when you met him?" she asked.

Without hesitation Vasilica responded, "I told him that I love him and have forgiven him and that Jesus loves him and has forgiven him too."

On Wednesday evening, when it was time for prayer requests, a thin hand shot up and a sweet voice implored, "Please pray for my daddy that he will remain faithful."

Oh, what faith, what forgiveness, what powerful love!

Chapter 8

Spring Joy

The building to house the Teaching Ministries Program was nearing completion. One of our trusted workers had brought us word of a property half a mile from the orphanage that had unexpectedly come up for sale when its owner died. Family members who lived in the capital wanted to quickly dispose of this old village home, which was situated on a large vacant lot right along the main thoroughfare. CAM had purchased the property, drawn up plans, obtained permits, and begun work.

Numerous volunteers had helped frame and roof a building nearly as large as the orphanage itself. Its upper floor would be used for Gospel literature translation and offices. Lamp and Light Publishers' Bible correspondence courses would go into circulation as soon as they could be translated into Romanian. Half of the lower level would provide storage for Bibles and Gospel literature.

The Nathaniel store would use the other half, which was within easy access of the street. Here we would sell milk and ice cream from the dairy, as well as bread and pastries from our bakery. The old German-style house would be adapted to accommodate families coming to help with the work.

On Tuesday evening we gathered at the Burdujeni train station. Numerous well-wishers were on hand to meet the incoming 10:30 train. Willis and Esther Bontrager with their two younger sons, Aaron and Andy, were returning from their six-week medical leave in the

States. We were so grateful that our prayers for Brother Willis's health had been wonderfully answered. We were overjoyed to hear that an operation had not been necessary. His condition had improved to the point that, with medication, he would be able to resume his pastoral duties and direct the Gospel literature department and Teaching Ministries Program for CAM in Romania.

Willis and Esther's three older children had returned to Romania several weeks earlier and were on hand to welcome the rest of their family. We waited impatiently, repeatedly glancing down the tracks toward Bucureşti. The church youth were there, as well as a number of children from the orphanage.

Venders pushed their way through the crowd, trying to sell handmade wooden spoons and fruit bowls. Beggars asked for handouts, and drunks tried to engage us in religious conversation. But our preoccupation with the incoming train left us with little interest for anything else. Marius, who was standing dangerously near the tracks, shouted, "Here she comes!" And sure enough, locomotive headlights could be seen in the distance. A worried adult cautioned those standing nearest the tracks to please step back.

We were strung out in a loose group as the train rolled in. We waved and craned our necks to look into the windows of each compartment as it flashed by.

"There they are!" shouted someone above the sound of the screeching brakes, and the entire crowd surged toward the slowing train. The train came to a complete stop, the doors burst open, and the train began disgorging its people and baggage. We gathered around wagon five. Through the windows we could see the Bontragers struggling with multiple large suitcases and trying to wave to us. Willing hands reached up to help as they passed their baggage through the train's open door. Finally the Bontragers emerged to the welcoming embraces of family. At last they were home!

Saturday dawned calm and still, but there was excitement in the air. Today Paul Yoder was going to help us cover the greenhouse with plastic. Working with careful patience among the fascinated children, he tied small pieces of wood to heavy cords and threw them over the steel framework. These cords were carefully fastened to the two waiting sheets of plastic, which were gently coaxed up and over the framework with assistance from several long poles and many willing hands along the way. The plastic was stretched tight and locked into the channel which ran all around the perimeter of the building, and the excess plastic was trimmed away. By evening the greenhouse looked finished, though there was much to do before it would be ready for the seedlings waiting to be transferred from the bakery garage.

The following Tuesday I welcomed Ionică and Vali (the orphanage treasurer) into my office for our morning meeting. Our main topic was the shipment of bicycles that had just arrived in the Pătrăuți warehouse. A youth group from Pennsylvania had labored to provide fifteen new, blue and white Schwinn bicycles for the orphanage children. What a gift!

"Which children will get them?" I asked.

"Well," said Vali, "I'm sure all the children would love to have one, but we have more than three times as many children as we have bikes."

"I was wondering if we couldn't come up with some plan that would put an incentive before the children," said Ionică thoughtfully. "If we don't, I'm afraid the children will not appreciate or take good care of the bikes."

"We don't have much time," I observed. "They will be delivered this afternoon."

"I think once we have them all assembled, we should lock them in the bakery garage. Then, after the children have earned the privilege, we will allow them to have the bikes," said Ionică. "How would it be if we set a small price—say, five dollars for each bike? Then two children could work to earn that amount and share the ownership of that bike."

"I like that idea," said Vali. "But don't you think it would be good to establish some rules before we turn them loose with bikes? Just think of the bumped heads and skinned knees from fifteen bikes whizzing around here and wrecking into each other. We will continually be taking the children to the hospital to have them patched up."

And so we decided to establish road rules for all bicycle operators and issue permits after they had passed a driver's examination. Ionică would be in charge of writing the laws and issuing the tests. Vali would collect the token payments from the children and make out titles for the new owners.

"Mama Ruth, Mama Ruth!" shouted Daniel as he ran down the drive, "I need a job for money. Do you have any jobs for me?"

"What's going on?" asked Ruth as Daniel drew near. "Suddenly everyone is asking me for work!"

"Because," answered ten-year-old Daniel, "we need bicycles, and Nenea Ionică said we have to pay for them. I have to make some money. Mama Ruth, did you see the bicycles up in the bakery garage? Are they ever pretty! And they are brand new!"

"I'll tell you what," said Ruth. "I have a storage closet under the steps. If you will clean that out and organize it, I will pay you fifty cents."

"All right!" said Daniel enthusiastically. "It's a deal!"

"Tata Johnny," pleaded Iliuță as he walked into my office, "do you have any work for me? How about down at the greenhouse? It's almost done, and I could sift some more dirt for you."

"I suppose you may if you stay out of Steve's way. He's hooking up the breaker panel and lights today, but if you keep your sifting operation at the far end, I think you should do fine. Get the screen from the bakery garage, but don't mix the sand with the dirt yet; I want to be there when you mix it."

"Can Costică help me?" Iliuță asked, looking out for his younger brother.

"Sure. Sifting goes best with two workers," I answered.

"I know—one to shake the screen, and one to shovel the dirt. How much are you going to pay us?" he asked. "We have to make enough to buy a bike."

"Let's see how you work, and I'll pay you accordingly," I responded.

Soon Ionela dropped by and asked if she could help sift soil in the greenhouse, but I explained that I had already given that task to the boys and we would have to find something else for her to do. I suggested that Mama Ruth might have a job for her. Later as I passed our house on the way to check up on the soil-sifting operation, I noticed Ionela happily washing windows. The atmosphere was so pleasant when the children were busy.

Sunday services often included children's presentations. This Sunday was no different. Following the Sunday school lesson, a group of children gave a mini program. They appeared to enjoy participating. At a prompt from Tanti Valentina, their childish voices swelled in beautiful harmony.

With longing we await the day of the Lord.
What a wonderful day, what a wonderful day!
There will be no more tears, only happiness there.
What a wonderful day, what a wonderful day!

Two ten-year-old girls trilled their high tenor, blending perfectly with the altos and sopranos. Younger children stopped fidgeting and stood on the benches beside their mothers to get a better view. The entire congregation spontaneously picked up the chorus and sang along. We couldn't help it; they just made us want to join them. The auditorium rang.

Oh, wonderful day, and how beautiful 'twill be,
When in heaven our Jesus we shall see.
Oh, wonderful day! Oh, happy the day,
When Jesus comes for His children!

The song ended and each of the children quoted a stanza of a poem from memory. The listeners smiled in love and appreciation. Marta, our tiniest girl, stood close to the mike, and in her sweet, clear voice shyly quoted the final verse. The program ended and the children resumed their seats.

Brother Willis fixed his gaze on the orphanage children occupying the first four benches on either side of the church. "Children, have you ever thought about what you would like to become when you grow up? You are growing, and you need to be thinking about this. Tell me, what would you like to be when you get big?"

There was a moment of silence, and then three hands shot into the air at once, followed by several more. All of them were waving to attract Brother Willis's attention.

"Ştefania," said Willis, acknowledging her spindly arm, "what would you like to be when you get big?"

"I'm going to be a doctor," she announced emphatically. I noticed several workers nodding at one another and grinning. They no doubt were remembering how hard they had struggled in coaxing Ştefania to eat. Hopefully she would major in nutrition.

"Very good," said Willis. "Then you can help sick people get well."

Glancing at our thin Gypsy girl, Willis acknowledged her hand and asked, "Yes, Florica, and what are you going to be when you grow up?"

Still waving her hand gracefully aloft with fluid motions as though she were conducting a chorus, Florica responded, "I want to be a choir director."

If a natural talent for singing counted, then Florica had a good start toward fulfilling her desire. Even though she had come to us at only five years old, her Gypsy culture had endowed her with a talent for music.

Several other hands were acknowledged. One wanted to be a forester while another desired to become a seamstress.

Gabi's hand was acknowledged. He hesitated and then blurted out, "I want to be a farm worker." As a little abandoned boy, Gabi had roamed the hills with the village animals. Very possibly those experiences had given him a deeper appreciation for farm animals.

Finally only one lonely hand remained raised. "Yes, Gigi, and what do you want to become when you get big?" asked Willis.

Little Gigi rose to his feet before the entire congregation with an air of importance belying his eight years and lisped his desire through his missing front teeth. "When I get big," he said with all seriousness, "I want to be a sponther."

Gigi had been rescued from a cradle orphanage at the request of an attending psychologist. He greatly appreciated the important role of a sponsor and wanted to help others even as he had been helped. The simple, honest heart of a child amazed me once again.

On Sunday evening there was no church service planned, and usually on such evenings we gathered in the orphanage living room for a story and singing. On this particular evening the weather was wet and dreary.

"Children, what would you like to do this evening?" I asked before dismissing them from the supper tables in the dining room. "Do you want to meet in the living room for singing and a story?"

"Let's go to your house!" shouted Mariana above the din.

"Yes, let's!" chorused a number of voices enthusiastically. "We want to sing at your house!" echoed several others. I looked questioningly at Ruth, and she smiled and nodded her approval. That was permission enough, and we made plans for the children to spend their evening in our tiny house. Even the childcare workers, cooks, and staff wanted to come.

At seven o'clock they all trooped down to our house through the drizzle. They entered the kitchen and removed their shoes, according to Romanian custom. In all, there were sixty-two pairs of shoes on our linoleum, and I wondered how they would all find their rightful owners when the time came for the children to return to the orphanage.

We gathered in the twelve-by-eighteen-foot living room of our little gray house. There wasn't nearly enough room for all to find seats, so we invited the adult workers and staff to sit on our sofa and chairs, and the smaller children nestled on their laps or sat on the arms of the chairs. A number of children chose to watch from the vantage point of the open staircase. The rest found seats on the living room floor. When all had found seats, there was no place left to walk and the singing began. What a singing it was! The children sang to their hearts' content! Their sweet voices filled our hearts with love even as they filled our house with harmony.

The beauty of those Romanian hymns touched our hearts as the children gave out selections two and three at a time: "Precious Jesus, I Want to Be Your Child," "He Builds Not on the Sand Who Builds With Faith," "Hear the Voice That Is Calling You," "My Heart Overflows With Unspeakable Joy," and many other old favorites of theirs. Finally, when we were all sung out, Ruth served a large tin of crunchy pretzels from Pennsylvania and individual cans of fruit juice which some thoughtful person had sent on a recent shipment from the States. From then until nearly bedtime we simply enjoyed talking together

Vasilica, Ida Jane, and Caroline join in the
singing at the little gray house.

like one big, happy family. Finally we stood for prayer, committing
these precious souls into the hands of our loving heavenly Father.

After the last of our great family had left for their dorms, I walked into
the kitchen and marveled that every last shoe had found its owner.

The following week our custodian, Aurel Ionese, painted bright
yellow directional arrows on all the sidewalks to indicate the bicycle
traffic pattern. Working for money became a top priority among the
children, and the ten bicycle safety rules were duly memorized and
recited to Ionică, who then quizzed the children on the meaning of
these rules. Cycling permits were issued to all who passed the test.
Any driver violating these rules or driving recklessly would be subject
to having his permit revoked for up to one week.

Vali drafted fifteen official-looking ownership titles. Evenings were
spent watching caravans of bikes circling the orphanage sidewalks
and driveway. I was so glad for the wisdom of planning out the routes
ahead of time. Even so, pedestrians had to take care.

A week after earning his permit, Manu was enjoying an evening ride on his new Schwinn. He loved the ease with which he could take the corners. Effortlessly he rode clockwise around the orphanage, carefully following the yellow arrows. Then he cycled on around the school building, making a huge figure eight. Earlier he had seen Nenea Ionică's car pull out through the gate and head toward town. Now he stood up and really began to pump, building speed. Then he sat down, leaned to take the corner, and whizzed out past the orphanage building and into the parking area. He loved the feel of the cool wind in his face.

Then Manu took a notion to see what it would be like to cycle around the orphanage the wrong way. After all, no one else was riding and it really wouldn't be dangerous. So away he went! The yellow arrows, pointing in the opposite direction, flew under his wheels. This was fun! He rounded the orphanage and shot out into the parking lot again, but gave a start, for there was Nenea Ionică's car coming through the gate!

Manu wondered if he had been seen, but he didn't have to wonder long.

"Manu," called Ionică as he strode from his car, "bring me your permit!"

"But . . . but . . ." sputtered Manu. "I thought you had gone home!"

"Just give me your permit and park your bike in the bakery garage. Be sure that you do not ride it again until you have your permit back," he warned. "Remember also that rules apply even when I am not here."

Manu hung his head. Why had he followed that crazy impulse?

Steve declared the greenhouse ready for occupancy. Eager boys and girls poured into the greenhouse to help. Several girls filled new flats and planted them with broccoli, cabbage, and cauliflower. Others were in charge of planting flower seeds to beautify the orphanage's many flower beds. Several of the boys took over transporting the flats of immature plants from the bakery garage to the new greenhouse. Wagonload after wagonload of carefully loaded Styrofoam cups and flats of seedlings were wheeled to the new greenhouse and placed on the raised stands occupying nearly a third of the structure.

Franklin, with the help of Nicu and Ionuț, took charge of finely tilling half of the greenhouse soil where the tomatoes were to be transplanted. Iosif and his brother Daniel deftly transplanted two hundred tomato plants in the rows I made to receive them. These plants would grow clipped to vertical twines supported by overhead cables and would be fed with fertilizer-laced water. We also prepared beds on the opposite side of the greenhouse to receive our cucumber plants just as soon as they were large enough for transplanting.

Children came by the droves to see our interesting little garden under its plastic dome. Most of them not only offered to help, but begged to be allowed to assist with the planting process. There is something so basic about children working with the soil and plants. It seems to touch something deep within them, as though they are being allowed to help God make things grow. The children had already experienced this with their assigned plots in our spacious flower beds along the front of the orphanage. Now we were experiencing a new dimension with the addition of the greenhouse.

Weeks sped by and our tomato plants grew at a tremendous rate.

"Tata Johnny, look!" cried Elena, who had wandered into the greenhouse as I was watering the plants. "Here is a baby tomato!"

Sure enough, she had discovered the first tomato growing in our new greenhouse. Soon there were hundreds of young tomatoes. They looked like miniature green faces peeping from beneath their yellow sunbonnets at the Nathaniel children. Tiny cucumbers were found swinging from their supported vines as well. The children felt compelled to finger them to see if they were real. Watching things grow is a balm to the human soul.

The head veterinarian of our *judeţ* (county) brought a prominent senator from the central government in Bucureşti to visit our orphanage. He came with several undersecretaries and attendants. Ionică and I were happy to give them a tour of our facilities and tell them about the wonders of our Nathaniel family. We began in the living room and showed them the fifty-five children's photos lining the walls.

"Allow me to introduce you to the Ciocan family. This is Manu, the oldest," I said, pointing out the photos, "and here is his sister Daniela. Their loving mother died of cancer, and their father was unable to care for his younger children without her. They came to be a part of our family here. Theirs was a Christian home with both father and mother being believers, and these children have a heart for God. They are also studious. This little fellow here," I said, pointing to another photo, "is their younger brother Adi.

"Over here," I indicated, "is Ovidiu, who has no brothers or sisters here. His mother and father died within three months of each other. His teenaged sisters tried to raise him, but they were so poor they found it impossible to provide for him. We welcomed him into our family about a year ago. He's a quiet boy and one who is willing to be taught.

"Then we have the Biţica family who needed a home after their father murdered their mother and was taken away to prison," I explained. Questions were asked as I pointed out the three little girls and their serious, fine-featured brother. I thought I saw a hint of tears glistening in the senator's eyes as I told them the story and described the scene of these children meeting their father after being separated for five years.

"And how is it now between the children and their father?" asked the senator.

"The children write to their father, and it is always special when he writes a response from prison," I answered. "They constantly remind him to remain faithful to the Lord."

Next I pointed out the photo of Beti, the little girl with unruly hair framing her round face and wide-set, dark eyes. "Beti," I explained, "was found roaming the streets when she wasn't quite four years old. No one knew where her mother was. Beti was hit by a car and wound up in a hospital. From there she went to live for a time with the family of the driver who hit her. Then she ended up coming to live with us."

We gave our visitors a tour of the dining room, kitchen, dorms, and the school. On our way to the farm we pointed out the new greenhouse. Both the veterinarian and senator showed interest and asked if they could look inside. I explained the useful function of the double-layered plastic and the small fan which maintained pressure between the layers. I pointed out the insulation value of those three inches of air. They were impressed not only with the mechanics of the greenhouse, but also with the lush, healthy plants.

Finally we ushered our guests down to the farm, where Alvin Stoltzfus took over and showed them our feed-making facilities, the donated cows that had been flown over from America, and the milk-processing laboratory. "Our dairy provides milk free of charge to fourteen orphanages and several church groups," he explained. The veterinarian and the senator exchanged glances and nodded approvingly. "But even more important," continued Alvin, "the orphanage boys are able to work right here beside us on the farm and learn many valuable life principles. We feel this will help them as they mature and eventually begin life on their own. Along with this is the opportunity to let them see the love of Jesus in action. We trust this will help them choose a godly direction in life."

Alvin wrapped up the farm tour with an invitation to gather in the orphanage dining room to try out a bowl of our farm-produced ice cream. We sat around the table discussing the orphanage, the farm, the children, and the Romanian government as we savored the delicious ice cream.

As the visit came to an end and our guests prepared to depart, they thanked us for the work we were doing to help these Romanian children. Then the senator said, "I sit on the Finance Committee. If I can ever be of assistance to you, please feel free to call on me."

Giving Directions

In working day in and day out with the Nathaniel children, we got to know their individual personalities quite well. As the children grew, it became a greater challenge to defuse tense situations or discipline the unruly. It also made us look for new and better ways to correct wrongdoing and guide their feet in a heavenly direction.

Florica had been giving us ongoing problems with her tongue. When others made her angry, she often responded by speaking horribly about them and at times even calling them vile names. Silvia had long talks with Florica, pleading with her to control her feelings and think before she spoke. She urged Florica to tame her tongue. I, too, had spoken with Florica concerning this problem; however, the problem persisted because she thought it was perfectly all right to say exactly what she felt.

One evening we had visitors who had just arrived from the States. We were visiting around the supper table at our little gray house as dessert was being served. Just then a call came over the intercom. "Tata Johnny," said our night-duty worker, Tanti Tatiana, "you must come up right away. Florica is very angry and completely out of control. She talks without thinking and is speaking disrespectfully against God."

"Okay, Tatiana. Have Florica sit in the conference room till I get there. I'll be up in a few minutes."

I could see no way to handle the situation without leaving my wife stranded with our guests, so I said, "I hope you folks can forgive me. I'm not sure how long this will take. Knowing Florica, this could take several hours." Our guests were understanding and forgiving, though my wife threw me an imploring look as I headed for the door.

I contemplated as I walked across the lawn in the darkness. How should I deal with Florica and her ongoing problem? She was getting too big to spank, and besides, spankings had never seemed to help her. She had been asked to wash out her own mouth with soap on occasion, but that hadn't helped either. *Dear Lord,* I prayed, *guide me with wisdom to help Florica.*

I entered the conference room and found Florica seated on a low stool. A sullen expression covered her dark complexion, and her dark eyes shone bright with pent-up anger. I pulled a chair close and sat down beside her. She averted her face with a haughty air and stared fixedly out the window, demonstrating clearly that I was not worthy of her attention.

I sat for awhile without saying anything, and her gaze eventually returned to her hands lying limply in her lap. Finally I broke the silence. "Florica, I am so disappointed in you," I said softly. "You know I am a Christian, and I love the Lord. They tell me you have been speaking disrespectfully of Him. Florica, what is wrong?"

Her head snapped up, and the words fairly flew from her mouth. "Tata Johnny, I didn't curse God. I didn't! They lie!"

"Okay, okay," I said soothingly, "but what you said—did it make Jesus happy?" She dropped her head and stared silently at her hands once more.

"Did it, Florica? Did it make Him happy to hear you say those terrible words?"

Her eyes snapped as she faced me and spoke between clenched teeth. "No, it didn't, but they made me so mad! I hate them!"

"You hate them? You really hate your tantis?"

"Yes!" she snapped.

"Florica, let me ask you a question. How much of this hate will you be able to take along to heaven?"

She sat in silence, staring at her hands. I sat quietly, waiting for her to process that thought and respond. The silence grew between us as the minutes ticked slowly by. Finally I reiterated my question.

"How much of this hate can you take along to heaven?"

Stony silence. After quite some time had passed, Florica gave a deep sigh and twisted about on her seat to find a more comfortable position. Her eyes no longer flashed fire. Her anger was abating.

I cleared my throat, and it sounded loud in the stillness of the conference room. "Florica," I said gently, "would you like to say anything more about this?"

For a long moment she was silent. Finally she shook her head, still staring intently at her hands.

In that moment I knew what God would have me do, but still I waited for Florica to say something more. She was silent. Finally I stood and, out of the corner of my eye, saw Florica tense as though she expected some punishment. I turned, knelt beside her, and began to pray aloud. The precious, personal words were for God and Florica alone, and for the battle that was raging in her heart.

The burden of that prayer reached into her soul. When I was finally prayed out, I stood and said softly, "Goodnight, Florica."

She glanced up at me with a look of shocked surprise, as if expecting something more. "Is . . . is that all?" she blurted.

"Yes, Florica, that is all. Goodnight," I repeated as I turned toward the door.

I left Florica in the conference room, still seated on the stool, with much to ponder as I walked down to our house and entered quietly so as not to disturb my sleeping wife and children. Our company had left long before. I was deeply troubled by Florica's failures, but I also felt God's peace resting in my soul.

Several days passed, and Florica seemed drawn closer to me than before. I entertained the hope that her heart had been touched by the finger of God. I prayed that He would help her be an overcomer, and I kept trying to encourage her whenever she dropped in at my office for a chat or I chanced to meet her in the hallway.

Several weeks later Ruth was walking toward the dining room when she heard a commotion. Florica stormed out of the kitchen in a fierce rage, cursing violently. Ruth cringed but stepped right in front of Florica and asked her what was wrong. Florica continued to spout off against the cooks and the tantis.

Ruth slipped her arm around Florica's shoulders and said, "I wonder how your mother would feel if she could hear you talking like this." Ruth knew that Florica's mother had been a believer but had died when Florica was only five years old.

"Do you know, Florica, your mother is in heaven, and my mother is also in heaven. Maybe they have learned to know each other up there and are talking about you."

"Your mother doesn't know me," retorted Florica, her eyes mere slits and her lips pursed into a sullen circle.

"Well," said Ruth, "when I visited my mother before she died, I showed her a picture of you, and I think she remembers. So, while you and I are down here talking about your problem of anger and bad words, they could be up in heaven talking about their daughters. Wouldn't that be something?"

A faint smile flickered over Florica's lips as the thought penetrated the storm clouds of her anger and illumined her heart.

"Mama Ruth, my mom was such a good Christian. I remember her," Florica said as a look of longing filled her eyes. "She prayed for me and talked to me about God. And before she got so sick, she could sing real nice. I like to sing because my mom taught me to love singing."

"My mother loved to sing too," Ruth said. "Perhaps in heaven they are singing together." Florica's face glowed. "But," continued Ruth, her arm still encircling Florica's shoulders, "you have to ask Jesus to help you overcome your anger and the horrible words you are in the habit of saying so that you can go to heaven to be with your mother."

"I will, Mama Ruth, I will," promised Florica. "I will pray and try really hard."

With that promise in her ears and a prayer in her heart, Mama Ruth released Florica who walked on down the hallway with new buoyancy in her step. It was a hope-filled bounce that replaced the heavy tread of anger.

I was sitting at my desk thinking pleasant thoughts about the orphanage children when Nenea Geo marched into my office gripping Leon's collar with his right hand and Costică's with his left.

"Tata Johnny," he said, and I could hear the exasperation in his voice, "these boys are constantly bickering and fighting. When I get them up in the morning, they make cutting remarks against each other. And when I leave their room for just a few moments to wake the other boys, they throw shoes at each other." He shook them roughly, released them with a shove, and turned on his heel. He shot over his shoulder as he left my office, "Take care of them!" And he was gone.

I glanced at Leon first, who was looking down and fingering the corner of my desk. He sniffed loudly but wouldn't meet my gaze. I looked at Costică who gave me a wry grin before dropping his gaze.

"Okay, boys," I said, "what is going on here?"

Leon came to life with plenty to say against his old enemy, Costică. But Costică was just as quick to defend himself against Leon's accusations. Both were talking at once, each trying to tell me his side of the story before the other could finish, and I couldn't begin to understand either of them. They talked faster and faster, louder and louder.

"Hold it right there, boys! Stop!" I commanded.

Reluctantly, they both fell silent.

"Both of you will have a chance to tell me your side of the story, but you need to respect each other. Let the other person say what he has to say, and then you will have your turn. Understand?"

I looked from one to the other. Both boys hung their heads, reluctant to say anything. "Come on," I insisted. "I want to know why you boys aren't getting along. Leon, tell me, what is the problem?"

Leon raised his eyes and glared at me, then at Costică. His lips curled contemptuously as he said, "Go ahead and let Costică talk first; he's just gonna lie anyhow."

I ignored the insult and asked Costică to tell me about the problem between him and Leon.

"Oh, I don't know," said Costică slowly. "He's just always picking on me—"

"Not true!" retorted Leon.

"Hey," I said, "let him finish. Go on Costică."

"Leon always throws his dirty clothes on my bed, and he won't leave the things on my dresser alone," complained Costică.

Leon's head snapped up and his eyes flashed. He took a deep breath and fairly shouted, "That's a big lie! See, I knew you wouldn't tell the truth. You never do!"

"Quiet, Leon!" I commanded. "You will get your turn to speak, but you must be quiet while Costică is talking." Leon looked at the floor, mumbling angrily under his breath.

Eventually I was able to extract the full story from both boys. I soon saw that they were antagonizing each other. How could I make them see that being kind was so much more rewarding than being mean, and that becoming friends was far more enriching than remaining enemies? We discussed their irritations, and I gave practical pointers on how to avoid being offensive to each other. However, Leon and Costică needed something to help them see their need for change. An inspiration hit me.

"Boys," I said, "in English we have a saying we sometimes use when two people have been fighting." Leon and Costică both looked at me wonderingly. "That phrase is, 'kiss and make up.' "

Costică shifted nervously. "What do you mean?" he asked, puzzled.

"I mean that I want you to shake hands, say you are sorry, and kiss each other."

"Oh, no!" said Costică, covering his face with his hands and turning toward the wall.

Leon looked questioningly at me. "You don't mean it, do you?"

"Oh, yes, I do mean it," I said. "You boys have been scrapping with each other for a long time, and we are all tired of it. You need to apologize and ask forgiveness of each other."

"But I'm ashamed to kiss him," said Leon.

"Please, Tata Johnny," begged Costică, "I—I just can't!"

"Oh, I think you can. Now you two just step a little closer and shake hands," I coached. The two offenders took a tentative step toward each other. "Go ahead," I urged. "Now shake hands." Leon waited and Costică offered his hand. Leon momentarily grasped it.

"I'm sorry," mumbled Costică averting his face and staring hard at the floor.

"Come now. That's no apology. I want you to look each other directly in the face and really apologize."

The boys shook hands and gave passable apologies while glancing into each other's eyes.

"Now, I want you to kiss each other," I continued.

"But I already said I would forgive him," said Leon hopefully.

"That won't pass. You need to kiss and make up," I repeated.

Grinning nervously, Costică came closer to Leon, and Leon offered his cheek. Costică planted a light peck on his cheek, and then it was Leon's turn. Costică closed his eyes tightly and waited. Leon took a deep breath and moved closer, but faltered. Finally he made a sudden lunge in Costică's direction. He closed his eyes at the last moment, made a smacking noise, but missed!

"Doesn't count," I said. "Try again."

"Oh, Tata Johnny!" exclaimed Leon in frustration. Costică grinned sheepishly.

"Come on," I prompted. Leon got a determined glint in his eye and took a step toward his old adversary. Costică averted his face slightly. Leon made another lunge and this time planted a legitimate kiss on Costică's cheek. Instantly they both exploded into gales of laughter. They laughed and laughed until the tears rolled down their cheeks, and I laughed until I was wiping my eyes right along with them.

Two days later, Nenea Geo asked me how I had made out with the boys. He told me they had been getting along famously. "What did you do to them?" he asked.

"Oh," I said, smiling as I remembered, "I just told them that they need to kiss and make up." Geo left, shaking his head and looking a bit puzzled.

Following this episode, Leon and Costică got along much better and often came down to find me working in the greenhouse. I showed them how to remove the suckers and unwanted branches from the tomato plants. They loved to help harvest tomatoes together.

Leon and Costică work together in the greenhouse, after their "kiss and make up" event.

We had planted seventeen double rows of peas in the orphanage garden, and they grew lush and tall as they climbed the four-foot chicken wire fencing we had placed between them. I noticed they were just about to bloom and asked Franklin to have several boys help him scatter fertilizer on either side of the pea rows and hoe it in.

"Sure, Dad," replied Franklin. "We'll take care of that for you."

I was planning to be gone for the day, and it felt good to know that Franklin and the orphanage boys could handle this job.

It was late afternoon when I returned, and I strolled down to the garden to see how the boys had gotten along with the fertilizing project.

"We're just finishing the last rows," said Franklin with a smile of satisfaction. "We were hoping to have it all done before you returned."

"Where did you get this fertilizer?" I asked, nudging a partial bag with the toe of my shoe.

"I found it down in the orphanage basement, back in the corner," was his reply.

I reached over and picked up a handful of crystals that had spilled from the bag and examined them closely. I had seen powdered and pelleted fertilizer before, but this was the first time I had ever seen fertilizer in crystal form. Upon impulse I placed one of those crystals on my tongue, and a grave realization dawned upon me. Franklin and his diligent helpers had fertilized our entire crop of peas with pure rock salt! An Old Testament passage pushed relentlessly into my mind. A king had sewn the land of a conquered city with salt so that it could no longer produce crops. What would happen to our peas?

I looked more closely at the bag. It was clearly marked in English with the name of the fertilizer company. Much lower on the bag, I finally found the words "rock salt" in small letters. I explained the situation to our boys, and many hands spent the next hour vigorously scraping the salt-laced soil away from the unsuspecting pea vines lest the coming rain dissolve the salt and destroy our winter's supply of garden peas. Franklin endured a bit of good-natured ribbing, and it didn't help to know that he was not fond of peas. In fact, he normally required several extra glasses of water whenever peas were on the menu. However, we were pleased to witness no ill effects to the peas themselves, and they bore bountifully.

Ruth and I inspected the orphanage basement and saw that it was in dire need of a thorough cleaning and reorganizing. We had been in Romania for nearly a year and a half and had amassed a jumble of canned goods and cleaning supplies.

"It's high time we take everything off the shelves and discard the things that are no longer usable," Ruth said. "Then we'll take an inventory and know exactly what we have on hand."

As much as I didn't want to attack this distasteful task, I knew Ruth was right.

We chose Saturday for our basement cleaning. A number of the children offered their help. Cardboard boxes had turned mushy in the high humidity of our basement, and what a mess they had made! Ruth found eight one-gallon tins of artichokes that were bulging from internal pressure because they were so old that they had spoiled. These the boys opened and carted down behind the barn in their wagons. They threw the spoiled artichokes into the manure pit and pitched the empty tins into the dumpster. They soon returned, pulling their empty wagons behind them and looking for more things to dispose of.

"Johnny," said Ruth, "what is in those boxes way back under the shelves?"

"I'm sure I don't know, but I'll find out," I answered as I got on my knees and tugged at a cardboard box. It disintegrated as I tried to extract it from its hiding place, and out tumbled several one-gallon plastic containers.

"What is it?" asked Ruth as I fished a container out from under the shelving. I brushed the cobwebs from my face as I handed her the jug. "Why, it's Thousand Island salad dressing—a whole gallon of it!" she exclaimed.

"And that's not all," I added. "It looks like there are two cases of the stuff."

"I don't know what to use it for," Ruth added. "Romanians don't like creamy salad dressings, and the children won't eat it, that's for sure. And look here," she continued. "It is way outdated! Open it for me, please."

I dutifully opened it and peeled back the seal. Ruth sniffed it with that expert cooking nose of hers. "It smells all right. I really hate to throw it away, but at the same time I'm afraid to use it. What should we do?" she asked, looking into my face questioningly.

"I know!" I said enthusiastically. "We'll turn it into pork chops!"

"How are you going to do that?" Ruth asked.

"Just watch. I'll show the boys how to top dress the feed for the pigs, and then it won't be wasted, even if it is outdated by several years."

"Hey, Iliuță," I shouted, "park your wagon at the head of the basement steps, and you and Gheorghe come on down. I have something for you to do."

When they arrived, I was dragging the last of the gallon containers from under the shelving, where they no doubt had rested for the past several years.

"What do you want?" asked Gheorghe.

"See these nine jugs of dressing?"

"What is it?" interjected Iliuță.

"It's really old salad dressing that we are afraid to use, and we want to feed it to the pigs. Here is what I want you to do. Load it onto your wagons and take it down to the little animal barn where the pigs are. Stack it in the alleyway against the wall and come back when you are done, okay?"

"Sure," they said in unison as they each grabbed two containers and struggled up the steps.

"Johnny," called Ruth, "can you move these cases of canned chicken up onto the middle shelf? They're too heavy for me."

We made wonderful progress. Several girls were scrubbing the shelving. Others had rags wrapped around brooms and were sweeping cobwebs from the ceiling. Still others were organizing canned goods in neat rows on the shelves. I was kept busy moving heavy things for the ladies.

"Here are a bunch of empty boxes that need to be taken to the dumpster," Ruth said.

"Fine, I'll have the boys take them out as soon as they return from the barn."

"What's taking them so long?" asked Ruth.

"I don't know," I responded. "You know how boys are. They're probably trying to catch sparrows or something."

Ten more minutes passed before Ruth said, "We really need to get these boxes out of our way so we can scrub the floor."

I crumpled several smaller boxes inside the larger ones and carried an armload up the steps. On my second trip I saw my delinquent haulers coming from the direction of the little barn. *Good,* I thought as I headed for the third load of boxes, *they can load up right away and get rid of these boxes for us.*

I dropped the next load of boxes onto the drive and glanced at the approaching boys. Their wagons were not empty, as I had expected, but were filled with one-gallon plastic salad dressing containers. What had they been doing? As the boys pulled their wagons up to me, I noticed to my consternation that every one of those jugs was empty! Instantly, I had visions of gooey, creamy salad dressing in a huge puddle running across the barn floor.

"Boys!" I exclaimed. "What have you done? I told you to stack those jugs along the wall. Where did you dump that stuff?"

"We gave it to the pigs," said Gheorghe innocently.

"You what?" I shouted, my voice rising to match my alarm. "You surely didn't give nine gallons of salad dressing to our four pigs!"

"Sure we did," smiled Iliuţă. "And they liked it very much!"

"Oh, no! We were going to mix just a little with their feed each day! Now I'm afraid they will get sick or maybe even die!"

"But we thought you wanted us to give it to the pigs now," said

Gheorghe apologetically.

"Did they eat all of it?" I asked disbelievingly.

"Every bit," said Iliuţă, grinning. "We stayed to watch."

I instructed the boys to take one of the containers down to Alvin at the farm so he could read the ingredients on the label, and then take the cardboard boxes and the rest of the empty salad dressing containers to the dumpster.

I hurried to the intercom and explained to Alvin what had happened. Alvin in turn called the vet, who reassured us that the worst problem arising from our overzealous feeding program would be a day or two of pig diarrhea.

Live and learn, I said to myself as I went back to helping the ladies in the orphanage basement. With so many willing workers the task was soon completed, and we all marveled at a job well done. The pigs survived their ordeal, and try as I might, I could not detect the slightest hint of Thousand Island flavoring in their pork chops.

Chapter 10

Hot Water and Cold

"Hello. Is this Tata Johnny?" asked the voice on the other end of the line.

"Yes, it is," I answered. "What can I do for you?"

"This is Dan from the Teaching Ministries Program, and I have a request," he said.

"Sure, Dan, how can I help you?"

"Well, about a month ago you had a group of visitors there at the orphanage, and you showed them your new greenhouse, didn't you?"

"Dan, I have lost track of how many people I have shown through our greenhouse."

"I know, but this was different," Dan continued. "These were officials, and one of them was a senator from Bucureşti."

"Okay, I do recall showing a senator and his group around."

"Well, he called and wants me to bring you to meet him at his place of business in Rădăuţi. Can you come?"

"When does he want us to come?" I asked.

"I can pick you up in about fifteen minutes, if that will suit you. I guess he was really impressed with your greenhouse and wants to talk over some possibilities he's been rolling around in his mind."

"I see. Well, I guess I'm free this evening. I'll be ready."

Dan arrived and we were soon on our way to Rădăuţi. As we traveled through the scenic countryside, we dodged an occasional horse-drawn wagon. Several times we gave a wide berth to a child leading the family cow to graze along the berm of the highway. Dan explained that this senator was one of the wealthiest men in northeastern Romania and owned numerous successful businesses throughout the country.

On the outskirts of Rădăuți we approached a large business complex. A guard opened the gate for us to enter. The senator and several attendants appeared from within and welcomed us. We stood in the parking lot through the formal introductions and, after some small talk, were invited to tour the plant with the senator leading the way.

We entered the first spacious room with its high ceiling. This room contained a setup for a bottling operation. The second room was filled with stainless steel pipes, covered vats, huge boilers, and tall, twin condensers with elevated catwalks. Next we were shown a vast warehouse where the entire floor was covered waist deep with shelled corn. The senator then led us to view his fields behind the warehouse.

"Here," he said, "are forty acres of land. When I was in Suceava and saw your greenhouse, I began thinking. If I erect greenhouses on my land, I could heat them with our hot wastewater. You see," he turned and addressed me directly, "every four hours we must dump several tons of hot water from our condensers and bring in fresh water. This cold water is used to cool the distilled alcohol from the boilers. Do you think it is feasible to heat greenhouses with this hot wastewater in order to raise vegetables? If I could raise vegetables, it would provide work for many people and produce nutritious food to sell. What do you think?" he asked.

"You have a wonderful idea there," I agreed. "Any time you can take a waste product and turn it into a salable item, it is certainly worth pursuing."

"Do you think there is enough wastewater to heat several greenhouses?" he wanted to know.

"Yes, I am certain this could be done. However, you might want to plan for some type of backup heat just in case the need should arise. It only takes several hours of freezing temperatures in a greenhouse to lose an entire crop."

We discussed the senator's plan at length. Finally my curiosity got the best of me and I asked, "Sir, what is it that you actually make here in your business?"

With obvious pride he replied, "Here we produce the finest medicinal alcohol in the entire country."

"I see," I replied innocently. "Then the rows of large brown bottles near the bottling machine in the first room were waiting to be filled with medicinal alcohol?"

"Oh, no," the senator replied. "That is the bottler for drinking alcohol, which we also produce."

"What percent of your finished product is for medical purposes?" I asked.

"Three percent of our alcohol production goes for medical purposes," was his ready response.

"But that must be terribly discouraging," I said.

"Why? What makes you say that?" he asked, trying to read the expression on my face.

"Well," I answered cautiously, "only three percent of your production is to make people well, and ninety-seven percent is to make them ill. That certainly must be discouraging."

The senator gazed down at the ground and began absently pushing the gravel around with the toe of his shoe. I couldn't help but notice the grin on Dan's face as we waited for the senator's response.

"Well," he said, lifting his head and changing the subject, "how many greenhouses do you suppose we could heat with our wastewater?"

"That depends whether you are planning to run the greenhouses year round or shut down during the dead of winter," I answered. "For now, if you're planning on shutting it down during the winter, I think you'd be safe planning on three, or maybe four."

We continued our discussion as we followed the senator back toward the parking lot.

"Say," said the senator, "won't you stop in with us for something to drink?" I wasn't sure what this brewery owner had in mind to drink, but I didn't wish to risk an embarrassing situation and kindly informed him that we do not drink alcoholic beverages. He changed his invitation and asked that we dine with him in his own restaurant. I protested that I had already eaten my supper, but the senator insisted.

The senator's attendants rode with him in his large Mercedes while I followed with Dan in his small Dacia. We had barely entered the restaurant when I noticed a scurry of activity among the waiters. One soon appeared at the senator's side with his favorite meal. He insisted that I try their fish platter, for which his restaurant was famous. I love fish, so it wasn't hard for me to accommodate him. When my order came, it was a trout done to perfection, and it totally filled my platter. It came complete with head and tail and a liberal helping of sauce made of pure garlic blended with sour cream. It was heady. But in spite of having already eaten, I found it to be very tasty.

We talked as we ate. The senator wanted to know more about America, where I grew up, and how I liked living in Romania. He was an interesting conversationalist, and I enjoyed the evening.

Near the end of our meal the senator turned to me and became very serious. I gave him my full attention as he spoke.

"I have traveled widely and have seen many inspiring things. In all my years there have only been a few times that I have been moved beyond words. However, when I visited your orphanage and saw those children and heard their stories, I was speechless. I was so deeply moved that I had no words."

I gazed into the senator's face. Even now, tears were glistening just below the surface.

"Again I want to say," he continued, "your people are doing a wonderful work in helping our people, and I want to thank you! Furthermore, as I told you when I was in Suceava, I sit on the Finance Committee in Romania's central government. If there is anything I can do to help your people, I will be glad to do so. Here," he said as he handed me his business card, "don't hesitate to call if you need me."

I thanked the senator for his pledge of support and invited him to visit us any time he was in our area. I also explained that God had prompted the hearts of many North American Christians to support CAM's work with the Romanian children. This was not a work of only a few, but there were many who sacrificed so this work could be a blessing to others.

Dan and I had much to contemplate as we traveled homeward together, and our trip was made in thoughtful quietness.

Our weather jumped straight from cool spring to early summer. The orphanage garden was beginning to look like a picture. Our greenhouse was doing great, and it was a joy to watch Cristi and Costel pull a wagonload of perfect, vine-ripened tomatoes up to the orphanage kitchen. Elena followed close behind with a bucket of fresh cucumbers with which to garnish the noonday salad.

Already this season the children had helped butcher and process fifty broilers hatched from our own incubators. One hundred more had already hatched, providing more work for the children.

Cristi and Costel haul a wagonload of tomatoes from the greenhouse.

Another batch of eggs was under the watchful eye of Loredana, whose attentiveness brought excellent results.

Although Beni had only been part of the Nathaniel family one year, he had already become my right-hand chick man by taking care of the newly hatched chicks until they were mature enough to place into their outdoor cages. Ionela and Rodica had asked for the job of

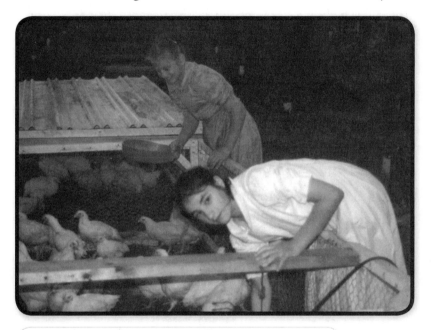

Ionela and Rodica tend the broilers.

tending the caged broilers outside. They fed and watered them and changed their cage locations to fresh areas of grass as needed, receiving a bit of spending money for a job well done.

Martha Esh, an American tanti, came up with a novel idea when she installed her "picking crew." A chosen few were invited to assist her in the garden at 7 a.m. They picked peas or beans and were amply rewarded by being invited into her apartment as soon as the task was completed. After washing up, they sat up to her table for a hearty breakfast, and they loved it! The children naturally asked Martha about her special friend, Nathan Bange. It was a splendid opportunity for them to observe a Christian courtship, and many valuable conversations were forthcoming.

One evening just before dismissing the children from the dining room supper tables, Martha announced, "Girls, the peas are ready for their second picking. I'd like for my special crew to be in the garden by seven in the morning. Can you do that?" she asked. "Don't eat breakfast, because I have a scrumptious brunch planned at my apartment as soon as we are finished."

"Tanti, Tanti," called Rodica, "are you going to make pancakes again?"

"Oh, do!" shouted Ionela. "We just love them! This is going to be such fun!" she confided to Oana, who was seated beside her. "I just love working in the garden with Tanti Martha."

All these activities had a purpose much deeper than merely providing food for our tables. As the children worked side by side with us in the garden, greenhouse, lawns, and farm, they were learning life-long lessons of good work habits. They were also deepening the roots of their own belonging and establishing good memories to cherish in years to come.

The peas were dripping with early morning dew as Martha surveyed the thirty-four rows of plants vining over the waist-high chicken wire. Wisps of mist lingered in the valley near the creek.

"Good morning, Tanti Martha," said Mihaela.

"Good morning!" Martha responded. "You are the first one here. Would you help me bring the buckets from the little red barn?"

"Sure," smiled Mihaela, glowing in Tanti Martha's praise.

When they returned with the buckets, the rest of the girls had just arrived and were eager to get started. Martha formed teams to pick on either side of the netting.

"Say," said Martha, glancing about, "where's Ionela?"

"She can't come this morning," answered Rodica.

"Why not? Is she sick?" asked Martha.

"No. Her tanti told her she couldn't come."

"But why?" Martha wanted to know. She always looked forward to Ionela's sunny disposition and ready hands.

"I know," volunteered Elena. "Last night she argued with her tanti and talked without respect, and the tanti punished her. So she can't help us pick peas."

"I'm so sorry," said Martha. "I was looking forward to her being with us this morning."

"Yes, and she cried too," added Rodica soberly.

In due time the peas were picked. A new crew of children began shelling as Martha took the picking crew into her apartment for that wonderful brunch.

Martha glanced about her table as the girls chattered merrily among themselves, and an overwhelming feeling of closeness threatened to choke her. It welled up from deep within her soul and made her wish that she could somehow keep these dear children with her always.

Later that day Martha had the opportunity to talk with Ionela.

"We really missed you this morning," Martha began.

Ionela stared off into the distance. "It's not fair!" she spouted as she blinked back her tears. "I didn't do anything. The tanti was just in a bad mood, and she took it out on me!"

"The others said you talked without respect. Is that right?" probed Martha kindly.

"Of course I got upset, but that was *after* the tanti treated me like dirt!" Ionela stated angrily.

"Well," said Martha in a kind, understanding voice, "we must learn that we cannot say everything we feel. We must also learn to guard our lips. Remember the song we sometimes sing, 'Set a watch, O Lord, set a watch! Set a watch upon my lips . . .'? You need to learn to be more careful with your words." Martha lovingly patted Ionela's shoulder.

Six excited little boys crowded into my office, all talking at once.

"What's that for?" asked Iosif, pointing to the long box I was holding.

"When Ruth and I were in America on furlough, we asked CAM to send this box on their next container," I explained as I carefully opened one end. I extracted the long wood-grained object and turned it over for the boys to see.

"Wow!" exclaimed Daniel. "What's the light for?"

"This is a special lid to fit on the top of an aquarium," I explained.

"So big?" asked Manu.

"But we don't even have an aquarium," interjected Iliuță.

"What's an aquarium?" asked Costică.

"An aquarium is a glass box filled with water for fish to swim in," I began. "When I was a boy your age, I loved going to my aunt's home because she had an aquarium. I sat for many interesting hours watching her fish glide about in their underwater world. I know you will love it too. I want to build an aquarium out of glass, and we will fix it up just as natural-looking as we can."

"How are you going to do that?" asked Manu.

I held up the tubes of silicone I had purchased in America. "These are filled with a type of caulking that feels like soft rubber after it has cured. We will stick the edges of the glass together and form a glass box. We will fill it with water, and then we can keep small fish in it. That will be our aquarium," I explained.

"Where are we going to get our fish?" asked Daniel.

"Would you boys like to go to the lake with me and help catch little fish, crawfish, snails, and water bugs to put into our aquarium?" I asked.

"Sure! Yeah! When?" They all began talking at once.

"Well," I chuckled at their immediate interest, "first we have to build the aquarium, and then we'll catch the fish."

A week later the six-millimeter glass had been cut to our specifications and delivered to the orphanage. Manu was helping me assemble it in the woodshop. Together we lightly ground down the sharp glass edges with a belt sander and fashioned a wooden framework to support our aquarium until the silicone cured. We positioned the glass bottom and set a wall in place on a bead of silicone. I smoothed the excess silicone as Manu steadied the glass wall. Next came the two ends and then the final wall.

"Tata Johnny," Manu exclaimed in alarm, "this wall is sliding in!" Sure enough, I had made provision to keep the walls from moving outward, but never thought that they needed to be prevented from moving inward as well. Gently we moved the errant glass panel back into its proper position and cleaned the smeared silicone from the end panels. Then, while Manu held it steady, I took careful measurements and cut a series of braces to fit internally. Finally, I straightened my aching back and surveyed our handiwork.

"How much water will it hold?" asked Manu.

"Well, it is forty-two inches long to match the light and lid. It is twenty inches wide so we can set it on the buffet in the living room. And it measures twenty-four inches high. Now, if I did my math correctly, it will hold eighty gallons of water," I responded.

"Wow, that's a lot of water!" observed Manu. "I sure hope it won't leak!"

"Don't you worry," I assured him. "We will test it thoroughly before taking it into the living room."

The following evening a group of children gathered as we carried our heavy glass aquarium into the bakery where there was a tile floor equipped with a drain, just in case. We set it on the flat wooden surface of the dough table and began filling it from a hose. The children chattered excitedly as they watched the water level creep higher and higher. We could just imagine the thrill of releasing fish and critters from the local lake to swim about in this little world we had created. When our homemade aquarium was full, we carefully placed the light on top and turned it on. The sparkling clear water was truly beautiful.

Next the boys wanted to see the water pump and air pump in action. After everything was thoroughly demonstrated and tested, we concluded that our aquarium had passed its test with flying colors.

We sent the children off to their beds that night with the promise that we would wait until school was out the next day before installing our new aquarium in the living room.

My office work was interrupted the next afternoon when Daniel burst in shouting, "Come on, Tata Johnny, it's time to set up our aquarium!"

"Hold on there," I replied. "You're not the only one who's interested in this. We don't want to begin until most of the children have finished their homework. We want everyone to enjoy watching. We must first collect the rocks and bring the sand to place on the bottom. We will not fill the aquarium until all is ready."

"Okay," Daniel said. "I'll go get the sand from the farm where they were mixing cement."

"That will be fine, Daniel. Just be sure it is clean. We'll need a full bucket."

Just then a group of girls announced that they had completed their school assignments and were ready to help with the aquarium project. "What can we do?" they asked.

"I'll tell you what. Why don't you run down to the creek and find six or eight nice, colorful rocks. Wash them really clean, and we'll place them in the bottom of the aquarium to give some of the smaller creatures a good place to hide."

"How big do you want them?" asked Ionela.

"Oh, maybe one about as big as a softball and the others about the size of your fists. I think that would look nice." The girls scampered off with Ionela in the lead and the rest following closely at her heels.

Several of the older boys helped me get the aquarium positioned on the buffet in the living room. Daniel returned from his errand, and under the watchful gazes of thirty pairs of eyes, I carefully covered the bottom of the aquarium with the sand he had brought. We placed a thin layer in the front and tapered it to several inches deep near the back.

The girls soon appeared with a bucket of freshly scrubbed rocks and offered them to me. They were colorful and would certainly add the needed touch to our aquarium. But as I lifted the largest from the bucket, I caught a whiff of soap. "Girls, did you wash these with soap?" I asked.

"We sure did," replied Rodica. "They were all covered with slimy green moss, and we had to wash them hard."

"It's fine that you got all the dirt off them," I said, "but you must go rinse them thoroughly. If we place these into the water as they are, the soap might be too strong for the fish and kill them."

Rodica headed for the kitchen with several girls to further scrub their rocks.

"Here, Tata Johnny," said Ionela as she held out a sizable drooping plant.

"What's this?" I asked.

"When we ran back to the creek for the rocks," she panted, "I found this underwater plant. I thought you might want it, so I dug it up from the bottom of the creek. Don't you think it will look nice in our aquarium?"

"I sure do," I answered in surprise. "Thank you so much!" I took the plant, still wet from the creek, and transplanted its roots into the sand near the back of our aquarium. By this time the girls had returned with the well-rinsed rocks, and I placed these over the sand-imbedded roots of our new aquatic plant. The plant drooped dejectedly, but I knew its leaves would rise when supported by water.

Nicu brought a hose and fastened it to the threaded faucet in the laundry room. He ran it out the laundry room window, down the flower bed, and back through the living room window, where a great crowd had gathered to observe the filling of the aquarium. I gave instructions for Daniel to turn the faucet only partially open so excessive pressure would not wash our sand out of place. After several inches of water had safely protected the sand, Daniel opened the valve farther, and we all watched with interest as our large aquarium began to fill.

"Why did you put sand in the water?" asked Florica. "Won't the fish get it stuck in their throats?"

"Why, no," I explained, "God has fish swimming in lakes, rivers, and oceans all over the world, and they don't get sand stuck in their throats, do they?"

"Can we girls go along to help catch the fish, Tata Johnny?" asked Larisa pleadingly.

"Why? Do you want to?" I teased.

"Sure we do!" chorused four little girls in unison.

"You always do more with the boys than you do with the girls, and that's not fair," pouted Ramona.

"Hey, I didn't say you couldn't go along," I said reprovingly.

"It's getting full, Tata Johnny, it's getting full!" squealed Vasilica excitedly.

"Well, we want it right up near the top," I explained. "We want the little fish to have plenty of room to swim."

Finally the aquarium was full, and I hollered for Daniel to turn off the faucet. I tossed the dripping hose back out the window and into the flower bed. The children crowded close, trying to see through the murky water.

"Why is it muddy?" asked Costică.

I explained that most of the fine dust from the sand was now suspended in the water but would soon settle to the bottom. The rest we would filter out as soon as we installed the pump and filtering system. Then the water would become completely clear.

"And the bubbles?" asked Elena. "When will the bubbles start? I heard that it is going to have bubbles!" she exclaimed as she squinted into the aquarium. I explained that we had a little air pump to install, and yes, we would have bubbles. I had to smile at her enthusiasm. Then I was reminded that this was the first time most of our children had ever seen an aquarium.

Leaving the aquarium under the watchful eyes of Ruth and the children, I hurried to the bakery garage where I had stored the lid, light, pump, filters, and aerator. Gathering an armload of gadgets and tubes, I headed back for the living room. I couldn't wait to see the children's expressions of delight when we had this all completed and the fish installed.

My thoughts were arrested by Lavinia, who ran into the bakery.

"Tata Johnny," she said soberly, "it broke."

"What?" I asked.

"I said it broke," she repeated.

"What are you talking about?" I asked, knowing full well how Lavinia was capable of teasing.

"The thing you put in the living room just broke, and there is water all over the place!"

"Come on," I replied, grinning. I watched for the smile she always gave when she was joking. But instead of the smile there was a look of grief.

A sick feeling rose in my stomach as she said, "It's true. Come see for yourself."

I suddenly realized that I no longer needed my precious gadgets, and dumping them all onto the counter, I rushed with Lavinia back to the orphanage living room.

The children were jumping up and down and squealing, "Tata Johnny, Tata Johnny, it broke and the water and sand all came pouring out. It was like waterfalls!"

"It ran all over the floor. Look, Tata Johnny!" shouted Daniel.

I couldn't believe it. I was stunned, dumbfounded.

Iosif walked over to stand close beside me and said, "Tata Johnny,

I'm so sorry, but you can make another one, yes?"

Manu asked, "Tata Johnny, why didn't it break when we tested it?"

The empty aquarium sat dejectedly on the buffet. A horizontal crack had split its back panel from corner to corner in a long, shallow arch which had flopped open like a large door. One third of our big living room was now a squishy mess. Ionela's water plant dangled limply through the break in the glass.

Well, it does no good to cry over spilled milk, or broken aquariums, I thought to myself. *We have work to do!*

The children all pitched in wonderfully with dustpans as scoops and formed a bucket brigade, carrying the reclaimed water outside to dump onto the lawn.

Ionela lugged in a Shop Vac to finish the job. Even then, and with fans blowing over the floor, it took several days to dry the carpet. Our homemade aquarium had to be discarded. Some time later, Ionică donated a smaller, commercially built one in its place. The children were delighted and watched the fish for hours on end.

Chapter 11
Corn Thieves

Private schools in Romania came under much
stronger governmental regulations than did their counterparts in
America. Thus the expansion of the Nathaniel Christian School to
include grades five through eight brought with it the need for numerous government approvals. Ionică filed all the appropriate paperwork
and applications nearly a year in advance and made many trips to
government offices seeking authorizations. Ionică made many trips
to his prayer closet as well. He had caught the vision of providing a
Christian-based education for the Nathaniel children, as well as others, and he worked tirelessly to bring it to pass.

We waited and prayed for authorization from the Romanian Department of Education. While we waited, we also applied to the
Building Commission for authorization to build a school to house
this expansion. With each passing year the oldest orphanage children
were moving into a higher grade and a new group of youngsters entered the first grade.

If the Department of Education granted us permission to operate
the Nathaniel School, we knew it would only be temporary. Additional tests on students' academic achievements and teachers' perfor-
mances would determine whether or not we could continue with our
school. If during any of the following four years we did not meet the
Department of Education's demands, our authorization to operate
grades five through eight could be revoked.

Our first orphanage building had been constructed with the needs of small children in mind. Several of those small children were now turning twelve years old, and we began making plans to renovate our present school building to serve as a dormitory for the girls. This would give all the children more privacy in less cramped quarters. But before we could renovate the current school building, we needed the coveted permit to build a new school large enough to accommodate all eight grades. Would the government grant us that permit? We prayed that it would.

Ruth had her hands in many things, and planning the orphanage menu was one of her areas of expertise. The season was wonderful for growing things. As the sweet corn began ripening, Ruth planned to serve early corn on the cob, which the children dearly loved. Right after breakfast and room cleaning, Ruth met with her helpers and gave them instructions.

"Iosif, Manu, and Ionuț," she called, "would you please each bring a wagon? And Iliuță, Nicu, and Ovidiu, I'd like for you to each bring a five-gallon bucket. Meet me at my house in ten minutes, and we'll go pick corn for our noon meal."

"Oh, Mama Ruth, I want to go too! Please?" begged Daniel. Ruth looked at his pleading eyes and didn't have the heart to turn him down, even though he was a bit young.

"All right," she said, "you may come too, but no one else. This will be enough."

Soon the excited boys congregated in front of the little gray house with their wagons, buckets, and their enthusiasm. Ruth joined them and led the way down the gravel road past the pasture and on to our two-acre corn patch. Several of the boys began pulling ears from the very first stalks they came to.

"Just a minute, boys. Some of those might not be ready. Come, let's have a look at them," Ruth patiently instructed. "See this blond silk? And notice that this ear isn't very fat." She took the ear from Daniel's hand and held it up for all to see. Deftly she peeled back the tough, green husk and revealed the small, white, immature kernels within.

"See," she said as she passed the ear around for the boys to view, "this one is too young and wouldn't be good to eat."

"I'm sorry," said Daniel.

"It's okay," Ruth consoled him, "but I think you would enjoy corn like this one much better." She took the ear that Ovidiu had picked and pointed to the dried, dark-brown silk on the tip of the fat-looking ear. "See," she said as she peeled back the husk. Its golden-yellow kernels gleamed in the bright sunlight. "Corn like this will make us a fine meal."

Leaving their wagons at the end of the row, the boys carried their five-gallon buckets among the rustling cornstalks as they followed Ruth. Here and there she paused and snapped off a promising ear and handed it to the closest boy, who dropped it into his bucket. But the boys were never content to simply assist. They enjoyed doing things on their own. They wanted to pick corn and not merely carry buckets.

"Mama Ruth, Mama Ruth, is this one okay?" asked Daniel, his hand poised to snap off an ear. "Is it?"

"Move your hand so I can see the silk. Yes, see how dark and dry the silk looks? And it's also nice and fat."

Snap, and off the stalk it came. Instantly Daniel peeled back the husk, gave Ruth a thumbs-up, and flashed her a quick smile as he viewed the full, golden-yellow kernels within. Daniel dropped it into his bucket even as his eyes scanned ahead for the next fat ear. This was delightful!

Snap, snap, snap. Ruth heard corn being harvested all about her. She felt a rush of love for these boys. If only she could protect them from all life's evils and teach them how to live godly lives! They seemed so willing to receive, and she had so much in her heart to give.

Several boys had already carried their full buckets to dump into the waiting wagons and rushed back to continue harvesting in their row. Ruth called to them, "Boys, we'll need about 250 ears for lunch."

"We already have about seventy-five," Iosif called back. Since it was early in the season, they had to search carefully for the ripened ears in order to find enough. The next twenty minutes passed with everyone working steadily toward their goal.

"Okay, boys, I think we have just about enough. Stop picking now and carry your buckets back to the wagons. I'll finish filling this bucket and then we'll husk it by the wagons. You may start husking right away if you like," Ruth instructed. Dutifully the boys lugged their buckets back through the rustling stalks to their waiting wagons. Ruth searched for the last few ears she needed to fill her bucket.

Snap! Snap! Ruth heard one of the boys pulling corn deep in the field off to her right. She was surprised and disappointed that one of her boys had not followed her instructions. Perhaps he was just being slow to respond and would quit at any moment. But no, he was at it again. *Snap! Snap!*

This was too much. Lugging her half-filled bucket so as not to lose it in the cornfield, Ruth made her way through the thick, lush cornstalks toward the sound of the culprit. Should she send him straight up to the orphanage or perhaps not allow him to have any corn for lunch? She wasn't exactly sure how she would deal with his disobedience, but she was determined to use this incident to teach a lesson!

Ruth broke into the row right next to the corn picker, and to her utter amazement found not a boy, but a full-grown man she had never laid eyes on before.

"Sir," she addressed him with a show of courage that she certainly did not feel, "just what do you think you are doing here?"

With a smirk, he nodded toward her bucket of corn and said, "Ma'am, I'm doing exactly what you have been doing—picking corn for my family." And with that he snapped off another ear and added it to his bulging sack.

Suddenly Ruth thought, *It might be best to allow this man to continue thinking I am also a corn thief.* Without another word, she turned and rapidly made her way back to the waiting boys. But as she went, she was irked to hear the mocking snap of more corn being stolen.

During lunch everyone savored the fresh sweet corn, but the story of Mama Ruth confronting the corn thief flavored the discussion around our dining room tables. Ştefi thought Mama Ruth certainly was brave, but Beti thought the man should have been punished for stealing our corn.

"Just look at that!" said one of the boys several days later as he stared toward the cornfield. I looked where he indicated but saw nothing unusual. Then the tall weeds began to move and two young men slipped through the creek and into our cornfield. Within moments the shaking tassels indicated they were picking our corn.

The nerve of them! And in broad daylight too! I thought to myself in disgust. I watched, fascinated as the boys struggled to climb the far bank of the creek, carrying a full gunnysack between them. As we watched, they returned and went to work in our cornfield again.

"Tata Johnny, let's go catch them!" chorused several boys who had gathered to watch.

"Well," I said, "I'm going to take a ride down there."

"Tata Johnny," said Manu, "I want to go with you."

"All right," I agreed. "Hop in!"

We quickly climbed into the gray Honda and drove up the drive in the opposite direction from the cornfield. We drove past the front of the orphanage and made a right turn onto the gravel road which led past the cornfield. I drove slowly, resisting Manu's advice and my own impulse to step on it. I wanted this to appear as calm and natural a drive as possible. Long before we reached the cornfield, two young fellows pushed their bicycles out of the tall weeds and began pedaling up the field lane ahead of us. At first they seemed to be moving at a fairly normal speed, but as the sound of our approaching car drew nearer, they stood up on their bikes and pedaled more vigorously. We were on a long uphill grade, and their legs were no match for our faithful old Honda. We soon overtook them and carefully passed them. I stopped the Honda and climbed out, motioning for the boys to stop.

"Where are you boys going?" I asked as calmly as I could. One of the boys was unfamiliar to me, but the other I recognized as Romică, our neighbor's fifteen-year-old son.

"We were just out riding," spoke up Romică.

"Fine," I said. "Why don't you boys come back with me to the cornfield and let's see if we can find the corn you were stealing."

Romică stood there on the road, straddling his bike. A look of shocked innocence crossed his face, and his hand clutched his chest involuntarily as he said, "Tata Johnny, you know I would never steal corn from you. Why would I do something like that?"

"Well, let's go see," I said as I laid my hand on his handlebars. Romică got off his bike and allowed me to push it back toward the cornfield as he walked along beside it. The other boy turned his bike around and headed back toward the cornfield as well, and Manu followed, bringing up the rear. I glanced toward the orphanage, and in the distance could make out a group of children on the lawn near our little gray house. Many eyes were watching.

"From my house we could see you boys carrying off our corn," I explained.

"Tata Johnny," said Romică, "you know me. I'm your neighbor, and I am a Christian. I attend the church in Ițcani, and I would never steal from you."

"Tata Johnny," spoke up the second boy, "we were riding by on our bicycles, and we saw some men taking corn from your field. We scared them off and were coming to tell you about it. Isn't that right,

Romică?"

"That's right," agreed Romică.

"Don't you boys think it is a bit strange that you would ride your bicycles away from the orphanage if you were coming to tell me that someone was stealing corn from our field?" I asked.

By this time we were quite near the cornfield and turned onto the footpath that bordered the creek. I looked about in the tall weeds, but could find nothing. All the while the boys insisted that they were not guilty of stealing our corn. Then to the side of the footpath I saw where the weeds were unnaturally bent and stopped to investigate. Pushing forward, I followed the tramped-down weeds and came upon two gunnysacks bulging with corn. They were carefully tied shut. Without saying a word, I dragged them to the boys, one at a time. Romică looked sick and couldn't meet my gaze. His partner also looked ill at ease.

"Come," I said as I dragged one bag toward the road. Manu brought the other, and the neighbor boys silently followed, pushing their bicycles. At the edge of the road I set the two sacks of stolen corn up against each other and instructed the boys to stand on either side of them. Reluctantly, they obeyed.

"Please stand a little closer together," I encouraged them as I focused my camera. "And raise your heads. I want people to be able to clearly see who you are." I snapped several photos before we loaded the corn into the trunk of the Honda. After delivering a sermonette on the evils of stealing, we returned to the orphanage, leaving behind two dejected-looking young men who soberly mounted their bikes and pedaled off in the direction they were headed when we had first arrived.

"Who were they?" asked Mihaela when we returned to the orphanage.

"Manu, what did Tata Johnny do to them?" Iosif wanted to know.

"Are you going to call the police?" asked Iliuţă.

"I really am not angry," I explained to the children who were crowding about us, "and I don't want to be mean to those boys. All I want is for them to understand that it is wrong to steal."

It was soon time for supper, and once again our children were chattering about the latest cornfield episode. They seemed to take it personally that someone had stolen their corn.

That evening, when it was nearly bedtime, one of the orphanage children informed me that a woman was out by the gate, wanting to speak with me. It was Romică's mother. I walked toward the gate with lagging footsteps, having no desire to tangle with an irate mother. How could I explain that I wished her son no ill, but only wanted to teach him that stealing is morally and spiritually wrong? I took a deep breath as I approached the woman standing in the shadows near our gate.

"Good evening," I said pleasantly as I drew near.

"Good evening, Tata Johnny," responded Romică's mother. She was dark and her thin features blended with the dim light. She looked frail. "I've come to talk to you about my son Romică," she began.

"Yes?" I responded, steeling myself.

"I understand that today you caught him stealing your corn." It was a statement, not a question. "Tata Johnny, I am so embarrassed. Please forgive him, will you?" she pleaded as she clasped and unclasped her thin hands.

She wasn't making excuses for her son or berating me for having accused him, but was trying to correct her son's wrong. My heart was moved with pity and admiration.

"My husband beat Romică severely for what he did, and I know he will never do it again. But Tata Johnny," she begged, and even in the darkness I could see her eyes filling with tears, "please destroy those photos you took. Don't give them to the police. Promise me!"

I was silent, thinking. "I'll tell you what," I said. "Have your son come at eight o'clock Monday morning. Tell him to bring his buddy with him. I have a job for them to do. I promise you that I will not give the photos to anyone."

"Oh, thank you, thank you!" she said. Then, laying her hand upon my arm, she added, "Please, please destroy those photos! I will be sure to have Romică here by eight o'clock Monday morning."

Romică and his buddy arrived on time, and I led them down to the pigpen that had only recently been emptied of its occupants.

"Here are two shovels," I informed them. "I want you to clean this pigpen for me, and when you are finished, please come up to my house. Okay?"

"Yes," they murmured. Several of the orphanage boys stood watching as Romică and his buddy took their shovels and turned to survey the task before them.

The assignment took Romică and his friend most of the day, but it gave them time to evaluate their actions. Along with the distasteful job came the blessing of a glass of cold milk and a plate of homemade cookies. Through it all, Romică and his family became trusted friends, and we were able to help his family during times of crisis in the years ahead.

A week later most of the corn was declared ready. Alvin took a group of single workers and older boys to the corn patch early in the morning. Soon the tractor was puttering up from the cornfield with its front-end loader filled to capacity. Fresh ears were piled on a large heap on the lawn beside the bakery, where they were immediately attacked by many energetic hands. Some were busy husking. Others brushed silk from the golden ears, while still others scalded and cooled the corn.

"Come, children," said Tanti Anişoara as she led her group of smaller children toward the cornfield. "I want to teach you how to help harvest the corn. Tanti Roza wants enough corn to serve for lunch today." She had to smile as eager little hands helped push one of the wagons while Neli guided it along. After some time they returned, pulling their little wagons laden with husked corn fresh from the field. The children were learning that they must all do their part. We were blessed with a dairy farm, a huge garden, and spacious lawns. We thanked God for providing these wonderful blessings for the Nathaniel children.

Our workers set up tables in the bakery garage where the corn cutting began in earnest. American families, youth, tantis, and children from the orphanage all pitched in and prepared corn for the freezer. It normally took two gallons of corn to supply the orphanage needs for just one meal, and we needed enough to last until the following season. One of the youth girls started a song, and soon we were having a wonderful time singing as we cut corn together.

Anişoara and the children bring back corn for lunch.

It proved to be a long day, but by evening four hundred quarts of corn were safely preserved in the freezer. Everyone felt tired, but along with our exhaustion came a sense of great accomplishment. Together we had worked, and together we would share the fruits of our labors.

A week later there was a commotion down at the farm, and Iosif came running to tell me that our farm watchman had apprehended a thief in our cornfield. *Got him!* I thought as I began walking toward the farm. *Maybe it's the same one Ruth bumped into ten days ago.*

My attention was arrested by a man's loud shouts and a woman's pitiful cry. *What is going on?* I wondered. Up the farm driveway came an elderly, bent grandma, crying and trying to talk. Right behind her came the farm watchman.

"You certainly *were* in our cornfield. I caught you there myself. What do you mean you weren't stealing? Just look, your bag is nearly bulging!" he shouted. His voice carried across the orphanage compound for all to hear. The woman stumbled along in front of him carrying her cloth bag by its homemade straps.

I stopped in my tracks. This certainly was not the thief Ruth had seen. This poor woman's back was permanently hunched over, probably from long years of hoeing on a communist collective farm. Her hands were coarse and rough from hard labor, and she twisted them together nervously as she stopped before me.

"Here," shouted the watchman roughly, "this is the orphanage director, and you can just tell him what you were doing in our cornfield. Go ahead and explain to him that you weren't stealing, and see if he believes you!"

Several girls had gathered and were watching to see what I would do.

"Please, Mr. Director," cried the woman, "you have to believe me. I am not a thief, and I never stole any of your corn!"

"Grandma," I addressed her in a respectful tone, "I certainly want to believe you. Now just be calm. No one is going to hurt you."

Turning to our faithful watchman, I said, "Thank you for being alert. I do appreciate it. And thank you for bringing her to me. I will take care of this."

The watchman nodded and headed back to the farm with the air of a man who had done his duty well.

More children had gathered. "Grandma, would you mind showing me what you have in your bag?" I asked politely. With effort she bent over stiffly and began unloading her bag. Out came a two-inch, broken point of an ear of corn.

"I picked this up off the ground where someone had dropped it," she said. Next came a puny ear of corn with husks that were dry and withered. "This was on the ground too," she whimpered. Another ear was white and immature, and another was curled and misshaped. "I never picked any corn from the stalks."

I rejoiced to see that her bag was indeed filled with corn which had been discarded by our workers as undesirable or unwanted. This grandma was no thief, but a gleaner like Ruth in the Bible. She had merely picked up the scraps others had tossed aside. I assisted her in placing her hard-earned corn nubbins back into her bag and asked her to come with me. "But I never stole!" she protested.

"I know, I know," I said reassuringly as I led the way to the bakery. There followed along a group of sympathetic children whose hearts had been touched by the plight of this poor old woman.

She stood near the entrance to the bakery, where I left her gazing into the sympathetic faces of the young girls surrounding her. Again she said as if addressing a jury, "I really only picked up the pieces of corn that were left lying on the ground," and the children smiled back their verdict.

I emerged with all the husked, full ears of golden corn I could carry in my hands and a bag of chocolate chip cookies still warm from the oven.

"Oh, thank you!" said the woman as I began trying to find room in her bag for these gifts.

"Girls," I said to the group who had followed us to the bakery, "would you be so kind as to show Grandmother to the gate."

"Sure," they responded, glad for the opportunity to show the kindness they felt.

"But, Mr. Director," interrupted the woman, "you don't believe I stole, do you?"

"I know you didn't steal; I know you are a good woman."

"Oh, thank you!" she said, and before I could stop her, she reached out her work-worn hands, clasped my hand to her lips, and kissed it!

"Thank you for believing that I am not a thief! May God in heaven richly repay you for your kindness!"

One girl took her bag, another took her hand, and others followed as they guided her tottering feet around the orphanage to the front gate. I stood watching from the bakery entrance, deeply humbled.

Chapter 12

Important Firsts

Lunch had just gotten under way when Lavinia blurted out excitedly, "Did you hear about the *logodna?*"

"You mean Martha and Nathan's?" I asked.

"Yes. If it's rainy, they are going to have it in the gym, but if it's nice on Saturday, they will have it outside on the lawn."

"What's a *logodna?*" asked little Liviu as he pulled another forkful of tender meat from the chicken thigh on his plate. His small, sharp face and dark eyes registered deep interest as he gazed up at me while chewing thoughtfully. I realized that his gypsy culture probably lacked this Romanian evangelical tradition.

"A *logodna,*" I began, "is a ceremony for a boy and a girl who plan to get married."

"Oh, it's a wedding with lots of food and music and dancing," he announced knowingly.

"But this is different than a wedding," I explained to Liviu and the other children who were leaning forward and listening intently. "When a boy and girl tell their pastors that they want to make plans to be married, the pastors come to the girl's home and both families are invited. Then the lead pastor asks the girl's parents if they agree that this boy marry their daughter. Next they ask the boy's parents if they agree that the girl marry their son. Then they ask the boy and the girl if they believe that God is directing them to be married. And if all are in agreement, then the pastors ask the boy and the girl to vow that they will keep themselves just for each other. When these promises have been made, the pastors give instructions and seal the engagement with a special prayer. Then on the following Sunday, the pastors announce to their congregations that these two are planning to be married soon. It is really quite a beautiful ceremony."

The children were impressed. Although they transferred their attention back to their plates of chicken and rice, their discussion remained centered around Nathan Bange and Martha Esh and their coming *logodna*.

The children had observed this blooming romance with the greatest of interest, as though their older sister were dating, and they felt privileged to share her joy.

Several of the older girls asked permission to go to Alvin and Lil's house. Martha's apartment was in their basement, and preparations were being made for her *logodna*. The girls just couldn't stay away! Martha and Lil somehow put up with these inquisitive children underfoot and even allowed several of the older ones to assist with the food preparation.

The adults couldn't hide their smiles when two of the girls sat up on stools and announced that one was Martha and the other was Nathan. Roxana impersonated Martha, perfectly mimicking her rapid speech, Lancaster accent, and expressive waving of her hands. Oana did a fine job of assuming Nathan's sober countenance as she spoke with a deep voice in a slow, thoughtful manner. Little Gigi sat on a chair, watching. He had to giggle at the girls' antics and was fascinated by the bustle of activity. Something important was in the making, and he wasn't about to miss it. As Nathan paused before him, Gigi innocently lisped, "I know what you are going to do tomowow."

"What are we going to do?" asked Nathan, smiling down at him.

Gigi quickly responded, "You're going to gib us ice queem and cake."

"But do you know *why* we will serve you ice cream and cake?" asked Nathan.

"Betause it's good!" Gigi answered innocently.

Saturday dawned a bit overcast, but as the day wore on, the skies cleared, and it turned out to be a perfect day. Benches were placed in a semicircle in front of Alvin's house. Adults and girls filled the benches, while many of the boys were content to sit on the lush grass. All were dressed in their Sunday best, and soon the singing began.

Following the singing, Ionică explained to the children what was about to take place. He asked that they be reverent and remain quiet.

A *logodna* normally takes place at the bride's home, and the parents are deeply involved in the betrothal. Since neither Martha's nor Nathan's parents were present, Alvin agreed to fill those roles.

Ionică's rich voice resonated as he addressed Alvin. "Brother Alvin, do you recognize and accept the churches from which Sister Martha and Brother Nathan have come?"

"Yes, I do," Alvin responded.

"Are you in agreement, and do you believe that God led these young people into this betrothal?"

"I am in agreement, and I do believe that God has led them."

"Have these young people been faithful, and are they walking with God?"

"Yes, I believe they are."

"Do you believe they are ready for this serious step in their lives?"

"Yes."

"Are you ready to release them, and can you add your blessing to their lives?"

"Yes, I release them, and I wish them God's richest blessings as they follow the Lord together."

Brother Sami, who worked closely with Nathan in CAM's food parcel distribution in the neighboring village of Pătrăuți, led a prayer of blessing as we stood together. Willis Bontrager shared a short message on the responsibilities and blessings of marriage.

Ionică gave the concluding message, bringing out a beautiful analogy from 1 Corinthians 11:7. He pointed out that man is too often like the sun, strong and at times harsh. "For example," he said, "you don't find people gazing at the sun. It has a beauty, but it is strong and overpowering. Just as the sun's light and glory are viewed and appreciated when reflected by the moon, so a godly man's light and glory are often better seen and appreciated through his wife. Together," he explained, "a godly husband and wife show God's glory in a very wonderful way." Ionică wound up his message with an admonition concerning the commitment of marriage and the seriousness with which we must approach it.

"And now," said Ionică as he brought his message to a close and turned to Martha and Nathan, "if it is your desire to proceed with this betrothal, you may come forward." A hush settled over the audience as Martha and Nathan stood before Ionică and he addressed them personally.

"Brother Nathan, do you of your own will and desire still wish to become engaged to Sister Martha?"

Nathan and Martha stand before Ionică at their *logodna.*

Nathaniel Orphanage family photo, 1998

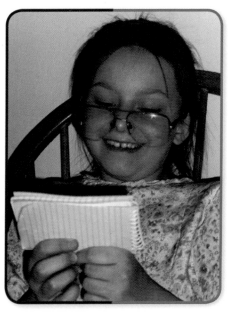

Beti pretends to be Tata Johnny.

Gheorghe and Liviu practice their
building skills.

Having their own birthday cake and serving it in the orphanage dining room makes each child feel special. Gheorghe helps
Maria serve her cake.

Four girls on one rope.
L to R: Ştefania, Roxana, Florica, Dorcas

Maria, Ovidiu, and Iliuţă exhibit their rabbits.

Happy to help, Daniela and Neli arm themselves
with donuts to transport from table to counter.

Lawnmower train—fun for all.

Roxana and Larisa pop in a few cherries
on cherry-preserving day.

Andi, thrilled to help with the
girls' dorm.

God's blessing on the
Nathaniel Christian Church.

FAMILY

ALBUM

Ovidiu Bădarau

Elena Bițica

Marian Bițica

Ștefania Bițica

Vasilica Bițica

Beni Bleoja

Monica Bleoja

Ionela Calancea

Laura Calancea

Loredana Calancea

Gigi Cimpoi

Adi Ciocan

Daniela Ciocan

Manu Ciocan

Larisa Cornea

Marius Cornea

MARINEL COZMIUC   PAVEL CRUȚ   COSTEL CUCUVEICA   ROXANA DICULOV

IOANA DICULOV   DAVUCU DOBREA   LAVINIA DOBREA   GABI FILAN

DANIEL GHEORGHEȘ   IOSIF GHEORGHEȘ   MARIANA GHEORGHEȘ   MIHAELA GHEORGHEȘ

ANDI IFROSE   SILVIU IFROSE   TINA IVANIOU   LEON IVANOF

RAMONA IVANOF   NICOLETA MIHALESCU   RODICA MIHALESCU   BETI MOCANU

FLORENTINA MUNTELE   ICA NICOLAESCU   CRISTI PADURARU   CRISTINA PADURARU

IONUȚ PADURARU   NICU PADURARU   BOGDAN PARNICA   GHEORGHE PARNICA

NELI PARNICA   MARIA PARNICA   MARTA PARNICA   EMANUELA PETRESCU

COSTICĂ SANDU   ILIUȚĂ SANDU   ȘTEFI SANDU   DANUȚ SAVIN

OANA SAVIN   FLORICA TURCAN   LIVIU CHERARIU

"Yes, I do," responded Nathan.

"Sister Martha, do you of your own will and desire wish to become engaged to Brother Nathan?"

"Yes," she responded with deep feeling.

"And do you both desire that this engagement should conclude in giving your marriage vows before God and the church?"

"Yes," they each responded in turn.

"Are you aware that the Bible forbids divorce?"

"Yes."

"And how long will you promise to be faithful to your marriage vows?"

"Until death," replied first Nathan and then Martha.

I glanced about at the Nathaniel children and tried to read their thoughts. Sober expressions covered their faces, and their attention was riveted to the trio before them. Gigi in particular caught my attention. I realized that he was seriously considering thoughts of far greater value than the ice cream and cake he had been contemplating earlier.

Ionică offered a prayer of blessing upon Nathan and Martha, sealing their betrothal to one another before God.

A basket had been prepared by Tanti Valentina and Caroline and was presented by little Marta, the youngest girl from our orphanage. It contained two cute, meowing kittens and two official-looking documents rolled up and tied with ribbons. The kittens brought smiles, and the documents brought instructions for Martha and Nathan to sing a Romanian song, *"Te-am Ales"* (I've Chosen You). Nathan took this opportunity to explain to the children that this hymn was about God's relationship with His children. Nathan expressed his thanks to God for having chosen them. However, on this special occasion, these words held dual meaning.

Martha and Nathan sang, their voices blending beautifully.

I've chosen you, I've chosen you;
From among thousands of thousands, I've chosen you.
Many voices have cried out, many hands have beckoned,
But from among them all, I've chosen you.

You have chosen me, you have chosen me;
From among the thousands of thousands, you have chosen me.
I want to thank you richly for your divine grace.
For I have come to understand your love;
I have chosen you, I have chosen you.

The second document asked Martha and Nathan to read to each other from the book of Ruth. Everyone listened closely as they read to one another these memorable words: ". . . whither thou goest, I will go; and where thou lodgest, I will lodge: thy people shall be my people, and thy God my God: Where thou diest, will I die, and there will I be buried: the Lord do so to me, and more also, if aught but death part thee and me."

Much to the children's dismay, but to the delight of the betrothed, the kittens made good their escape during this portion of the ceremony. Chairs were brought forward and Martha and Nathan were asked to be seated. The children began filing past to add their blessings to those of the adult well-wishers. Each girl presented Tanti Martha with an embrace and a kiss and laid a long-stemmed carnation at her feet. Each of the boys did the same for Nathan until there was a beautiful carpet of flowers before them. Perhaps these represented the many colorful years God would lay out before them.

We went to our homes that night with a deeper appreciation for the *logodna* and the seriousness of the betrothal.

June 21, 1998 dawned clear and bright. It was an exceptionally beautiful Sunday morning, and we had good reason to be glad. This was the day seventeen-year-old Mihaela Sveduneac was to be baptized.

Mihaela came from a broken home and lived with her mother and two brothers in their modest apartment in Suceava. Her sincere testimony of living her life for Jesus was a blessing to the church. I had been privileged to meet with her for weekly Bible studies in preparation for this day.

Friends and relatives filled the church to capacity in their eagerness to witness Mihaela's baptism. This was the first baptism for the Nathaniel Church, and we rejoiced. I glanced over the audience and was pleased to see that Mihaela's grandparents, Victor and Caterina, were present. They were dedicated believers from a local Pentecostal church, and we deeply appreciated their faith, commitment, and walk with the Lord. Mihaela's estranged father was also present and sat near the front. *What thoughts must be going through his mind?* I wondered as the singing began. *What feelings are coursing through his heart and soul?* He was about to witness the believer's baptism for his daughter, symbolizing her commitment to Christ, while he continued fighting a battle with alcoholism. I felt compassion for him.

Mihaela's cousins and friends from high school sat together right behind her mother and paternal grandmother. For some, it was their first experience in attending an evangelical church, and we were happy to have them.

The service progressed through the Sunday school lesson. Then I preached a message on the need to willingly obey Christ's commands, one of which is water baptism.

When the sermon ended, Mihaela was asked to come forward. She looked beautiful in her simple, white dress as she knelt facing the congregation. Her countenance was radiant and her testimony pure.

The orphanage children stopped wiggling, and a holy hush filled the auditorium as Pastor Willis presented her with the baptismal vows. The microphone was positioned so that the entire congregation could hear her responses. When the vows were completed, Mihaela was baptized with water, publicly testifying that she had repented of her sins and had committed her life to following her Saviour.

I glanced toward her father and saw that he was deeply moved. As the baptismal waters dripped from his daughter's face, tears of longing dripped from his own. Then his only daughter was received as a member into the Nathaniel Christian Church.

Following the benediction, family members and friends pressed forward to congratulate Mihaela. Christian friends quoted passages of Scripture and spoke words of encouragement. The pastor's wife, Esther, presented Mihaela with a beautiful bouquet of flowers. An invitation was extended for close friends to join the family in the church basement for a fellowship meal.

The overflowing crowd made it difficult to freely move about. Many wanted to make their way to the front of the church to greet Mihaela.

"Tata Johnny!" someone called. I looked about. It was Silvia. She motioned for me to join her at a window and pointed. "Look, there goes Mihaela's father. He's leaving!" Sure enough, he was walking up the road and was already passing the bakery on his way toward the main highway. "Please try to stop him and have him join the family meal," she begged. "I know it would mean so much to Mihaela if he stayed."

I made my way outside and rushed up the road toward the receding figure. "Wait, Mr. Sveduneac," I called. "We have a meal prepared for family and close friends, and we want you to join us. Will you?"

He hesitated, undecided. His own loneliness, suffering, and longing played across his face. Seven years had passed since his divorce. Did they really want him?

Seeing that he was weighing the possibility, I quickly added, "Please do it for Mihaela's sake. You are her father, and it will mean so much to her! Will you?"

"I would," he said with carefully measured words, "but you see, I have to be at work by four o'clock, and the bus leaves in half an hour.

I'd better go." He turned once more toward the main highway.

"But wait," I said, laying my hand on his shoulder, "it is only 12:30. I promise to get you to your job before four o'clock."

He hesitated.

"Please come," I said. "It will make Mihaela so happy!"

Reluctantly he followed me back into the church, where Silvia warmly greeted him.

Soon we were seated around the banquet tables in the church basement, enjoying a delicious meal together and learning to know Mihaela's extended family.

Observing Mihaela's baptism opened the hearts of the Nathaniel children to ask many questions about faith and practice. This became a wonderful opportunity, and we pointed them to the Bible as a guide for their lives.

Another first occurred that evening when we gathered to celebrate the death and suffering of our Lord by breaking bread and sharing the cup. Here again, the Nathaniel children showed a strong interest in watching the congregation share the Lord's Supper. We were from several different communities in America and Romania. We were not all from the same background, but we all had one common interest, and that was remembering the Lord's sacrifice for us and pledging anew our commitments to Him. This was indeed a blessed time as we felt the closeness of the Lord. His hands were drawing us together as a congregation of believers.

The Nathaniel children watched with undisguised fascination as we broke bread and passed it to each of the participants and also shared the cup. The children were sure they had never been to a more interesting church service in their whole lives.

The account of Jesus washing His disciples' feet was read and explained from John 13. Following Christ's example, we made preparation to wash one another's feet, symbolizing our desire to help each other maintain a pure walk before the Lord. Our sisters retired to the privacy of the nursery to wash one another's feet. The brethren paired off two by two and washed each other's feet in basins of water that had been set near the front of the church. This was too much for our inquisitive Nathaniel children. At first they stood and looked over the benches as best they could. Adults tried to get them to sit, but to no avail. They had to see what was going on! More and more children stood in order to see. Still they couldn't see well because all those from the front benches were also standing. Several groups of smaller children got up from their seats and walked determinedly to the front, where they could observe unhindered. We were happy to afford them this privilege of witnessing firsthand a practical application of God's Word.

The following week one of the tantis checked on the girls assigned to her. She was amazed to discover five of them holed up in a bedroom. Roxana seemed to be the preacher and had just wrapped up her sermon. Two other girls were gathered near a basin of water. One was seated with her foot in the water while the other knelt, tenderly washing her foot. It is so amazing to see how readily children learn by observing adults. May we ever be true examples of His righteousness and grace.

Ruth and I were busy putting the children to bed. We had finished tucking the boys in and now had most of the girls quieted down for the night. Peace finally reigned.

Eleven-year-old Rodica and her nine-year-old sister, Nicoleta, had been with their mother for the evening, but had just now returned to the orphanage. Rodica was crying uncontrollably, and Ruth didn't know how to comfort her. Rodica, completely beside herself, was determined to run out the door and follow her mother to her home an hour's drive away. She wailed as Ruth placed her arms about her and tried to console her. In desperation Ruth called for me to intervene.

"Rodica, stop it!" Ruth pleaded as Rodica pulled her toward the door. "This is no way to act. You are a big girl. Your mother will come to visit you again."

"I don't care. I am going home with her now!" wailed Rodica.

"But you can't," Ruth reasoned. "She has already caught a ride and is headed toward Rădăuți. You can't follow her now."

Rodica wailed and attempted to pull free from Ruth's grasp.

"I go! Mama!" she screamed as she shoved Ruth hard, jerked her hands free, and darted toward the steps.

I arrived just then and stepped into her path. "Now just a minute, young lady," I commanded. "You are not going anywhere!" I saw at a glance that Rodica had worked herself into an absolute frenzy. Her hair was disheveled and wet with sweat, her eyes were wild, and her breath was coming in great gasps as she covered her mouth with the back of her hand.

I spoke soothingly as I took her arm and attempted to lead her back into her room. She fought me with the strength of a person totally out of control. I had to become quite firm with her. After thirty minutes of conflict, reason finally prevailed. Peace was restored, but not before awakening nearly half of the sleeping girls.

At first I was tempted to be quite harsh in my judgment of Rodica. But then I wondered how I would respond if I had never met my father. Or if over the years there had been numerous men in my mother's life. How could we best minister to Rodica's need? Oh, if only she would know the love of Jesus, what a difference it would make! That night we prayed for wisdom, and we prayed for Rodica's peace.

Weeks passed and we found Rodica drawn closer to us. She found excuses to spend more time at our house. Ruth related that her conversations with Rodica were becoming deeper and more personal.

"You know, Ruth," I said one evening as we were discussing Rodica's situation, "I've been thinking that she might be under conviction from the Holy Spirit. If she comes, wanting to talk, let's drop whatever we are doing and talk with her right then and there. No duty can possibly be as important as helping a soul who is seeking peace with God."

"Tata Johnny, are you going along up on the hill?" asked Tina as she entered my office.

"I sure am," I responded. "We are all going together. I wouldn't miss it for anything! Did you see all the corn I prepared to take along?"

"You mean in the big white trash cans?"

"Right. Last evening I stacked those two thirty-gallon containers full of sweet corn with all the ears pointed up. Then I filled the containers with salt water."

"Why did you do that?" Tina wanted to know.

"Well, I've opened those tips a little, and this will allow the salt water to work its way down inside the husks. Then this evening, when we roast them on the grill, the steam will cook the roasting ears, and the salt will make them absolutely delicious. They will also have a hint of smoke flavor from the open fire."

"Oh," said Tina with her gentle smile of understanding, "that sounds so good. And we're going to play games too, aren't we?"

"I'm sure we will."

Later that evening smoke burned my eyes as I bent over the grill, turning the roasting ears. There was a swirl of activity about me. I was somewhat distracted by the interesting conversations flowing among staff gathered around the neighboring fire. The hill and forest behind Burdujeni, a suburb bordering Iţcani, had been assaulted and conquered by orphanage children, workers, and the entire American staff from our different departments. The woods resounded with the happy noise of a game of dodge ball and shouts of children climbing trees or playing tag.

"Mama Ruth, Mama Ruth, look at me up here! Look, Mama Ruth!"

Ruth momentarily stopped arranging food containers on the tables and looked about for the owner of the voice.

"Here," Paula waved from her perch high in a tree.

Mama Ruth smiled and waved back, but added a warning, "You be careful!"

Workers drew closer to the campfires as the shadows lengthened. They stood together in groups of twos and threes and talked of their work experiences. It was just good to be together.

The last of the roasting ears were nearly done. Ruth was scurrying about over at the tables, helping the other ladies with last-minute food preparation.

"Mama Ruth?"

"Yes, Rodica?"

"I want to talk with you."

"Right now?"

Rodica nodded solemnly.

"What do you want to talk about?"

With a sober expression Rodica replied, "I want to talk about God and my heart."

Ruth heard the Holy Spirit's gentle whisper in her soul saying, "Go!" But where should they go? There were people everywhere! Then she spied the big orphanage van.

"Come," she said, and together they walked to the van and climbed into its spacious second seat.

"Let's pray," Ruth suggested. "Dear God, look down upon us tonight and help us to know your will. Help us to yield our hearts to you. I know you have been speaking to Rodica. Help her be willing to open her heart completely before you. Dear Father, you know her need; you love her and want her to love and obey you in return. Be with us and guide us, we pray in the name of Jesus. Amen."

The carefree shouts of the children pursuing their games penetrated the van where Ruth and Rodica sat. But they were tuning their ears to hear another voice, the voice of the Holy Spirit.

"Rodica," Ruth began, "I am here to help you in any way I can. What do you want to share with me?"

At first there was no response. From the light of the flickering campfires, Ruth saw Rodica's eyes fill with tears. She waited. Then in a voice that quavered with deep feeling, Rodica said, "I want to confess my sins and ask Jesus to come into my heart."

"But Rodica, I know that you have not been living a holy life. What are you going to do about that?" Ruth gently probed.

"Oh, Mama Ruth, I want to confess all my sins!" cried Rodica with deep conviction as the tears flowed freely down her cheeks.

God in heaven reached down into that van. He heard the cry of Rodica's penitent heart as she confessed her sins and invited Jesus to come into her heart and change her life. Her eyes cried and her heart cried. Mama Ruth sat with Rodica in the van, listening and praying as the Holy Spirit accomplished His work of ushering Rodica to her Father.

Outside, the children had been called to stop their games and gather around to ask the blessing on the food. Soon long lines of hungry people were filing past the loaded tables.

Following the prayer, I raced back to attend the last fifteen roasting ears still on the grill. Squinting through the smoke, I sensed someone approaching. I heard Rodica's low voice intone, "Tata Johnny, I want to tell you something."

"Sure," I responded absently.

There was a pause.

"I'm listening," I said as I deftly rolled another ear of hot corn and jerked my hand back.

"I repented and asked Jesus to come into my heart," Rodica said in a matter-of-fact manner.

"Oh, really? That's good," I said rather disbelievingly.

Then a thrill shot through me as she continued. "I talked about it with Mama Ruth, and we prayed together, and now I am a Christian."

The corn suddenly lost my attention. With a rush of feeling I exclaimed, "Rodica, this is truly wonderful!" She smiled at me through the haze of smoke and walked toward the food tables and Mama Ruth.

That evening Ruth recounted all that had taken place, and we rejoiced together.

The very next day Rodica brought Vasilica down to our little gray house to talk with Ruth about God. Together they discussed the wonderful way we can live with Jesus in our hearts, and how He gives us power to resist temptation. When that precious conversation drew to a close, Vasilica, with all of her eight-year-old understanding, said, "Now I'm closer to Jesus than I was."

In our morning meeting I joyfully shared these spiritual encounters with Ionică and asked him to also talk with the girls. Ruth and I were keenly aware that when it came to spiritual matters, our language limitations still hindered us. Also, he knew these children better than we did and possessed a keener insight into their personalities. We wanted to do everything we could to help them become firmly established in the Lord.

God's Authorization

"Johnny," said Ionică as he stopped by my office after spending the entire morning in Suceava, "I have good news from the Department of Education."

"Really?" I asked, eager to hear his report.

"I was told unofficially that Nathaniel Christian School has been granted authorization to include grades five through eight."

"Praise the Lord, Ionică! That is a direct answer to prayer! But what about the authorization to build the new school building? Has any progress been made on that?" I asked, hoping against hope that we could move ahead with the necessary building.

"Whenever I speak with the mayor personally, he seems favorable, but there has also been some pretty strong opposition from his undersecretaries. So at this point, we really don't know. Still, this authorization to operate is one answer to prayer. Let's just believe God will help us with the building department authorization also," said Ionică encouragingly.

Ten days later Ionică explained that he had a meeting with the mayor and that we could begin digging the basement for the new school building. But the mayor instructed us not to begin on the actual school structure until we received final word from him.

We rejoiced that God was bringing things together for the Nathaniel Christian School.

Our married children, our grandchildren, and our son John had come to Romania for a visit, and we were overjoyed to have them. Vali found a simple house in the foothills of a quiet mountain village about an hour's drive from the orphanage. There we rested and reconnected as a family.

The country folks followed their daily routine without regard to the foreigners camped among them. Our twenty-eight-year-old son Dwight was fascinated by the hand scything, raking, and stacking of hay that was going on in the meadow right next door. Being the enterprising person that he was, he hopped over the fence and bridged the language barrier as best he could. He indicated that he would like to join them with their haymaking. The villagers were most accommodating, and an elderly lady handed him her handmade, wood-tined rake. I smiled as I watched. Dwight struggled to keep the freshly cut hay raked up as fast as the lady was forking it onto the drying rack. The rack was made of a ten-foot fir sapling that had been cut and dried. Its branches were trimmed to about two feet. The butt end of the sapling had been sharpened and driven into the ground. I watched, fascinated, as the elderly woman deftly forked the hay onto its supporting branches. It was evident by her movements that she had grown up forking hay. Her husband and sister formed another team nearby.

Ten minutes of this vigorous exercise caused Dwight to more deeply appreciate the lives of these hard-working Romanian villagers. In twenty minutes Dwight realized that he was completely winded and conceded defeat. He shook his head as he handed the rake to the sixty-three-year-old lady and climbed back over the fence. "I can't keep up with her," he panted as he joined me in the cool shade of a spreading maple.

As we hiked through the rugged mountains, we found trails and uprooted areas where European wild boars had roamed. We drank in the quietness of the mountain beauty, played games, rested, and had cookouts. But mainly we just caught up like a family who had been separated for a year and a half.

Our three days soon ended, and we packed up and headed for the orphanage. We entered the orphanage compound and parked beside the little gray house. Children came running from several directions to welcome us home. They surrounded the van and chattered excitedly.

"Where did you go?"

"Was it fun?"

"Did you go swimming?"

"What did you do?" they all wanted to know at once.

"Mama Ruth, we missed you so much!" cried several of the girls, all trying to hug her at once.

"Tata Johnny, Tata Johnny, you know what?" called Costică above the din. "Florica let Papagal out!"

"What do you mean?" I asked. "She knows she is not supposed to open his cage without permission. Has she put him back?"

"She took him outside and let him go!" insisted Costică.

I shook my head in disbelief. Surely there must be some mistake.

"It's true, Tata Johnny," said Mihaela. Her serious voice and sad, dark eyes confirmed what Costică had just said.

"Well," I said, "I am very sorry. This is quite a disappointment!"

"I bet you're going to spank her," interjected Beti. "Aren't you?"

I pushed the thoughts of Florica and Papagal out of my mind. I would have to deal with that later.

In spite of many willing helpers, it took a bit of effort and time to clean out the van and properly stow the items from our trip. Once that task was accomplished, I walked up to the orphanage and called Florica into my office.

"Florica," I began, "tell me what happened to Papagal."

"I was just giving him a ride, you know, and, well, he just flew away and I couldn't catch him," she explained with a shrug, raising her hands in a gesture of helplessness.

"What do you mean, you were giving him a ride? Did you have him on your shoulder, as Daniel sometimes does?"

"No, I was holding him in my hand, and I just took him outside for a little walk, you know, and he sort of flew away." She laughed nervously.

"You mean to tell me that you took our parakeet out of his cage without permission, and then you took him outside while you were holding him in your hand?" I asked in disbelief.

Florica nodded. "You see, I didn't want to squeeze him too tight, and he just gave a quick wiggle and flew right out of my hand. I didn't mean to, Tata Johnny, it just happened."

"Florica, tell me, what is the rule I made about you children taking the parakeet out of his cage?"

"You said we shouldn't take Papagal out of his cage until we get permission from you," answered Florica.

"That's right! And Florica, if you had listened to me, he would be safely in his cage right now. But because you didn't obey, he is outside somewhere and will freeze and die as soon as the weather turns cold. So your disobedience will cause Papagal's death," I admonished, trying to appeal to her sense of reason.

"But the other birds don't die," countered Florica.

"That's true, but parakeets come from the tropics where it is warm all year long," I explained. "They can't survive the cold winters in Romania."

"I'm sorry, Tata Johnny, I really am! But you weren't here, so I couldn't ask permission, and I just knew that Papagal wanted to go outside! I wasn't going to let him go. He just went. I couldn't help it."

I knew that Florica hadn't intentionally let our parakeet go, but her love for animals was greater than her desire to be obedient. Disgusted with her disobedience, but uncertain what measures to take, I dismissed her.

Our son John stayed with us for several weeks longer than the rest of our children. He assisted Franklin in being a big brother to the boys. Franklin had acquired a beautiful German shepherd named Jessica and worked extensively to train her. He had taught her amazingly well. John added several new dimensions to her training program, and Jessica was an apt student. However, the many hours working together with Franklin and the orphanage boys proved to be the greatest blessing of all. I felt sorry for Jessica as I watched her respond to the command to lie still. She patiently awaited Frank-

Jessica's obedience and strength is tested to the max.

lin's command to be released, even though the children whistled and called imploringly. She had been taught to jump a four-foot fence on command, climb a ladder onto the roof of a building, and, much to Ruth's dismay, leap through our house window. I thought I had seen it all until I looked out the window and saw Jessica dutifully pulling a wagon weighted with a heavy block of wood. Then, to prove his dog's worth, Franklin had a couple of children hop on and ride also. The children were delighted with the ride, and Jessica endured it all with loving patience. The boys were learning that much could be accomplished through patient training.

Several of the boys began training their rabbits. Pavel trained his to jump when prompted, and it would leap a full three feet, much to the boys' delight.

However, not all of this training knowledge was being put into legitimate use, as we discovered several weeks later. As Franklin approached the little animal barn, he heard a loud bang followed by gales of laughter. He hurried to see what the boys were up to this time. Daniel was watching from the open doorway with a big grin on his face.

"What are you guys doing?" asked Franklin.

"Oh, Franklin," laughed Daniel, "you have got to see this! It's the funniest thing!"

Franklin peered into the alley just outside the barn where Marius was dancing about in front of our big Russian ram. There was a mischievous grin on Marius's face and a murderous gleam in the ram's eye.

"Watch, Franklin! Just watch this!" shouted Marius as he pranced a little closer to the ram. At that moment the ram arched his neck high and uttered a guttural *baaa!* as he reared slightly. When his forefeet hit the ground, he was in full forward motion. Marius darted ahead of the ram toward the gate, glancing over his shoulder as he ran. It looked like Marius was in trouble, but suddenly he gave a mighty leap and vaulted over the gate a split second before the ram hit the gate with his thick, curled horns. *Bam!* The boys were in stitches of laughter as the ram backed off several steps and shook his head wonderingly.

"Pavel," the boys cried, "you do it! You do it!" It was a challenge Pavel couldn't resist. He eased out into the pasture, keeping a close eye on the ram. Out there he was a bit farther from the protection of the gate. The ram eyed Pavel and took several menacing steps in his direction. Pavel danced closer to the ram and then ran back several steps. The ram made several false starts, pausing each time as if trying to figure it all out. Suddenly he gave a half *baa,* half-grunt battle cry, reared, tucked in his chin, and took off after Pavel with all the body language of a warrior intent on killing his enemy. Pavel obviously didn't think this was a battle worth dying for and made a beeline toward the pasture's chain-link fence. Franklin held his breath. Pavel leaped, grabbed the pipe along the top of the fence, and flung his legs out of harm's way just as the infuriated ram hit the fence at full tilt. The spring action of the fence simply tossed the ram right back the way he had come. Howls of laughter erupted from the boys.

"Franklin, you do it! You do it!" they cried next.

Two lessons had been learned down at the little animal barn. One was that the ram was an impossibly slow learner, and the other was that the ram now hated anyone who crossed his path.

"Dad," said John one evening as we sat in the living room, "I am determined to teach these boys to pick up the things they use and put them away when they're finished. I told Marius that if he leaves the feed bucket out in the pasture one more time, I'm going to make him crawl on his hands and knees to put it away. Well, today he did it again, so I marched him out there and told him to get down on his hands and knees and crawl with that bucket all the way back to the barn and put it where it belongs. He begged, saying he had forgotten to put the bucket away. He wasn't at all happy with me, but I made him stick to it, and I believe it will help him remember next time."

I had to smile as I visualized this scene. "You know, John," I reminisced, "I so well remember when you were a boy. Over and over again I had to remind you to go back, pick up things, and put them where they belonged. I wish you would have taught yourself then as you are teaching the orphanage boys now," I chuckled.

The paperwork finally came from the mayor's office, authorizing the construction of the new Nathaniel Christian School. A voluntary masonry crew from the States came to assist in this mammoth work project. Ionică informed me that it was largely through the mayor's persistence that we had finally been granted our building authorization and suggested that we acknowledge his assistance and thank him for his help. We decided to invite the mayor and his family to join us for a cookout at our little gray house.

John marinated steak and pork tenderloin. Later he started a fire and set up the grill. The orphanage children helped us set up tables on our lawn, and the ladies worked hard all day to prepare for the coming of Suceava's mayor and family. I was excited and my wife was on edge. We were all busy. It wasn't often that the mayor came to our house for supper.

Finally all was ready. Our entire family was present. Ionică was there with his wife and daughters, and John began grilling the meat. Ionică had warned the orphanage children to stay up near the orphanage and play quietly to make a good impression on the mayor.

The mayor arrived with his family, much to the excitement of the children as well as the adults. We enjoyed the meal immensely. As the meal progressed, I noticed a steady stream of children walking to and from Alvin's house just across the garden from where we sat. They had become experts at inventing questions they just had to ask Lil right then. Others remembered some borrowed item that needed to be returned immediately. As each child walked slowly across the lawn, he cast longing eyes in our direction.

Ionică sat with his wife and daughters near the mayor, and their talk naturally gravitated to the new school building. The meal was nearly ended when the mayor began telling us just how he had gone about obtaining our building permit.

"I presented the proposal to the building commission," explained the mayor. "Immediately there arose opposition among the commissioners. One raised the question whether we should allow evangelical people to build their own school. Several others instantly supported him. 'Okay,' I said, 'let's forget about this school; here is a different problem.

" 'As you know, many of our young people have left for other countries to find better-paying jobs. This has left us with a growing problem. Who is going to take care of the elderly villagers? Some are old or infirm and can no longer work. They cannot care for themselves. We need to build facilities and care for these elderly folk as they live out their days. We need to buy land, draft the design, and build the buildings. We need to find qualified staff to operate these homes for the elderly.'

"One of my commissioners protested. 'Why are you even talking about this when you know how low we are in funds? We could never finance such a project with our budget.'

" 'Well, then, how are we going to resolve this problem?' I asked. I allowed them time to think this through, and then I told them about a group of private citizens who would be willing to take on this work. 'These people are evangelicals, and they have a vision for helping the elderly. Furthermore, these people have the means to build and maintain such a facility.'

"One of the commissioners suggested, 'Why don't we authorize these people to go ahead and build and allow them to care for these older people?' The rest of the commissioners soon agreed and the proposal carried. The permit was given to the evangelicals to build a home for the elderly.

"With that out of the way, I came back to the issue of the Nathaniel Christian School. I told the commissioners, 'Here are some evangelicals who are willing to build their own school. They will pay for the land and the construction. They will pay the teachers' wages, and they will pay for the books. They have already received authorization from the Department of Education to operate grades five through eight in addition to the first four grades they are already operating. Why are you willing to authorize private citizens to build a care center for the elderly, but you hesitate to give authorization for the Nathaniel Christian School building?'

"You see," said the mayor, "it is so important to know your people and to understand how they think. I had to shame them into giving in and signing the papers."

Dessert was being served when the mayor's cell phone rang. He excused himself and left the table to take the call.

No sooner had he gone than the mayor's wife took up where her husband had left off. "You heard everything my husband said about getting that building authorization for you? Now let me tell you something. It wasn't so much my husband who obtained that authorization for you; it was the Lord!"

With supper ended, the women began taking care of the dishes while Ionică took the mayor on a short tour. He didn't get too far because the mayor saw the orphanage boys playing foot tennis in the gym and joined them. He was surprisingly agile and gave the boys stiff competition.

Soon it was bedtime for the boys, and the mayor prepared to leave. He seemed to appreciate our work with the children, and we certainly appreciated his friendship and support.

Crews of dedicated workers flew over from America and donated their time to build the new school building. Several local men were hired to carry on the school's construction. Through working closely together, lasting friendships were forged between the Romanian brethren and the visiting American volunteers.

The race was on to see whether the new school could be enclosed before winter weather set in. In a short time the masonry walls of the basement were completed and the floor joists set in place and covered with plywood.

"Tata Johnny, we want to see the new school," begged Ionela. "May we go look at it?"

"Please, Tata Johnny, you'll let us, won't you?" pleaded Daniela.

"I'll tell you what," I told the girls, "the workers will soon go to lunch, and I'll take you down after they leave so we won't get in their way. Tell the boys, and we'll all go together."

"All right!" squealed Tina, clasping her hands together.

A very enthusiastic group of children gathered outside the orphanage. I led the way as we walked down past the little gray house and the church. We carefully picked our way down the hill and over the mounds of soil excavated from the school basement. Gingerly we inched our way over the plank spanning the excavation and gathered on the huge plywood deck.

"Tata Johnny, where's first grade going to be?" Beti wanted to know.

"Where are you going to have the fifth-grade classroom?" Laura asked imploringly. I pointed out where I thought each of the classrooms would be but explained that several classrooms would be in the basement as well.

"But, Tata Johnny, how will we get to the basement?" asked Cristina.

I showed them where the staircase would be placed near the front entrance.

"Is Nenea Ionică going to have an office here in the school?" Iosif asked.

"Yes. A wide hallway will run through the entire length of the building. Classrooms will open to the left and right of the hallway. Nenea Ionică will be the principal of the school, and we are putting his office near the center so he will be near all the classrooms."

"Can we help build the school?" Ionuț asked.

"Well, perhaps some of you bigger boys can help in the morning when we set up the walls," I suggested. "These walls are framed with two-by-sixes and are ninety-six feet long. They are very heavy. Early tomorrow morning they are going to need many willing hands to set up the walls. If you bigger boys want to help, I'm sure you would be welcome."

"But what can we girls do?" asked Lavinia.

"Later, after the heavier work is done, there will be work for you girls to do as well," I promised.

Many willing hands raise the new school wall.

As the children walked back toward the orphanage, I took one last look around the construction site and thanked God for allowing this to become a reality. I realized anew the great truth spoken by the mayor's wife, "It wasn't my husband who obtained this authorization for you; it was the Lord!"

Chapter 14

Schooling

July's afternoon sun beat down relentlessly upon Tanti Anişoara and the ten girls under her watchful eye as they labored together to pull weeds from the bean patch. Some of the larger weeds were deeply rooted, and the heat made this job even more distasteful. They pulled, they sweated, and they itched together. Tanti Anişoara was determined that her girls would learn to stick to a job until it was finished. She was casting about in her mind how she might reward them for their diligence—that is, all except Ioana. She had reminded Ioana over and over to get busy and help, but every time she turned to check, Ioana was just standing there, refusing to pull a single weed.

"Come on, Ioana," she called. "Come work beside me; then, if a weed is too big, I will help you."

Ioana took a reluctant step in her tanti's direction but paused, grabbed the top of a weed, and gave it a half-hearted jerk. The weed snapped off just below her grasp. She fumbled with the remainder of the weed, but only succeeded in snapping it off a little lower, allowing the roots to continue growing. *What does it matter, anyhow?* she thought.

All around her the other girls were bending low and grasping the weeds just above the roots. Leaning back on their heels, they pulled and uprooted them, piling them together to be picked up with wagons.

Tanti Anişoara straightened and placed her hand on her aching back as she surveyed the remainder of the bean patch. "Girls," she announced with a practiced eye, "if we all work steadily, we'll be finished in another forty-five minutes, and then I'll have a surprise for all who have done a good job."

"Oh, good!" exclaimed Cristina as she grabbed a weed half her own height. "Come on, girls!" she said enthusiastically as she leaned back hard. Nothing happened. She jerked with all her might. Suddenly the roots gave up their hold in the hard-packed soil, and Cristina toppled over backward and sat down with a plop, laughing. She glanced toward Ioana, who was toying around with the top of another weed. "Tanti," she complained as she scrambled to her feet, "Ioana isn't helping."

"Really?" said Tanti Anişoara without turning to look.

It's not fair! thought Cristina as she watched Ioana give a disdainful sniff and turn her back toward Cristina, who was already reaching for another weed.

The girls worked diligently, and soon their section of the patch was weeded. They clustered around their tanti as she led them toward the orphanage. "What's our surprise?" Mariana wanted to know. Her hands were stained green, and her face was hot and sweaty. Her sandy-colored hair stuck fast to her forehead.

"Go wash your hands and faces, and I'll tell you." All ten girls crammed into the bathroom to wash while Tanti Anişoara walked down the hall to my office. Tapping lightly at the open doorway, she announced, "Tata Johnny, my class of girls has helped me so well in the garden, I'd like to reward them."

"Sure," I said. "What do you have in mind?"

"We are all pretty warm from working in the hot sun, and I thought they might like wading in the creek below the meadow. Could we?" she asked with a pleasant smile.

"It's certainly all right with me," I said. "All I ask is that they dress modestly since it is near the bridge where people from the village pass by."

"Oh, of course. Thank you, Tata Johnny." She paused at the door and announced, "I'll have them back in plenty of time for supper."

I smiled when I heard squeals of excitement and thundering footsteps as the girls scrambled up to their rooms to put on their "creek clothes." Moments later the back door banged repeatedly as the girls ran to catch up with Tanti Anişoara, who was already advancing toward the creek's refreshing waters.

However, the girls' excitement turned to dismay when Tanti Anişoara stopped purposefully at the edge of the garden. "Ioana, please come with me. The rest of you stay right here until I return," she said as she marched off in the direction of Martha's apartment. Ioana followed.

"Uh-oh," exclaimed Cristina. "I think Ioana is in trouble."

"You think?" said Mariana. "What's Tanti Anişoara going to do?"

Tanti Anişoara soon returned, without Ioana, and the girls resumed their march toward the creek.

Martha emerged from her apartment a few minutes later and entered the garden with Ioana. "This is how you do it," demonstrated Martha as she bent over and pulled a weed from the soil. "Grab it down low and lean back. There you go!" she said encouragingly as the weed came up in Ioana's hand. Again and again Martha bent close as Ioana pulled yet another weed.

Ioana's face looked very sober as Martha explained that, because she had refused to listen to her tanti and do her share of work along with the others, she now had to pull weeds alone while the others cooled off in the creek and enjoyed their fun together.

Ioana reached thoughtfully for another weed. Just then peals of laughter and squeals of delight echoed up from the creek bottom, and big tears welled up in Ioana's eyes.

"Just keep pulling weeds so you can go along next time," Martha encouraged her, hoping the discipline would not only rid our garden of weeds, but would also extract the weed of stubbornness from Ioana's heart.

The blackboards in the Nathaniel School were far from satisfactory. They were made of large sheets of glass. The back sides of these glass panels were painted black, and the face side was etched with a strong acid solution. This gave the surface a slightly roughened texture upon which one could write with chalk. However, the acid did not do a thorough job of etching, and there were random slick areas on our blackboards where the chalk refused to leave its mark. Teachers and students alike were used to keeping a wet rag handy with which to swipe the glass in the area where they intended to write. The wet surface allowed the chalk to write reasonably well. So the swipe-and-write method became the order of the day.

I had ordered a special chalkboard preparation with which to paint the glass chalkboards in each of our five classrooms. This meant that the glass had to be dismounted from the wall, placed horizontally, and carefully painted. After several coats were applied and the slow curing process was completed, the glass panels were ready for reinstallation. It was tedious work, but the results were well worth the effort. But now I began to wonder if we would be able to locate a more satisfactory chalkboard material for the new school. I visited several schools in the Suceava area, but found that they, too, were using glass chalkboards.

Preparations were made for the first day of school. Teachers who had the credentials to teach fifth grade were interviewed and hired. The law required no less than three fifth-grade teachers for the different subjects.

Brother Willis had moved the Teaching Ministries Program with their Gospel literature distribution to the newly completed office above the Nathaniel Store. This allowed the Nathaniel School to utilize the vacant office for the fifth-grade classroom till the new schoolhouse could be completed.

With school starting soon, Ionică and Vali wanted to do something special for the children. Included in their plans was an excursion to visit a village school, a village mayor's office, and a village bakery. The big van was crammed to capacity with excited children. Like all children, they dearly loved to go to new places and see new things.

At the school the principal welcomed them into a huge, two-story brick building. The bare concrete stairs and hallway resounded with the steps of many feet as the Nathaniel children followed Ionică, Vali, and the school principal. They entered the high-ceilinged classroom filled with fifty seats, a teacher's desk, and many glass cases with biology exhibits. Glancing about the room, it was easy to see the school's acceptance of the theory of evolution. The walls held posters and diagrams depicting evolving animals and epochs of time far exceeding the Biblical account. Yet prominently displayed at several places were icons of saints revered by the Orthodox believers. One had to wonder how students were to reconcile these opposing beliefs.

True to form, the blackboards were made of acid-etched glass and situated at the head of the room. Spacious windows were positioned to the left side of the students. This was a never-to-be-challenged rule in all Romanian schools to keep the natural lighting from casting the shadow of the student's right hand on the work he was performing. All students were right-handed. Should a first-grade child show signs of being left-handed, he was quickly broken of the habit.

On the way to the next village, Ionică wanted the children to enjoy a bird's-eye view of the village sprinkled in the valley below. He stopped the van on a prominent knob, and the children got out to view the beauty of the village. There was the spire of the Orthodox church standing head and shoulders above its fellows. The village flourmill could be seen with a number of horse-drawn wagons waiting patiently for the wheat to be ground. The air was crisp and clear and the view breathtaking. When the order was given to get back into the van to go visit the village bakery, the children happily scrambled to get back to their favorite seats. The doors were closed and the driver tried to start the engine, but try as he might, the key would not turn. Again he tried, but the big Ford van's ignition switch refused to budge.

"What's the matter?" chorused several boys. In desperation the driver gave a mighty wrench, and the stubborn ignition turned with a snap, but the engine didn't make a sound. In surprised disbelief the driver turned the ignition back and forth, but the only sound was a peculiar grinding from within the steering column.

When the driver pulled the key from the defunct ignition, he was surprised to find that only half of the key was in his hand. The other half had snapped off deep within the lock.

"Maybe we could push the van," suggested one of the older boys. But the driver explained that the steering column was locked and the wheels sharply turned, so pushing it was out of the question.

"Well, we will just have to walk from here," Ionică announced.

"Way down to that village?" asked one of the smaller girls.

"You want to stay here by yourself?" asked her seatmate.

"Everyone walk on the left side of the road," cautioned Vali, "and watch out for oncoming vehicles."

Soon a happy group of children marched two abreast toward the distant village, while Vali called to inform me of their problem. He gave me precise directions to the van and told me where they would be waiting with the children. I ran over a list of tools that might be useful, gathered them along with a spare key, and set off.

I found the van and examined the frozen ignition. With my flashlight I could just make out the shiny stub of the broken key buried nearly an inch in the heart of the lock. With needle-nose pliers I was able to bend a sharp hook on the end of a thin wire. But try as I might, I couldn't get it to grab the broken key stub. Again and again I tried reshaping the wire, but to no avail. What a tedious task! I would have to come up with something better.

I found a bobby pin and cut it to length. I was able to fashion a sharp V-hook on its end, and with a prayer on my lips, I inserted it into the lock. I felt the bobby pin slide past the end of the stub. Holding my breath and concentrating, I gingerly pulled back. Something within gave slightly, but the bobby pin slipped off the stub. I tried again. This time the hook held, and I breathed a prayer of thanksgiving as the key stub dropped onto the floor.

I inserted the spare key, but it refused to turn, and I paused as the thought hit me, *Perhaps the ignition is damaged. Where in all of Romania will we be able to find another one?* Again I tried turning the key, but to no avail. I sat there, utterly defeated. Then the Lord nudged me with another thought. *Maybe the steering has too much tension on it.* Again I tried to turn that stubborn key, this time with my other hand rocking the steering wheel. The key suddenly turned, and the most gorgeous engine sound filled the van. "Praise the Lord!" involuntarily shot from my lips.

I found the children waiting at the village store, thirstily drinking bottles of pop. When we tried to pay the storeowner for the drinks, he refused, saying he wanted to give the children a treat. We thanked the kind storeowner profusely as we said our goodbyes and headed for the village bakery.

The baker explained their routine for baking bread. I was curious to see how they operated their huge brick oven. It was fully ten feet deep, and as wide, yet its opening only measured sixteen inches from top to bottom.

Asking the children to stand back, the owner took a fuel-oil-fired flamethrower and propped it in the opening of his oven. The roar of the two-foot flame made it difficult to hear as he explained that this flame would heat the bricks. Once they were hot enough, he extinguished the flame and allowed the draft to pull the oil fumes up the chimney. Then he used a long-handled paddle to place the pans of bread deep within the oven. As I left the bakery, I couldn't help but wonder what our inspectors would say if we fired fuel oil directly into the oven space where we placed edible products.

Three days later Ionică stopped in at my office. "Johnny," he said, "I am going to interview a potential teacher, and I want your opinion. Would you have time to join us?"

"Sure, I'll be there in a couple of minutes."

I entered the conference room, and Ionică introduced me to Mariana Leonte, a pleasant-looking twenty-two-year-old with two years of teaching experience.

"We are interested in hiring Christian teachers to fill our needs here," began Ionică. "The children from the Nathaniel Orphanage have suffered devastating situations in their homes. Some have experienced the death of their parents. Others are still grappling with the pain of having been abandoned by their father or mother, and we have a number of children who were abandoned by both of their parents. Some of our children are as much as two years behind in their schooling because of these traumatic circumstances in their lives. They were unwanted and unloved until they came here, so we are looking for teachers who are willing to do more than just teach. We need teachers who will love these children. They are behind in their learning and need teachers who are willing to sacrifice their time and go far beyond the call of duty in order to help them catch up. Are you willing to do this for these children?"

I glanced at Mariana Leonte's face and then averted my gaze as I saw tears glistening in her eyes. "I have prayed about this," she said with a tremor in her voice, "and I feel that God has prepared me."

"But I must be honest with you," continued Ionică. "If you come to work for us, and we for any reason fail to obtain the final approval to continue the Nathaniel Christian School, then the Department of Education might not be willing to hire you back to teach in their public schools. Do you understand how this could affect your teaching career?"

Mrs. Leonte was well aware that this could mean all her schooling and teacher preparation would be wasted, but she responded, "I'll just have to trust the Lord about that."

"Mrs. Leonte," continued Ionică, "we are looking for a dedicated teacher. We do not want you to teach for us if your decision is based only on the salary or upon good working conditions. We do not want you to even consider it unless your heart and soul are in this work."

Tears were now coursing down Mariana's cheeks, and she could barely speak. Finally she was able to say, "If you will hire me, I will come."

Word spread quickly throughout the community that the Nathaniel Christian School had been granted authorization to proceed with grades one through eight. There was a rush as Christian parents enrolled their children.

The Nathaniel School had originally been designed to serve the educational needs of our orphanage children. We wanted to provide a well-rounded education in a safe Christian environment. Now we were accepting selected children from Christian families in our community. This would be a blessing as it broadened the horizons of our Nathaniel children through their interaction with others from normal home settings. It also gave us greater contact with the people of our community.

The orphanage workers' children were given first chance to enroll in our school. Other enrollees were given consideration as space permitted. We had purposely designed our classrooms to accommodate a maximum of fifteen students in order for the teacher to give more individual attention to each student.

The opening day of school couldn't wait for the new building, which was still several months from completion. Seventy-three children were assembled in the gym with their teachers. There was an air of excitement as they formed straight lines, each class standing with its teacher. Every child was dressed up for the occasion, and many students carried bouquets with which to honor their teachers.

Ionică asked me to have a devotional for the student body. I read from Isaiah 40:12-15, "Who hath measured the waters in the hollow of his hand, and meted out heaven with the span . . . ?" I pointed out that in this passage we find mathematics, astronomy, geology, geography, and sociology. "In fact," I explained, "an education devoid of God is an incomplete education."

Ionică addressed the assembly with challenges for teachers and students alike to do their best. I glanced over the rows of children, and mixed emotions flooded my heart. The boys looked so serious and grown-up in their white shirts and dark pants. The girls appeared especially sweet in the matching dresses our seamstress had sewn.

There was Liviu standing at the very front of his class. He was quick and would learn easily. I caught an infectious smile on his upturned face as his teacher walked by.

Monica and Beni were standing with their respective classes. My mind went back to the horrible conditions of abandonment from which we had rescued them. Here they stood with a new life and new opportunities opening to them.

Little Ica looked a bit worried standing at the head of the line of first-grade girls. I gave her a reassuring nod and acknowledged her

Lined up for the opening day of school.

timid smile in response. In spite of the fact that she was approaching her ninth birthday, Ica was only now entering the first grade.

Ionică's strong voice echoed in the gym as he encouraged the teachers to give themselves for these children. He challenged them to be godly examples for the students to follow. A child and a teacher from each of the five grades led in prayer. A teacher spoke briefly on the need to impart knowledge in order to equip and prepare these students for life ahead.

Ionică asked a father from the community to share his vision and blessing for the Nathaniel Christian School. A quick glance at my watch confirmed that these seventy-three children had been standing quietly for nearly forty-five minutes, and I was sure they were wishing they could be dismissed to their classrooms so they could sit down. Ionică finally closed with prayer, and the teachers marched off, leading their students to the classrooms. Nathaniel Christian School officially began its fifth year.

Two days later, as I sat in my office preparing a fax for CAM's Ohio office, Manu appeared in my doorway.

"Well, Manu," I greeted him, "how do you like being in fifth grade?"

"It's great!" came his enthusiastic reply. "Tata Johnny, every teacher is perfect, just perfect!" Here Manu closed his eyes and tilted his face upward as though he were savoring some tantalizing aroma. Then, pointing heavenward with his eyes still screwed tightly shut, he said fervently, "Thank you, Lord!"

His words echoed the sentiment of my own heart. Certainly the Lord was watching over these children, and He had blessed us with a Christian school.

Chapter 15

The Surprise

I rang the bell for silence when the meal was finished and asked if Ionică had anything to announce.

"Yes," he said as he rose to address the children still seated around their tables. "I want all of you to have your homework finished by four o'clock this afternoon. Then come to the living room, because I'll have a surprise for you."

Murmurs of excitement ran through the dining room as the children guessed what the surprise might be. "I'll bet it's a new soccer ball," said Nicu.

"Oh, I hope it's chocolates!" exclaimed Ştefania.

"Or maybe a big fish for the aquarium," guessed Iosif.

I rang the bell a second time to restore order. "Marta," I said, glancing at the wall chart, "it's your turn to pick the song."

She thought for only a moment before saying, "Jesus Loves All the Children."

It was one of her favorites and had an English verse as well as a Romanian one. The children sang enthusiastically, and they left no room for doubt that they were indeed loved by their heavenly Father. I hoped they could also feel my love for them as I walked from table to table, dismissing each group with a *ding*.

At four o'clock, when nearly all the children were assembled in the living room, Ionică pulled up in his car. Those sitting closest swished back the curtains, and faces filled the windows trying to see the surprise. Ionică walked to the far side of his car and opened the passenger door. An elderly man climbed out. His shoulders were stooped with age and his legs were bowed. With the help of his cane and Ionică's guiding hand, he entered the living room and looked about at all the children.

Ionică introduced him as an eighty-four-year-old brother in the Lord whom he had met years before. "And," continued Ionică, "our brother has a story for you."

If there was one thing the children loved, it was a good story. I watched as the smaller children wiggled in here and there among the older ones to find a comfortable seat. Little Gigi sat with his full attention upon the old man. This was a wonderful surprise!

"Well . . ." The old man rubbed his shiny, copper-headed cane and cleared his throat. "My wife and I had six children and were expecting our seventh. Some of our children were about the size of you older ones back then," he recalled. "That was over forty years ago, and our country was under strict communist rule. The winters were cold and long, and it was difficult to find time to cut enough firewood for the winter after working all day on the collective farm.

"One sunny Friday in December, I was off work. I hitched up my horse to the wagon and took my two oldest boys with me. They were eleven and twelve years old at that time. We took our crosscut saw and ax along to cut the wood. There were no chainsaws in those days," he explained. "We really had to work hard in order to survive."

I glanced at the brother's heavy wrists and well-rounded shoulders, no doubt developed through long years of heavy toil. He was clearly a man of unusual strength and determination.

"We drove our horse and wagon way up into the mountains, looking for dead trees that we could legally cut. You see, in those days the law forbade anyone to cut live trees, but you could cut the dead ones for firewood if you had a permit. We had to go a long way because so many other people had been looking for firewood that it was difficult to find a dead tree. Finally we found a nice one that would make lots of firewood for our family.

"My boys and I took turns as we cut through its trunk with the ax and saw. Finally the big tree crashed to the ground. Then my one boy helped me saw the larger pieces of wood while my other son cut up the smaller limbs with the ax. We began loading the wagon. I was careful to set the brakes so that it wouldn't roll down the steep mountainside.

"We had the wagon half loaded when my youngest son ran up to me all excited, saying he had seen a bear. I didn't pay too much attention to him, because I knew bears were usually afraid of humans and would run away if we left them alone. So I said, 'Just keep cutting wood and the bear won't bother us.'

"But my son was afraid and soon returned saying, 'Dad, look! The bear is coming this way!' I looked to where my son was pointing. Sure enough, a full-grown bear was digging around an old stump. I figured he was hungry and was looking for mice.

"Soon, however, he moved closer to us. I wondered why he didn't run away. My sons said they were scared and begged me to take them home in the wagon. I told them that if they were scared they should climb a tree. If we left the firewood now, someone else would come and take it. 'I'll just keep chopping wood,' I told them. I was sure the sound of my ax would keep the bear away.

"My sons quickly found tall, skinny trees to climb. When the bear came uncomfortably close, I shouted to scare him away, but instead of running, the bear began walking in my direction. I was glad my boys were safely up in their trees, and for a moment I wished I had climbed a tree too, but now it was too late!"

I glanced about the room and saw worried looks on the listeners' faces. Gigi's eyes were large with interest and shining with excitement. He rested his chin in his hands and his elbows on his knees, eager to hear more of the old man's story, but at the same time dreading the outcome. Marian had a frightened look on his face and swallowed hard as the old man continued.

"There was no time now to release the brakes and ride the wagon to safety. My horse was getting nervous; he could smell the bear. Perhaps the bear had also smelled my horse and would attack him. But I took a firm grip on my ax handle, thinking, *No, we need our horse. I will never let that happen!*"

The old man stood to his feet in the middle of the living room, and his gnarled hands took a firm grip on his cane to demonstrate how he had stood forty years earlier.

"The bear didn't run toward me; he just walked without stopping. When he was only ten feet away, he paused for just a moment. I could feel the blood pounding in my ears, and for a moment I forgot everything except that bear. Then, with a savage growl, he lunged at me. In a split second, I drew back my ax and swung it with all my strength. I felt the shock in my arms as the ax made solid contact with the bear's skull. I was shocked when the bear fell at my feet, leaving me standing there, trembling all over. I heard my boys crying and looked around to see they had slid down their trees and were running down the mountainside as fast as their legs could carry them.

"I wondered what I should do next. It was illegal to hunt bear, but I hadn't been hunting. I was simply trying to protect myself. Surely the police would understand. I quickly threw the rest of the cut firewood onto the wagon, but left the uncut portion since I no longer had my boys to help me. I had a chain with me which we sometimes used to pull dead trees to a more level spot where we could cut them more easily. I took this chain, hooked it around the bear's neck, and hitched it to the back of the wagon. Then slowly, carefully, I started down the mountain.

"When I dragged the bear into town, it was almost dark, but the news spread, and people came from all around to see my bear. A great crowd formed and wanted me to tell them what happened. A policeman also showed up and wanted to know why I had killed the bear. So I told him my story all over again, and he wrote everything down on his notepad.

"While I was talking to the policeman, a sophisticated lady stepped out of the crowd to see the bear. She was dressed in fashionable clothes and wore a long fur coat. Maybe she thought my bear would make her another fine coat. Anyway, she stepped right up to the bear and leaned over to get a good look at the bear's head. Perhaps she wanted to see the wound where I had hit him with my ax. I don't know. But at that very moment, the bear opened his mouth and let out a loud *woof!* It scared that poor lady so badly that she staggered backward and her knees wouldn't hold her anymore. Others had to grab her and pull her away or she would have fainted."

The children were leaning forward, drinking in every detail. Tina had involuntarily placed a finger in her mouth, and Beti's big brown eyes were wide and sober.

"As soon as the crowd realized the bear wasn't dead as we had thought, they backed off. One man begged the policeman to shoot the bear. But the policeman refused, saying he couldn't do that since all wildlife was strictly the property of the communist government. Finally they decided to tie the bear with ropes and transport him to a veterinary clinic where they would try to save the bear's life.

"Three days later a policeman came to my house and arrested me, saying the bear had died and I would have to go to prison in Bucureşti. I explained that my wife was soon to have our baby and I couldn't leave my family just now. We had no one else to stay with our children. I reminded him that it was winter. 'I'm sorry,' said the policeman, 'but orders are orders. Come along with me.'

"So they took me to Bucureşti, where they locked me into prison. I had been there two weeks when someone sent word that my wife had gone to the hospital to have our baby and no one was at home to care for the children. The jailer was a kind man and allowed me some freedom to walk about without being locked up all the time. He also informed me that the bear's head had been sent away to a medical laboratory where tests were being performed. I would have to stay in prison until we learned the results.

"One day, while I was free to walk about, I told the jailer that I was going home to my family because they needed me. If there was further legal action against me, they knew where to find me. I told them that I would not run away or hide. The jailer just shrugged his shoulders and looked the other way as I walked out. I made my way home to my family. When I arrived, there was much rejoicing because God had blessed us with a beautiful baby girl and Daddy was back with his children again!

"About a month later we got the results from the tests. The bear that had tried to attack me had rabies. This highly contagious disease causes animals to lose their fear of humans and eventually is fatal to the animal as well as to anyone it bites. Finally the courts decided I was not guilty because this bear would have died anyhow. I still had to pay a fine, but I didn't have to go back to jail. God certainly was good to us!" he concluded.

The old man finished his story and was soon ready to leave. The children stretched their cramped arms and legs as they came back to reality after having lived in his story for forty-five minutes. I knew this elderly brother had made a deep impression on the children when I observed one of the smaller boys with a faraway look in his eyes several days later. He had a firm grasp on a make-believe ax as he swung it purposefully at an imaginary bear. I just hoped he wouldn't wind up in an imaginary prison.

I had just returned from town and was informed that we had visitors. I was surprised to find Beni and Monica seated in the orphanage living room beside a woman they introduced as their mother. When I shook hands and welcomed her, the unmistakable smell of alcohol confirmed the rumors I had heard concerning this woman's drinking problem.

I left them alone to catch up. The children had been rescued nearly two years earlier from a house that would have hardly been fit for livestock. Monica and Beni had nearly frozen after their mother had abandoned them in the dead of winter. They had survived by breaking down the wooden fence outside their shack and burning it in their little tin stove. They had come to us gaunt, hungry, and full of lice. Now that they had developed into beautiful children, loved and cared for, their mother had shown up. Where had she been when they needed her? The rumor was that she had found another man and abandoned the children for him.

I tried to go back to my work, but couldn't push Beni and Monica from my mind. The mayor had declared the children abandoned and in need. A judge had signed them into our care, and an evangelist working in that remote village had rescued Monica and Beni and brought them to us in the middle of the night. Unless the mother could convince the authorities that she had become a competent parent, there was no way her children would have to suffer her neglect again.

Later that afternoon Ionică and Vali walked into my office wanting to know what they should do. "Monica and Beni's mother is begging for the school allocation funds the government gives to families sending children to school," they explained.

"What are you talking about?" I asked in surprise. "She abandoned her children and left them with no money, no food, and no means to keep from freezing during the bitter winter. Then she disappeared and no one knew where she was. They were legally given into our care, and we have fed and clothed them properly. We have loved and provided for them these two years. We have sent them to our private school and paid for their education. We have taught them Bible truths, and they are doing well. They are well adjusted and want to be good. They love being at our orphanage. So now their mother comes, wanting to cash in on the government handout. No way!"

The government had allocated six dollars per child per month to help families of school children buy schoolbooks and clothing. This mother was hardly entitled to those funds, as we provided everything for her children.

"If we give her this money, she will leave the children alone," Ionică said. "I don't really believe she wants the children. We have seen the horrible conditions and neglect they lived in."

"I think she is looking for easy money to buy more alcohol. We have never accepted government money for any of our children, and I see no reason why we should make it available to her. This is a matter of principle," I said.

We agreed that it would be best to maintain our position to not accept government handouts for the Nathaniel children.

Late that afternoon Monica and Beni's mother finally left for the train station. I didn't like the way she had taken Beni and Monica aside and spoken to them in low tones for hours. I didn't trust her, and I felt relieved when she finally left.

On Wednesday I was watering and tying up tomato plants in the greenhouse when the door opened and Cristina rushed in. "Tata Johnny," she panted, "Nenea Ionică wants you to come up to the orphanage. He says he wants you to meet someone."

"Okay," I responded. "Thanks for telling me. I'll clean up and be there in a jiffy."

Several minutes later I entered the orphanage and found Ionică in our big living room, talking intently with a dark man who appeared to be in his mid-thirties. The visitor was dressed in worn clothing and spoke rather coarsely through gaps in his front teeth. A large, ragged scar ran across his cheek. His nose was crooked and appeared to have been broken at least once. He looked like a person who drank heavily and fought easily.

"This is Liviu's father," said Ionică. "He was recently released from prison and has come to see his son." Glancing at his watch, Ionică continued, "It's almost time for recess. Would you please run over to the school and bring Liviu to meet his father?"

"Liviu," I said as we walked toward the orphanage, "your father is here and would like to see you."

"What does he want?" little Liviu asked, a shadow of worry crossing his face.

"He was in prison for a long time and now he wants to see you, that's all," I said reassuringly. *Poor little chap,* I thought. *His mother spent months in the hospital after nearly being killed by this man, and Liviu is scared.*

"Here he is," announced Ionică as we entered the living room together.

"Come here, my son," the visitor said softly. "I've come to see you."

Liviu shuffled over beside the visitor and stood with downcast eyes. His father's rough hand stroked his head. Liviu stood gazing at the floor, no doubt recalling the blows he had often endured from that very same hand.

"So, where are you going to live now?" Ionică addressed the visitor.

"In Arbore where my mother-in-law lives," said Liviu's father. "And there's lots of room for my son there too. I can now take him with me."

Startled, I looked at Ionică, but his face was a mask. Liviu suddenly looked for all the world like a slave on an auction block as he shifted his weight from one foot to the other. He wrinkled his nose and gave a deep sigh.

This just cannot be! I thought. *Surely Ionică would never give little Liviu into the care of this violent man!* I didn't care if he was Liviu's father; he had forfeited his right to have custody of his child. Suddenly I felt just how much Liviu had come to mean to me. I had become very attached to him as he sat beside me at the dining room table day after day. I had used all my persuasive powers to help him overcome his aversion to foods that were new to him. He had chattered his way right into my heart in the ten months that he had been a part of our Nathaniel family. I realized that I couldn't bear his leaving, much less his being given into the hands of his abusive, alcoholic father.

My thoughts were arrested by Ionică's voice. "Liviu, come here," he commanded.

Liviu left his father's side and walked to the chair where Ionică was sitting.

"Liviu," continued Ionică, putting his arms about him, "you understand that this is your father, don't you?" Liviu stared at the floor and didn't respond. Ionică reached out and gently lifted his chin, forcing Liviu to meet his gaze. Then, looking him directly in the eyes, he repeated the question. Liviu nodded.

"Look," interrupted the visitor impatiently, "I was away when they brought him to this orphanage, and I couldn't do anything about it. But now I'm back, and I'm taking my son with me!"

"You understand that he is now eight years old and has started school here, don't you?" inquired Ionică.

The visitor shrugged.

Why wasn't Ionică telling this visitor that he would have to prove to the Child Protection Agency that he had become a competent father before Liviu could legally be restored to him? Why wasn't he telling him that we have papers in our files giving us responsibility for Liviu? What was the matter with him?

Ionică's heavy voice penetrated my thoughts. "You haven't asked your son if he *wants* to go with you. Perhaps he would rather stay here."

Surprise registered on the visitor's face at this thought, and he took a step toward Ionică's chair. He leaned close, and his scar and crooked nose appeared bigger than life. Then in a controlled voice he said, "Liviu, my son, you want to live with your papa, don't you?"

Liviu's only response was to move closer to Ionică's chair. His little hand reached up and sought Ionică's big one.

"Answer me, son. You want to come live with me, don't you?"

Liviu swallowed hard and stared at the floor.

"Answer me!" commanded the visitor, an angry edge creeping into his voice. But Liviu continued to stare at the floor as if he had heard nothing.

"Speak," commanded Ionică.

Liviu continued to gaze fixedly at the floor, but this time quietly said, "No."

"What did you say?" asked Ionică as though he hadn't heard him clearly.

"No!" repeated Liviu, louder this time.

"You mean you don't want to come live with your papa and your own people in Arbore?" asked the visitor roughly.

"No," spoke Liviu, lifting his gaze for the first time. "I want to stay here." His little fingers were firmly entwined in Ionică's.

"Well," said Ionică, rising, "I guess that settles it. Liviu wants to stay here at the Nathaniel Orphanage."

"But," sputtered his father, "he needs to live with his relatives."

"You may visit Liviu whenever you like, but Liviu wants to live with us, and he will stay with us," said Ionică, a note of finality in his voice. He glanced down at Liviu. "You've been out of school long enough, and it is time you get back to your class. Tell your father goodbye."

"Bye," said Liviu simply, and a moment later he was out the door, heading back to his classroom.

Chapter 16
Blind Help

"Please, Ştefania," begged Roza, "I made this especially for you, and you must eat it. Look how skinny your arms are becoming. You're going to get sick if you don't eat!"

I wondered if I should intervene in this contest of wills, but I chose to watch, listen, and allow Tanti Roza to handle the situation.

"But Tanti," whined little Ştefania, "it's too much! I can't eat all that."

"But you must. Next year you will be starting school, and you won't be strong enough to keep up with the others," replied our dedicated cook.

I watched Ştefania out of the corner of my eye. She had placed one knobby elbow on the table and rested her face in the palm of her hand. Her unmanageable hair formed a fuzzy frame about her face. She poked her fork half-heartedly at the roast beef and potatoes on her plate. Ştefania looked gaunt and hollow-eyed, yet she dawdled with her fork. Finally succeeding in filling it with potatoes, she raised it halfway to her lips, but then paused. "Tanti," she asked with her fork in midair, "could I please have more water?"

Always the servant, Roza asked that the pitcher be passed, and she filled Ştefania's glass. I watched, fascinated, as Ştefania laid her full fork back on her plate, wrapped her long, boney fingers around the glass, and raised it to her lips. There it stayed for a long moment as she looked over its rim and surveyed the other children in the dining room. The water level had hardly diminished at all when she finally placed it back on the table.

Mihaela asked for a second helping of potatoes, and before any-one else could respond, Ştefania's thin arm shot out across the table, picked up the bowl, and passed it in Mihaela's direction. She turned and asked her sister Vasilica, seated next to her, "Do you like your new teacher?"

"Oh, I like her!" responded Vasilica enthusiastically.

"But isn't she kind of bossy?" probed Ştefania, trying to keep the conversation going as long as possible.

"No, not bossy, but her students do respect her," Vasilica explained.

Our nurse, Sora Viorica, came from the far end of the table and stood beside Ştefania.

"Ştefania, why aren't you eating? I am ready to take you to see a doctor. Something is wrong with you," she cried in agitation, her voice rising. The children from the other tables stopped their dining room chatter and watched. Ştefania looked embarrassed and hid her face in her arms.

"Here," said the nurse as she scooped up a forkful of food from the plate. "Now open your mouth and eat this." But Ştefania only hid her face deeper in the crooks of her gangly arms and refused to take even one bite. "Look at you," scolded the nurse. "The other children have cleaned up their plates and are almost finished eating their fruit, and you've hardly eaten anything!"

Ionică, who had also been watching, appeared at Sora Viorica's side. "Here," he said, "I believe this little girl needs to learn to eat all over again." He picked up Ştefania's plate and carried it to the empty table near the entrance of the dining room. Then he marched Ştefania to the table, where he whispered instructions into her ear. Ştefania still covered her face with her arms, but she nodded.

The meal was soon finished and we closed with a song. The children filed out past the skinny little girl standing forlornly at the table with her plate of food in front of her. She absently licked a stray piece of potato from her fork as she turned a wistful gaze toward those who were leaving. She stood first on one foot, then on the other. She sipped a little water from her glass, gave a deep sigh, and picked up her fork once more.

Food, ugh! Ştefania picks at her potatoes.

Several weeks passed, and Ştefania came down with the measles. She had to be quarantined. For the following ten days she had to stay in a room we designated as the sickroom. Life was very boring for her there, and she longed to be with the other children. As she lay upstairs in her bed, she could just make out the soft voice of Tanti Maria, the cook, mingled with Tanti Roza's richer tones, floating up from the kitchen. She visualized what was happening as she heard the clanging of pots and pans, and she knew they were preparing food. She shuddered involuntarily. Food! Ugh! She couldn't stand the thought of eating.

On Wednesday evening as the girls were preparing to go to Bible study, Tanti Valentina heard Paula storming angrily about in her room and went to investigate. "Now just what is your problem, young lady?" she asked.

"Somebody put beans in the pockets of my nice blue dress," Paula wailed.

"Well, don't cry about it. Dump them out and put your dress on. And hurry, or you will make us late."

"I can't shake them out. I tried. They are sticky and won't come," she sniffled.

Tanti Valentina strode to the closet where Paula stood shaking her dress. "Let me see," she demanded as she held out her hand. She reached her fingers into Paula's dress pocket and jerked her hand out again. Her fingers had encountered something soft, cold, and slippery. Moving directly under the light, Valentina held the pocket open and peered into its depths. Then she threw back her head and laughed. "Paula, you must have been wearing this dress when we had green beans for lunch and you didn't like them. Did you hide them in your pockets so Tanti Roza wouldn't see that you hadn't eaten them?" she inquired.

"No, Tanti! I didn't hide any beans in my dress pockets. I didn't!" she insisted.

"Then who did?" asked Valentina. "Well, we will have to wash this dress before you can wear it, so pick out another dress, and hurry!"

On Friday, as Tanti Lenuṭa was getting the girls ready for school, she heard a wail from Rodica's room. "Tanti," Rodica yelled, "someone played a mean trick and put mashed potatoes in my school uniform pockets! What am I going to wear for school?"

"Bring it to the bathroom and maybe we can clean it enough for you to wear today. Then we will wash it tonight and it will be fine for Monday morning. Come, I'll help you," she called reassuringly.

On Tuesday during the monthly staff meeting, Valentina brought up the problem.

"It's not only in dress pockets," interjected Tanti Lenuṭa. "Some of the older girls reported that they found stale bread and wilted salad folded into their underwear."

"Who has been taking food upstairs?" demanded Ionică.

Sora Viorica answered, "Ştefania eats her meals upstairs in the quarantine room, but she is forbidden to leave that room, so it can't be her."

"Well, we can't have this," Ionică said. "Can you imagine what the health inspectors would say if they found mashed potatoes in the girls' underwear drawers? Sora Viorica, would you please look into this and have a talk with Ștefania to see if she's been stashing food in the girls' clothing."

Tanti Lenuța spoke up, "I already asked her, but she declares she doesn't know anything about it."

"Okay," Ionică suggested, "let's be especially observant in the dining room and see to it that no one takes food upstairs. When one of you takes food to Ștefania, stay with her until she is finished eating. That should eliminate all possibilities."

"But Ionică, we have too many responsibilities to sit for an hour and a half while Ștefania plays with her food!"

"That's right!" chimed in several other workers.

"Do you think her measles are still contagious?" asked Ionică.

"Probably not, but we should give her another day or so just to be sure," replied the nurse. "We don't want a major outbreak of measles among the children."

I stood at the head of the table on Wednesday and rang the bell for silence. The chatter diminished to a soft murmur and finally subsided altogether. We bowed our heads as the blessing was asked. My attention turned heavenward, but was immediately sidetracked by the patter of feet dashing across the floor directly above me. I lost my prayer as the thought invaded my consciousness, *Which of the children is missing from the dining room?* When the prayer ended, I remained standing, searching table by table for a gap that would indicate someone missing. Sora Viorica was also on her feet, and her gaze met mine as she strode purposefully toward the stairs.

In my mind I turned this problem over to our competent nurse. She would take care of it.

"Here, Tata Johnny," said Davucu as he passed me the plate of baked chicken. It was done to a golden brown and looked delicious. Next came the mashed potatoes and gravy, followed by green beans and garden salad. What a delightful meal! The cooks had outdone themselves once more. Happy talk enveloped every table as the meal progressed, but suddenly a hush settled over the dining room, and I looked about in surprise. Sora Viorica was striding toward me with a very determined look on her face. She held a frightened little girl firmly in her grasp. It was Ștefania, and I rightly guessed that her quarantine had come to an abrupt end.

"Tata Johnny," sputtered Sora Viorica, her eyes flashing, "this little girl was supposed to stay in the sickroom and eat the plate of food that had been brought to her just moments before we had prayer here in the dining room. When I heard footsteps, I rushed up and found Ștefania in the sickroom with her plate completely empty. I asked her, 'Where did your food go so fast?' She told me she had already eaten it. I knew that was impossible, so I asked her what she had done with the chicken bones."

Here she pushed Ștefania, forcing her to stand directly in front of me. Ștefania looked scared and ashamed and tried to hide her face from the curious gazes of the other children.

"This little girl had the nerve to tell me she had eaten the chicken bones too," Sora Viorica continued, "and then I knew for sure she was lying! Come, Tata Johnny, come! Ștefania has something she wants to show you." Viorica swung open the back door and motioned for me to step outside. "Show him, Ștefania. Show Tata Johnny what you did with your food!"

I looked questioningly at Ștefania as she made a half-hearted motion toward the flower bed under the fire escape. There, nestled among the assorted flowers, was a mound of mashed potatoes, chicken, green beans, and salad all mixed together.

Pointing up to the doorway leading to the fire escape, Sora Viorica explained, "Ștefania brought her plate to the fire escape and dumped all her food into the flower bed without eating one bite!"

Ștefania sniffled and tried to slip from Sora Viorica's grasp, but was shaken for her efforts and commanded to hold still.

I couldn't help but smile as I looked down at Ștefania. "So, you have been eating chicken bones, have you?" I inquired. "Are they good?"

Order was finally restored with Ștefania sitting beside Sora Viorica, where she stared in dismay at a fresh plate of food. She glanced at Viorica, picked up her fork, and jabbed dejectedly at her plate.

Ionică informed me that an evangelist had called and would like to bring a visitor from England to the orphanage. Could he come this evening after supper?

"Sure," I responded, "we often have visitors and we enjoy them."

"Oh, but there is one thing you should know about this visitor. He is blind."

"This will be a new experience for the children. I don't recall ever having a blind visitor before. I'm sure he will be more than welcome," I responded.

Soon after supper our guest arrived. We ushered him into the big living room and sat him on a chair near the center post where Ionică usually sat. It was the place of honor. Now it was time for introductions.

"My name is Jim," began our guest. "Because I am blind, I cannot see your faces, so come close and let me know who you are. But you cannot all speak at once or I will get mixed up."

Beti stepped in front of our guest and announced, "I'm Beti."

Jim stretched out his hand and said, "Hi, Beti. Let me shake your hand, and tell me how old you are."

"I'm seven," Beti replied.

Jim was disarmingly friendly and soon was engulfed with children, each wanting to become the blind man's friend. The news of our visitor spread throughout the orphanage, and the living room quickly filled with children. Ștefania stood close by but said little. Her face was the picture of compassion as she gazed into the man's sightless eyes.

"What happened that you can't see?" asked Iosif.

"Could you ever see?" asked Marius.

"Yes. I was able to see very well until four years ago."

"Why don't you tell the children how you lost your eyesight?" I suggested.

Anticipating a story, the children scrambled to place themselves right in front of Jim. They kept scooting up closer and closer until they were practically against his knees.

The children scramble to get a better view of blind Jim's eye.

"Well," Jim began, "when I was little, like some of you, I could see just fine. I went to school and studied my lessons like most of you. And in time I grew up. I married a beautiful young lady. I had a wonderful job and was making lots of money. I owned a nice home and a very expensive car. My wife had an expensive car all her own. But there was one thing I didn't have. Can any of you guess what that was? I did not have God. I was living only for myself, and that is all I cared about in life.

"About four years ago when I was coming home from my job, I drove through an intersection, and in one moment, there was a terrible crash. I still do not know exactly how it happened."

I looked into the faces staring up at the speaker and wished fervently that Jim could, for just one moment, get a glimpse of the compassion and rapt attention on the listeners' faces.

"Yes, there was this terrible crash and that is all I remember. When I woke up in the hospital, I was blind. I couldn't see one thing—all was black. My facial bones and my skull were broken in numerous places. My right eye had been wrenched from its socket and couldn't be saved."

"You mean . . . you mean your eye popped right out of your head?" asked Beti, twisting up her face.

"That's right. They told me my eye was just hanging by its muscles and nerves. My left eye was still in its place, but it was also damaged beyond repair, and so I became blind in both eyes.

"About a month after the accident, my wife informed me that she was going to divorce me. Then the place where I worked told me that because I was blind, I couldn't work for them anymore. I had an operation to remove both eyes, so what you see now are not really my eyes. They are artificial eyes made of glass."

"Can you see with your new eyes?" asked Ştefania.

"No, darling," said Jim with deep feeling, "I cannot see anything at all.

"So," continued Jim, "one day I had everything this world had to offer. I had a beautiful wife, an expensive car, a high-paying job, an elaborate home, and a secure career. Then came the crash, and I lost it all. But I had some friends who were Christians. They were praying for me, and do you know what? I gave my life to the Lord Jesus. And even though I lost everything down here, I have something so wonderful to live for. I began living for Jesus, and my Christian brothers and sisters found me a job where I could work even though I couldn't see. Isn't that wonderful?

"Now I would like to have a glass of water. Is there someone who would bring me a glass of water, please?"

Iosif sprang to his feet and said, "Sure, I'll get you one."

I glanced at my watch and realized it was bedtime for the children. However, what our visitor was sharing with them was so valuable I felt it would be well worth the extra effort of pulling sleepy children from their beds in the morning.

Iosif returned with the glass of water, and the visitor thirstily drank all but the last inch.

"I'll take the glass for you if you've had enough," offered Iosif politely.

"Actually, I'd like to keep it," replied the visitor. "Would you children like for me take my eye out so you can see it better?" Jim asked.

"Yes! Yes!" chorused the children. "Let us see it! We want to see it!" As if by some unseen signal, they all jumped to their feet and crowded closely about Jim.

"Well," said Jim, "First I will need a napkin."

Before he could say another word, Ionela raced for the kitchen and soon returned with a napkin. "Here, here," she said as she thrust it toward him.

"Place it in my hand," Jim invited as he extended his hand in the direction of her voice. "Is it a clean one? It has to be a clean one."

"Oh, yes," answered Ionela. "It's a new one I got from the kitchen just now."

"Thank you. Okay, children, now I will take out my left eye for you to see."

An awed hush swept over the children as they craned their necks to get a better view. Working the glass eye from its socket took but a few seconds. Carefully, Jim wiped his eye dry on the clean napkin. Then he held his eye up for all to see. Most of the girls gasped to see an eye looking back at them from between Jim's fingers. The boys grimaced, and I was glad for Jim's sake that he was unable to see the children's faces.

"Did everyone get to see it?" asked Jim, turning it this way and that. A number of heads nodded.

"He cannot see you nodding," I quietly informed them. "You must speak so that he understands."

"Who would like to hold my eye?" asked Jim. Those who were standing closest to Jim took an involuntary step backward, distancing themselves from the staring eye. Ruth saw the children were fearful and said, "I'd like to hold it." She took it from Jim and held it aloft for the children to see. The children scrambled to get a better view, but none wanted to touch it. Then she gave it back to Jim, who dropped it into the water remaining in the glass he was holding.

"You see," he explained, "God made your eyes so they are always wet. When I get ready to put mine back in, I must moisten it. That's why I placed it in this water." He held up the glass and swished the eye about for the children to see.

Then, with the children watching intently, our visitor reached into the glass and wiggled his fingers in a vain attempt to catch his elusive eye. "Oh, no!" he cried. "I can't get my hand into this small glass. My hand is too big. What am I going to do? Is there anyone here with a small hand who would be willing to reach in and give me my eye?"

The children involuntarily shrank back and made faces. No one wanted to touch Jim's wet eye.

Ştefania, who stood only inches away, had taken it all in with deep soberness. She felt so sorry for him! "I'll get it for you, Jim," she offered.

"Who offered to help me?" asked Jim as he turned in the direction of the voice.

Ştefania swallowed and gazed up into Jim's sightless face. She raised her hand and said, "I will."

"Who said that?" Jim asked again.

"Me."

"Okay, give me your hand," coached Jim.

Ştefania slowly laid her thin little hand in Jim's big, strong one as he asked, "What is your name?"

"I'm Ştefania," came her soft reply.

"And you want to help me get my eye out of the glass of water?"

Ştefania nodded.

"Ştefania," whispered Ruth, "you must say 'yes' because he cannot see your head nodding."

"Yes," said Ştefania dutifully.

"Okay, I will hold the glass and you see if you can get the eye out for me. But please don't drop it," he cautioned. "It cost very, very much."

The children all held their breath as Ştefania slipped her thin little hand into the glass and carefully extracted the eye. She cupped it gently in her hand and gazed upon it even as it seemed to gaze back at her.

"Did you get it?" asked Jim.

"Yes," said Ştefania.

"Can you place it in my hand?" he asked.

After feeling it over carefully, Jim repositioned his glass eye back into its socket and blinked several times to realign it. An audible sigh of relief escaped the children as they gazed at their friend.

It was past time to put the children to bed, and I announced that we would pray together before the children went up to their beds. I invited the children to pray as we stood in a circle around Jim. Five of the children prayed for Jim with heartfelt words. Every child bid him goodnight before heading up the stairs to be tucked into their beds.

Ruth and I stayed with Jim and answered his questions. He wanted to know all about the orphanage and the children, but he showed a special interest in the little girl who had been brave enough to get his eye out of the glass of water. We told him how her father murdered her mother and how he had been sent away to prison. We explained how he accepted the Lord in prison and truly became a changed man. We also explained our worries about Ştefania not eating properly.

"If it's not too late, I would like to talk with that little girl again," said Jim. "Do you think she is asleep already?"

Ruth hurried upstairs while I continued talking with Jim. Soon she returned with Ștefania.

"Ștefania," said Jim, "I would like if you would lead me to the kitchen and back. Would you do that?"

"Yes," said Ștefania as she reached out to take his hand. It was a beautiful sight, the big blind man being led up the hallway by the skinny little girl. *And a little child shall lead them,* I thought.

Upon their return Jim said, "Thank you, Ștefania. Thank you very much! I shall never forget you. And now I would like to ask if it would be all right for me to offer a special prayer for you."

"Yes," said Ștefania shyly.

Jim knelt and placed his arm about Ștefania. As he began to pray, Jim was overcome with tears. He prayed brokenly, "Dear heavenly Father, bless this little girl! Take the troubles in her life and let them shape her for your glory. Feed her, dear Father . . ." His voice became too choked to continue. Tears streamed from his sightless eyes as his sense of touch registered her knobby frame with so little flesh upon it. "Cause her to become hungry, and feed her, heavenly Father. Yes, feed her with your bread from heaven, and may she grow up to serve you. In Jesus' name. Amen!"

Jim bid Ștefania goodbye and Ruth led her back upstairs to her waiting bed. Just then the people who had brought Jim to us came to pick him up. I embraced Jim as I bid him farewell, with the promise that we would pray for each other. I have faith that someday God will give Jim a new body with new eyes, and He will wipe away every one of his tears.

Chapter 18
Gone

"Johnny," said Ionică as he and Vali entered my office for our morning meeting, "what do you think of us taking the children who are from the Vaslui area to visit their families? It's been a year and a half since Neli, Bogdan, Andi, Silviu, and Marta have visited their relatives."

"You have a good idea there!" I agreed enthusiastically.

"What about Beni and Monica? They're from the same village. Have they ever been back to visit their family?" asked Vali.

"No, they haven't, and of course we would take them too. You want to know something?" Ionică asked. "For the past twenty weeks Beni hasn't received one bad mark on his behavior report. He's a little man, and he certainly deserves to go," he said with obvious affection.

I recalled the special glow in Ionică's eyes whenever he rumpled Beni's hair, met him in the hall, or talked with him at the table. I was sure he missed having a son of his own.

"Perhaps this would help convince their mother that we are not her enemy and that we really do care about the welfare of her children. And, if it's raining, you should take a four-wheel-drive vehicle," I suggested as I recalled the horrible dirt road to Hreațca.

"Could you arrange that for us?" asked Ionică.

"Sure. When would you like to go?" I asked.

"I was thinking about leaving early Thursday morning."

"Sounds like a good plan to me. I'm sure the children will be most delighted! I'll arrange for you to take the four-wheel-drive Suburban. Who are you planning to take with you to help oversee the children?" I asked.

"I've been thinking this would be a good chance for the new volunteer, Brenda Sommers, to see what rural village life is really like. Do you think she would want to go?" he asked. "She could help Jean and Veronica care for the children, and James Mullet is used to working with the boys. Could you spare him too?"

"I'm sure we could work around that if you would like to take them with you. Why don't you go ahead and ask them."

There was excitement in the air, and the Vaslui children could hardly wait until Thursday. They talked of little else. Brenda and Jean helped our cook Lăcri pack a huge lunch for everyone, and Veronica prepared large sacks of used clothing to share with the needy families they would encounter.

On Thursday morning the children scrambled out of their beds, dressed hurriedly, and gulped a hasty breakfast. They stood by the Suburban and watched with anticipation as the space behind the third seat was packed with several large sacks of clothing and a cooler filled with their lunches.

"Beni, what's with the winter coat?" asked Veronica. "And you, Monica, why are you bringing your coat?"

"It's cold," murmured Beni.

"It might be cold there," Monica added.

Ionică slammed the back door of the Suburban and announced, "All is ready!"

The children wiggled into their choice positions among their favorite workers. Ionică smiled as he looked back over the seats filled with excited faces. This was going to be a trip to remember.

"Children," said Ionică, "let's be quiet; we want to pray." After praying for protection and blessing, he expertly guided the loaded Suburban through the orphanage gate and headed south. As the miles slipped by, the children became quiet. Their minds raced ahead, contemplating how it would be when they reached their homes. There were no phones in their village, so this was going to be a big surprise. It was exciting, and yet it seemed so strange, as though they were driving into a dream. They were going home—and yet, not really home.

Neli wondered about her little brother whom she hardly knew. She couldn't remember what he looked like. He'd been so young when she had come to live in the orphanage. Would he know her? Would he come to her? Could she hold him? Perhaps now he was too big to hold!

Andi thought of his cousins. It shocked him to realize that he hadn't even thought of them in a long time. He could hardly wait to show them all he had learned about playing soccer with the bigger boys in the orphanage.

Marta smiled shyly to herself as she gazed at the passing scenery and thought of her mother. Somehow, though she was drawing nearer home, Marta felt like her mom was far away. It was like going to meet a distant relative instead of her mother. With a sigh Marta closed her eyes. The rumbling vehicle soothed her mixed emotions and made her feel drowsy.

Thoughts and miles intermingled as the hours sped by.

The road to Hreaţca was well rutted and filled with chuckholes, and the passengers were shaken together relentlessly. They would be most happy to reach their destination. As they neared the village, Ionică glanced back at Beni, who was sitting forward, taking everything in. "We'll drop you off at your mom's house, and I'll be back for you at three o'clock. You'll be ready?"

Beni answered "yes" absently as he gazed at a herd of sheep grazing in the distance.

As they entered the village, children and adults ceased their activities and stared with open wonder. They hung over the board fences which lined the dirt track as it wound its way among the village houses. They were awestruck. Most of them had seldom seen a motorized vehicle other than a tractor. Jubilant children raced along behind the Suburban as it made its way deeper into the village.

Brenda was deeply moved at their obvious poverty. The houses were extremely small and made of mud bricks. Some were thatched with long-stemmed, coarse grass. She was shocked to discover that outhouses were made of closely set cornstalks, forming three walls without the benefit of a door, roof, or seat—just a hole in the ground. *How do these people survive?* she wondered.

"Here we are," sighed Ionică as he stopped before one of the poorest houses. Large tarpaper patches covered rotted areas of thatching. However, there were unpatched holes where the rain no doubt poured right through. Faces strained to see them through translucent plastic tacked over the window frames. A black hen scratched for insects in the bare earth in front of the house, and off to the side a half-grown pig paused from its rooting long enough to survey the newcomers. Grunting its mistrust, the pig ambled out of sight behind the house. A crowd immediately surrounded them as the visitors extracted themselves from the Suburban and stretched their cramped limbs.

"Come on!" Beni called to his sister. They quickly covered the short distance between the dirt street and the house. Children, youth, and adults had emerged through the doorway and stood staring from the narrow, raised ledge that served as the front porch.

Ionică strode to the porch as an eighteen-year-old mother with a toddler clinging to her skirt threw her arms about Monica and cried, "Oh, you have come! We have missed you so much!" She laid her hand on Beni's shoulder and, turning to Ionică, asked, "How long may they stay?"

"We will take Neli and the others to their houses and come back in about two hours," instructed Ionică. "Have them here so we will not have to wait on them."

Monica's sister-in-law caressed her head affectionately. Monica glanced up, flashed a broad grin, and then held out her arms toward the toddler.

Neli and Bogdan were engulfed by their family members the moment they entered the small courtyard through the little green gate. Their mother couldn't get done hugging them, and her face was wreathed in smiles. "What a wonderful day this is! Praise God, my children have come!" she cried as she shook hands with Ionică and the rest of the adults. Quickly she ordered one of the older boys to run to the field and find Papa. Then she instructed one of the girls to start a fire in the cookstove and put water on for tea. Several children carried stools from the house for the visitors. "Come," their mother said, spreading her hands wide in a gesture of genuine hospitality, "come sit down."

Brenda glanced about. A horse-drawn wagon was parked near the wooden fence. Several plump hens pecked contentedly beneath it. Lush grapevines formed a canopy over a trellis that stretched all the way to the eaves of the whitewashed house. *There is a homey feel about this place*, she thought.

"Veronica, how is Neli's condition?" asked her mother after Neli had followed her sisters into the house. "Is her arthritis medication helping her? Does she still have days when she has to stay in bed?" Concern clouded her countenance.

"A visitor from America saw how Neli suffered," Veronica answered. "He sends processed aloe vera for her to take as a supplement. She has been taking it daily along with her standard medication. This spring she has had only three days when the pain and swelling were severe enough that she stayed in bed. Praise the Lord she is improving, and this year she has missed very little school."

"Oh, I'm so thankful!" responded her mother. "Neli suffered terribly when she lived here and at times could hardly get out of bed for a week at a time. But tell me, how's she doing in school?"

"Neli is a very bright child," said Ionică delightedly. "She learns easily and isn't afraid to study hard. She is even learning English from our American workers."

Tea was served and conversations flowed freely. Time passed rapidly as they discussed the children, their behavior, and their progress. The children gathered in the house, where Neli and Bogdan told all about life in the orphanage. Their brothers and sisters explained all about life in the village. Soon they wandered up the street and joined Andi, Silviu, and Marta at their house.

Ionică rose. "It's time I go pick up Monica and Beni," he announced as he walked toward the gate. "We need to start back soon. Just stay and visit. I won't be gone long. Try to have everyone together when I get back."

They finished their tea as they waited for Ionică's return, and the conversation turned to the clothing Veronica had brought. "When Ionică brings Monica and Beni, I will give you the bag of clothing we brought for you," she explained. "Use what you can and share the rest with your neighbors. Some are heavy winter clothes that you can use to a good advantage in several months."

Ionică was gone for a considerable length of time, and James found himself listening for the return of the Suburban. Finally he announced, "Here they come!"

Moments later Ionică walked through the gate and joined them. He looked pale. His tense face appeared pained. Then he blurted out, "Beni and Monica don't want to go back!"

"What are you saying?" asked James in disbelief as he rose and looked over the fence. The Suburban sat on the village street, empty.

Ionică pursed his lips and clenched his jaws like a man trying hard to maintain control of his emotions. "I did everything in my power to persuade them that there is no future here for them. There is no father in their home, their mother is . . ." He broke off speaking and shook his head. Ionică turned away as he ran his fingers over his forehead and through his hair as though trying to brush away some unwanted thought. He turned and faced the group again. "I don't know what horrible stories that woman has been feeding them. She probably told them we are going to cut out their organs to sell, or that we plan to sell them to some far country. I don't know. But they absolutely refused to come with me!" He threw up his hands in a gesture of utter helplessness. "O Lord, help us!" he groaned.

"I asked Beni if anything happened at the orphanage that made him want to leave," Ionică continued in despair, "and he said 'no.' I asked him if I had wronged him in anyway, and he said that's not it either."

"What are we going to do?" asked James. "We can't leave them here! Why don't we just go get them?" he asked.

Ionică sadly shook his head. "I explained the law to them. I recounted the wonderful opportunities they have at the orphanage. I reminded them how happy they were two years ago when the evangelist rescued them from nearly starving and freezing to death. I reminded them how he brought them to us in the middle of the night and how happy they were. I talked with them about their schooling, their Biblical teaching, and their tantis who love them so dearly. I told them how hurt the rest of the children will be. But James, they don't care. They didn't even want to listen! I'm finished. I have nothing more to say." He walked toward the fence like a man in a dream and stood there staring across the village, slowly shaking his head in disbelief.

"What is happening?" asked the children, who had returned just in time to catch the tail end of Ionică's speech. In hushed tones Veronica quickly informed them that Beni and Monica were determined to stay in Hreața and not return with us to the orphanage.

"But why?" asked Neli.

"They're stupid!" exclaimed Bogdan.

"I would never want to do that," said Marta, unconsciously moving closer to Veronica.

Andi said nothing, but his set jaw showed the news had affected him deeply.

James walked out the gate and headed back toward Beni and Monica's house, praying that he would be able to talk sense into Beni. They enjoyed a close relationship. Surely Beni would listen to him.

After dropping off the promised bag of clothing and loading the children into the waiting Suburban, Ionică drove everyone to Monica and Beni's house. Veronica and Jean reasoned kindly with Monica to please return with them to the orphanage. "Who knows what will happen to you if you remain here in this village? What will Mama Ruth and Tata Johnny say if we return without you?"

Monica sat on the edge of the bed. "I'll go if Beni does," she finally said.

"You will?" asked Jean.

Monica nodded and smiled.

Brenda had only been in Romania several weeks and had difficulty with the language, so she left the negotiating up to others. She watched in surprise as a hungry chicken entered the front door, looking for crumbs. There appeared to be only one inhabitable room. Brenda saw no kitchen table and wondered where they ate. There were two couches and a bed, but not nearly enough space for the twelve people she was told regularly slept there. How would Monica survive in this environment? She prayed that Monica would listen to reason. It wasn't safe for her here. Who would protect her? Who would love her, and who would teach her?

Outside, James continued to talk with Beni. "But why don't you want to go back to Suceava with us?" he asked, a pleading note in his voice.

"It's better for me to stay here," Beni answered as he pushed a twig around in the dust with his shoe.

"But how is it better?" James asked.

Beni shrugged, "It's just better."

"Look, school will soon begin, and you won't go to school here in this village. Think of all you have been taught during the past two years at the Nathaniel School. Think of your classmates. Do you want them to start the next grade without you?" James reasoned.

Beni paused and took a deep breath. "You can say anything you want, but I am staying right here, and nothing is going to change that. My brother told me it's better for me to stay, and I'm staying, so leave me alone!" Tears of frustration filled his eyes.

James walked to the house with a heavy heart. The others looked at him expectantly as he entered. James swallowed the lump that was rising in his throat and shook his head. "It's no use," he said. "He will not come."

"Then I am going to stay with my brother," announced Monica.

There was more talk, reasoning, and pleading, but the outcome remained the same.

Monica stood on the narrow ledge and waved as the Suburban started up the village street. Beni was nowhere to be seen.

All was quiet as the Suburban left Hreaţca and started over the dirt track across the vast fields. Their hearts were too heavy for words. The Suburban eventually slowed and stopped. Ionică leaned forward. He laid his head on the steering wheel and wept. The sound of a grown man weeping was almost more than Brenda could bear. Her own eyes were too filled with tears to be able to watch.

"I was going to pick him up, and he turned against me and hit me with his fists. I cannot believe this is our Beni. At the orphanage he was such a good boy. What have I done wrong?" he asked as tears coursed down his cheeks.

"I wonder if this wasn't something Beni and Monica had planned since their mother's visit," ventured Veronica. "Did you notice they both wore their winter coats even though it was warm? I think they remembered how nearly they froze during the winter their mother abandoned them. No doubt they wanted to bring their coats along because they planned to stay."

"You are probably right," replied Ionică, "but how could we have been so blind? What is going to happen to them? This village is filled with drinking, wickedness, and immorality. Who will guide their feet on the path to God?"

A sober group found a shaded area beneath apple trees growing by the roadside where they ate their packed lunch. On another day and under different circumstances it would have been a delightful picnic spot. But today the trees' shade seemed dark and dismal.

It was nearly dark when the Suburban finally pulled into the orphanage compound. Ionică dreaded having to tell me that they had returned without Monica and Beni. He could hardly bring himself to talk about it, but explained briefly what had happened. "I'm sorry, so sorry!" he said, as though blaming himself.

"Ionică," I responded, "you cannot take the blame for this. If you had forced Beni to come back against his will, he no doubt would have caused more problems. What he needs is a change of heart."

Ionică left for his home and a much-needed rest. I turned and walked toward the orphanage.

"Tata Johnny," called Rodica from her second-story dorm window, "did you know that Monica and Beni didn't come back with Nenea Ionică? Oh, I feel so sad!"

"Tata Johnny," came a voice from the boys' dorm, "did you find out that Nenea Ionică couldn't make Beni come back with him? We are going to pray for him and write him to come back and be good."

"That's a good idea," I called back to Iosif. "Let's pray and see what God will do."

This was hard on the Nathaniel children. Partings tore at their hearts. It was like a close family member rejecting them and leaving. This was their family, the only real family most of them had ever known.

The next day many of the children voluntarily joined the adults as they fasted and prayed for Monica and Beni. Manu and Iosif asked if they could accompany Mihai (the evangelist who had brought Monica and Beni to the orphanage two years before) to Hreațca for a weekend of ministering. Permission was granted, and they carried no less than forty notes, cards, and letters written by the Nathaniel children and workers, begging Beni and Monica to return.

There was great disappointment when Manu and Iosif returned Sunday evening and announced that Beni was rude to them, used bad language, threw rocks, and even offered them a cigarette.

Mihai reported that Beni and Monica's mother was trying to get her hands on the government handout money offered to the guardians of abandoned children, but which we had refused. She was also demanding that the Nathaniel Orphanage pay her for the chores Monica and Beni had performed during the two years we had fed, clothed, educated, loved, and taught them.

Ionică was so despondent over the radical change in Beni's character that he found it very difficult to discuss the situation with anyone. Beni and Monica were gone. Though our hearts bled, life at the Nathaniel Christian Orphanage would have to continue without them.

Chapter 17

Mystery Eggs

Elena Bițica heaved a deep sigh as she flopped down on the living room sofa of our little gray house. "Mama Ruth," she said with painful longing in her voice, "is it true that if you adopted me, it would cost $2,000?"

"Yes," replied Ruth thoughtfully, "at least that much and maybe even more."

Elena gave another wistful sigh and murmured softly, "I love your family so much. I wish I could be a part of your family."

"Well," replied Ruth, "we love you very much too, and you are always welcome in our home."

"Oh, I know that, Mama Ruth, but . . ."

We were beginning to realize just how deeply God had implanted into each child's heart the need to be loved, to be wanted, and to belong. Elena's heart was no different. She was constantly aware that her family was forever shattered. If only she could be part of a real family!

Several days later I called Elena into my office. "Elena," I said as I glanced across the desk to where she was seated, "I have a fax here from Sam and Danielle Wray, your sponsors. They are planning a trip to Romania next spring to visit you, and they want to stay for several weeks. What do you think about that?"

"Really?" exclaimed Elena, suddenly sitting forward with interest. "Are they going to bring their children? When are they coming? Oh, I can hardly wait!" She rubbed her cheeks in excitement.

"They wrote to ask us when would be the best time to come and how they might help us while they are here," I explained.

"But Tata Johnny, I'll be in school and won't be able to be with them . . . But that's all right," she rushed on. "I don't go to school in the afternoon, and we can be together then. Oh, I'm so happy! I can't believe it!" she squealed. "Thank you, Tata Johnny, thank you!"

"Don't thank me. Thank God, who is making all this possible."

"Oh, I will!" she gushed as she rushed from my office to share her wonderful news.

"Tata Johnny," asked Davucu at the dinner table, "when are the new chicks going to come out?"

"They should begin hatching on Friday," I responded.

Davucu was momentarily preoccupied, counting on his stubby little fingers. Suddenly his face lit up as he exclaimed, "Just four more days!"

"You're going to put more eggs in the incubator after these hatch, aren't you?" asked Roxana.

"I don't think so," I responded.

"Why not?" asked Mariana.

"I'm afraid the weather will turn cold before they mature," I explained. "How would you like to be kept in an outdoor pen when the weather is really cold? Also, I will be gone during November."

"Are you going to leave us?" asked Mariana, her deep blue eyes clouding with apprehension. "Where will you go?"

"I am going to CAM's open house in Pennsylvania, where I will show slides of you children to your supporters and tell them about your lives and experiences."

"Then you and Mama Ruth will come back, won't you?" asked Mariana, seeking reassurance.

Oh, how my heart went out to these precious children! First they had been torn away from their families through no fault of their own. They had made adjustments and bonded with workers in our orphanage. However, those whom they had come to love and trust had left one by one to move back to America or had married and moved away, leaving their little hearts broken and bleeding once again. Would this procession of painful partings never cease?

Nine-year-old Costică looked up into my face and asked the question burning in his little heart. "You're going to open house?"

"Yes," I replied, wondering if he would ask to go along.

"How long will you stay there?" he asked, struggling to understand.

"Costică," I explained gently, "we are going to take our family furlough during this trip and spend some time visiting our married children. We will be gone one month."

Costică digested this for a moment and then blurted out his thoughts. "I think open house is very bad!"

"Maybe if you are all good while we are away, we will bring you a small gift from America when we come back," I said, trying to direct their focus to our return rather than our departure.

"What a delicious supper! Thanks!" I complimented my wife on Monday evening. "Ionică will begin report in ten minutes," I added as I glanced at the clock, "and we don't want to be late."

"I can't come to report right away, but I'll be there later if I can," Ruth informed me as she began clearing away the supper dishes. "I feel I have been neglecting our own children, and I need to be here for them."

"Okay." I headed toward the orphanage. On my way, I decided to duck into the bakery garage for a quick check on the incubators. Loredana had been doing a fine job. She wrote on a chart each time she turned the eggs. *Her dedication will serve her well in other areas of life,* I thought.

I opened the first incubator expectantly, sure I would find everything in good order as usual. But to my utter dismay I found three broken eggs. *How could this have happened?* I wondered. *Has Loredana become careless? Perhaps she dropped the lid as she was finishing and never noticed. I'll have to talk to her about this.* I lifted the lid from the second incubator and almost dropped it in shock. Five more broken eggs! A total of eight eggs broken only four days from hatching! Something had gone terribly wrong. I examined a broken egg with its doomed chick more closely. I noticed that the break was not flattened as though it had been dropped. Instead it was a long, narrow break as though it had been struck with a long, thin object. I observed that each of the eggs was broken in a similar manner. I could not imagine what had happened, but I had to hurry or I would be late for report.

Ionică was already sitting in the brown overstuffed chair near the center post of the living room as I entered. He tapped a sheath of papers in his open palm as he waited patiently for the children to form a huge semicircle around him. Some sat on the sofas and chairs while others nestled themselves comfortably on the living room carpet.

Ştefania snuggled close beside Tanti Valentina while Larisa and Maria argued to sit on her other side. "But it's my turn," insisted Maria. "You have to move and let me sit there because you sat here at the last report."

"I don't care. I was here first and I won't move. You can just go sit somewhere else! Tanti, wasn't I here first?" asked Larisa.

"Yes," replied Tanti Valentina. "Maria, you are mistaken. I wasn't on duty last Monday evening, so Larisa couldn't have been sitting beside me."

Maria's cute little rosebud mouth turned into a sour frown, and a flush of color crept between the large freckles sprinkled across her high cheeks. *Uh-oh,* I thought. *Maria is going to cry.* But at that moment Tanti Valentina came to the rescue. Her arm encircled Maria's shoulders, and she whispered into her ear, "Come sit here in front of me and I will rub your back."

With pure delight shining from her eyes and her mouth no longer frowning, Maria sat at Tanti Valentina's feet. She savored the loving touch as her tanti rubbed her back and shoulders, and all was right with the world once more.

"Okay, children," announced Ionică as his eyes swept over the faces before him, "some of you are showing improvement in your conduct, but some still need to try a bit harder. No one has reported food hidden in their clothing," he said as he glanced knowingly in Ștefania's direction. She avoided his gaze and stared at the floor in embarrassment. But she couldn't help but smile as Ionică continued, "Ștefania has found that it is actually better to eat her food than to hide it in her friends' clothes. And the nurse tells me that our little girl is starting to gain some weight." I remembered our blind visitor and his special prayer for Ștefania. God was answering Jim's prayer.

"Marta," called Ionică in his no-nonsense voice. Five-year-old Marta scrambled to her feet and stood at attention while Ionică stared gravely at the papers in his hand. "Marta," he asked, "what have you been doing?"

Little Marta met the big man's gaze with her eyebrows raised in question, but with a shy smile on her face. She loved and respected Ionică, and she wasn't afraid of him. She knew that as long as you didn't do wrong, you needn't be afraid of Nenea Ionică, and she was sure she hadn't done anything wrong.

Ionică's bass voice carried into the farthest corners of the living room. "For all of this past week you do not have one mark of complaint from any of the tantis. Are you really that good?" he teased. All eyes were on Marta as she modestly smiled, shrugged her shoulders, and waited. Then came those two most coveted words from Nenea Ionică. "Very good!"

"Ioana."

Ioana stood and glanced at Ionică with her dark, penetrating eyes.

My mind flashed back to exactly how she had come to be a member of our Nathaniel family.

Tanti Silvia had been helping at the orphanage and was a favorite among the children. She told them stories from her own childhood and kept them spellbound with accounts of her brushes with the communist secret police while smuggling Bibles and teaching children about God.

Silvia had been sitting right here in this living room talking with a small group of children when the front door had burst open. Glancing up, she had seen a short, trim woman struggling with a little girl not more than three years old who had striking, dark eyes and a head full of silky brown hair. Silvia had watched wonderingly as the little girl had grabbed the edge of the doorframe and held on.

"No! No!" little Ioana had shouted. "I don't want to! I don't want to!"

"Yes," her mother had said firmly as she tore the little hands from the doorframe and shoved her into the room. "You have a sister here."

"No, Mama! I want you!" the little girl had wailed.

"Tanti Silvia," several girls had cried in surprise, "that woman is Roxana's mother!"

Two of the smaller girls had dashed off to inform Roxana, who had returned just in time to see her little sister being thrust into Silvia's arms.

"I've brought her here!" her mother had said. With that, she had turned and dashed out the door. It had happened so fast that Silvia hadn't had time to think. In shock she had glanced at the little girl kicking and screaming in her arms. Silvia had released her, and little Ioana had run wailing after her mother.

"No, Mama, no! Don't leave me here!"

How could a mother turn a deaf ear to such a desperate cry from the heart of her own child? But in spite of Ioana's cries, the door had banged shut.

Roxana's heart had been moved at the plight of her little sister, although she hardly knew her. She couldn't remember ever having lived together, but she ran to her screaming sister and tried her best to comfort her. Little Ioana resisted all her efforts and broke from her embrace. She screamed, "Mama! Mama!" as she flung herself against the closed door again and again.

Somehow three-year-old Ioana had been able to grasp that her mother was walking out of her life. From that day forth, Ioana had found her home in the Nathaniel Christian Orphanage. Yes, this had become her home, but it was a home without a mother.

Ionică's voice brought me back to the present as he said, "Let's see if you can do better next week, Ioana. You may sit down."

"Gigi," called Ionică, and Gigi slowly rose to his feet. Marius caught Gigi's eye and winked. Gigi grinned his infectious grin and winked back. But then he sobered, at least outwardly, as Ionică read from the paper. "Gigi," he asked, "why does it say here that on Wednesday you failed to show up to set the supper table?"

Gigi was the picture of innocence. He raised his eyebrows, shrugged, and replied, "I don't know."

"Do you mean to tell me," said Ionică, "that you didn't know you were supposed to set the table for supper?"

"Well, yeah, but I was busy at the farm, and I guess I forgot."

"What were you doing at the farm?"

"Helping," said Gigi.

"Helping what?" asked Ionică.

"I was helping the workers put the young bull into the horse pasture," Gigi replied.

"Did you lead the bull?" asked Ionică.

"No."

"Did you chase the bull?"

"Not really."

"Then what were you doing that you forgot your assignment in the dining room?"

"I guess I was sort of watching," mumbled Gigi guiltily.

"Okay, Gigi, look at me." Gigi raised his gaze until it met Ionică's. "You knew you were supposed to set the table for supper. But you decided it was more interesting to watch what was happening at the farm than to do your duty. Is that right?" he asked.

Reluctantly, Gigi nodded as he nervously twisted his fingers together.

"Let's see," said Ionică. "If I remember right, it was just last week that you slipped away to watch the big boys play soccer when you were supposed to be wiping the dining room tables."

Ionică sat back in his chair and grew thoughtful. I knew he had Gigi's best interests at heart and was searching for a good way to convey it. Then he leaned forward and addressed Gigi once more. "If I let you get by with this kind of irresponsibility while you are young, what kind of man will you be when you grow up?"

Gigi shrugged.

"Gigi," continued Ionică, "on Saturday I want you to work in the kitchen for three hours. You clean vegetables, set tables, or do whatever the cooks tell you. After you have worked to their satisfaction for three hours, you may go down to the farm, but not before. Do you understand?"

Gigi's dark eyes were blinking back tears, but he answered respectfully, "Yes, Nenea Ionică, I understand."

"Roxana." She stood nervously, glancing about the room and chewing her lip. "Roxana, it says here that you skipped out from helping wipe the dishes at noon on Tuesday. Why did you sneak away?" Roxana chewed her lip a little harder and stared into space. She made no comment. "Answer me!" commanded Ionică, his voice rising.

"I was tired," Roxana responded, blinking her innocent blue eyes and glancing nervously at the other children as if searching for support.

"Tired?" said Ionică. "I suppose you were tired! The tantis told me you have been running from room to room waking the younger children when all of you were supposed to be taking your afternoon naps. They also reported that you even spanked the smaller girls when you commanded them to get out of their beds and they didn't want to. What's the matter with you?" he demanded.

"I was just playing," murmured Roxana.

"You call that playing?" asked Ionică.

"Well, yes. I mean, I was pretending that I was the mom and my children wouldn't get out of bed," she replied lamely.

"So you were spanking them?" asked Ionică in amazement.

"Not hard," said Roxana. "It didn't really hurt."

"Perhaps I should give you a spanking to see if it hurts. How would you like that?" he asked.

Roxana shifted her weight onto her other foot and sighed. She continued to chew her lip.

"Is that what you want?" asked Ionică.

"Want what?" asked Roxana.

"A spanking," replied Ionică.

All eyes were now on Roxana. She blinked nervously and shook her head ever so slightly. She swallowed, and her lips formed the word "no," but no sound came out. Again she tried, and this time she was successful. "No," she said in a strained voice.

"Roxana," said Ionică, "I am going to give you the blue qualification for this week, and I think you understand what that means. No bike riding, no playing in the gym, no going to town, no rollerblades for you. And I really want you to think about two things. One is that when you are scheduled to work, don't you dare sneak away. And the other one is that if I hear you have been waking or spanking the younger children while you are playing mother, you will know what my spankings feel like. Do you understand me?"

"Yes, Nenea Ionică," she meekly replied.

"Good," said Ionică. "Be very sure that you do not forget! You may sit down."

Then Ionică called out, "Loredana."

She stood, and Ionică commended her for the good marks she had received. He thanked her for being a good example to the younger girls, gave her the highest qualification, and released her to sit down. He was just getting ready to call on her twin sister Laura when I interjected, "Excuse me, Brother Ionică, but I have a question for Loredana." Loredana respectfully stood once more.

"Loredana, I deeply appreciate the careful attention you have been giving the incubators. I know how careful you have been in making sure the eggs are turned on time. You have kept a close eye on the humidity, and I really do appreciate that. Have you been having problems with the incubators lately?"

"Problems?" repeated Loredana. "What do you mean?"

"Have you been having a problem with eggs breaking?" I asked cautiously as I watched her countenance.

"Why, no," she said, her eyes big with surprise, "I haven't broken any eggs. Why do you ask?"

"Well," I continued, carefully choosing my words, wanting deep in my heart to believe her, "I just checked the incubators on my way here and found some broken eggs."

"No!" said Loredana in disbelief. Her hand stole to her throat and a look of horror crossed her face. "I rolled the eggs just before supper and didn't break any!" she exclaimed.

Either she knows nothing about the broken eggs, or she is putting on a very good act, I thought to myself. "Yes, Loredana," I said deliberately, "there are eight broken eggs."

"Not eight!" gasped Loredana in surprise.

"Did you drop an incubator?" asked Ionică.

"Nenea Ionică, I didn't break one egg. Why are you accusing me?" cried Loredana as she burst into tears.

Ionică thought for a moment before speaking. "Loredana, do you always write down the time when you roll the eggs?"

"Yes," came her muffled response.

"Where do you keep that paper?"

"In the cupboard drawer by the incubators," she sobbed.

"Paula, would you please run to the bakery and bring me that paper from the drawer?" asked Ionică.

The children fidgeted nervously; then all became still as they waited for Paula's return. There was no sound except for the heartbreaking sobs of the lone figure standing before us. I felt sure now that she was not the one who had broken the eggs. But then, who had?

"Loredana," said Ionică, "you may sit down. And stop crying."

Paula returned and presented the paper to Ionică, who glanced over it quickly and then focused on the last entry. "It says here that the eggs were turned at 6:40 p.m. Loredana, is this correct?"

"Yes," answered Loredana brokenly as she rose to her feet. "I turned the eggs just before supper." I admired her, for even while she felt she was being unjustly accused, she still had the presence of mind to show respect by standing when responding to a superior, according to Romanian etiquette.

"Please sit down," said Ionică.

"Okay, children," he addressed them all. "Someone in this room knows about these broken eggs. Someone in this room did this cowardly deed, and I want you to simply confess what you have done. Who did it?" he demanded. His eyes traveled slowly from face to face as though trying to read their thoughts. Someone was guilty, and he intended to find out who it was. "Whoever did this, stand up and confess your wrong!" he implored. "God sees our hearts, and God sees all that we do. You cannot hide your wrongdoing from God. The only way you can find forgiveness is to confess your sins."

No one moved, no one spoke, no one stood, and no one confessed to having broken the eggs.

"Johnny," Ionică turned to me, "what time was it when you found the broken eggs?"

"It was about 7:45 when I checked the incubators," I replied.

"That means that someone went into the bakery garage during the one-hour period between the time Loredana rolled the eggs and you went to check the incubators."

Turning back to the children, he asked once more, "Did any of you see a child entering the bakery before supper? If you did, raise your hand." He glanced slowly about, but again all was silent and not one hand was raised.

"Okay," said Ionică, "if anyone remembers something later that will help us resolve this problem, please come tell me."

Report was soon over and there was a buzz among the children as they speculated among themselves who might have broken the eggs and whether it was done on purpose or accidentally. Ionică went with me to examine the eggs. We agreed that the eggs had been hit with a long, thin object rather than dropped. We were quite certain it was an act of vandalism and not an accident. "But Ionică, who could have possibly done such a thing, and why?" I asked as I removed the last broken egg from the incubators.

"I don't know," he replied. "At times I feel like I do not understand these children at all. Let's just pray and see what the Lord brings out of this."

Two days later Ionică walked into my office with a wry grin on his face and closed the door. "Well, the egg mystery has been solved!" he exclaimed as he moved his chair closer to my desk.

"Tell me about it," I said.

"I asked the children if they saw anyone entering the bakery between the time Loredana rolled the eggs and report, and a boy came to me saying he had seen Raluca* entering the bakery garage just after supper. That was all he had to report. I asked him why he hadn't raised his hand and told all of us while we were together, and he said he just hadn't had the courage."

"And then what?" I asked encouragingly.

"Well," continued Ionică, "I called Raluca into my office and be-

*Name changed.

gan questioning her about the broken eggs, but she denied knowing anything about it. When I told her that she had been seen going into the bakery garage at 7:30, she couldn't meet my gaze. I began talking to her about lying and covering her wrongs, and I asked her how she expects God to bless her. Then she began to cry. She really was sorry for what she had done, and she apologized with tears. However, I wanted to know *why* she had done this thing, and little by little I was able to get the story from her. It seems that Raluca has a crush on your son Franklin."

"Really?" I asked in surprise. "But she is only eleven years old!"

"Since Loredana was given the responsibility of caring for the incubators, Raluca imagined that this would give Loredana an advantage."

"What advantage?" I asked, still not understanding.

"Raluca thought that if Loredana did a good job caring for the hatching eggs, you would speak well of her in Franklin's presence. She was afraid this would give Loredana favor in your son's eyes."

"Ionică," I exclaimed, "they're just children! They have no business even thinking about such things for years to come!"

"I know, I know. But we must face things as they are, not as they should be," he reminded me.

"So, what have you decided to do about this?" I asked.

"First of all I told Raluca how serious her offence was. I also explained how wrong it was to break the eggs in order to make someone else look bad. And I spoke to her about her jealousy. I explained that her actions cast a shadow of suspicion upon all the orphanage children. She therefore owes all the children an apology. I insisted that she go to every child and confess what she did and ask them personally to grant her forgiveness."

"Whew!" I responded. "It's going to take a lot of humility for her to go to Loredana and ask for her forgiveness."

"That is exactly what she needs," Ionică concluded.

Ionică left, and I was alone with my thoughts. Poor Raluca. Her father had died while she was quite young, and her mother had placed her in our orphanage because she was unable to care for her. She missed her mother terribly and often wrote her letters. Her soul was hungry to be in a family. Had she wanted so desperately to be loved and appreciated that she was willing to do wrong just to belong?

Chapter 19

The Unexpected

Daniel was only ten years old, but he loved the farm. He had lived with his nine brothers and sisters in a small city apartment in Bacău. Due to his father's bout with alcohol and mental illness, Daniel had come to the Nathaniel Orphanage when he was only three years old. He had grown up learning to care for animals. Whenever he wasn't in school, you could find Daniel making himself useful down at the farm. Today was no different.

"Nenea Alvin," he said with deep concern in his voice, "did you know the bull is sick?"

"What bull?" asked Alvin.

"The young one they moved into the horse pasture last week," responded Daniel.

"Why, what makes you think he is sick?"

"Because he has a cold," Daniel explained. "You'd better call the vet."

When Daniel saw Alvin's smile, he felt hurt because Alvin wasn't taking him seriously.

"It's true," said Daniel, his eyes wide and serious. "He's making a funny noise, like this." Daniel lowered his voice and made a deep, guttural, drawn-out sound.

"Well," said Alvin in surprise, "that doesn't sound like a sick bull to me. He is simply growing up and is changing his voice. That means he thinks he is big now and doesn't want to be messed with. You boys stay away from that pasture until we move him into another pen. Do you hear?"

Martha Esh and Nathan Bange had gone back to America on a leave of absence to be married and begin their lives together. Jean Mullet had come to fill in for a year. She helped in the bakery, the garden, the flower beds, or with whatever needed to be done at the moment. The girls loved Jean's sunny disposition and took to her readily. Rodica in particular loved to help her. It became a common sight to see Jean working in the flower beds or garden with Rodica voluntarily working right along beside her. As they worked together, they talked. Rodica looked to Jean as her mentor.

Today they were pulling weeds from the flower bed that lined the long white fence from the road down toward Alvin's house. It was a hot, unpleasant job, and Jean was grateful for Rodica's help.

"When can I go visit my mom and sisters again?" asked Rodica.

"I guess that will depend on when Tata Johnny and Ionică think you deserve to go," replied Jean.

"Tell them you want to take me," begged Rodica.

"No, I told you I will not take you again because it was so upsetting to you the last time you went," Jean reminded her.

"But I won't be upset this time, I promise," said Rodica in a wheedling tone.

"No, Rodica," Jean said firmly. "You must learn that when I say no, that is exactly what I mean. You can beg all you want, but it will not change one thing."

"But it's not fair," countered Rodica. "I help you a lot, and now you won't help me!"

"That isn't the point at all, and you know it," Jean explained patiently. "You know we have thoroughly discussed this before, and you are just trying to make me change my mind about it."

"I thought you were my friend," pouted Rodica, "but you won't even help me."

Rodica had mastered the art of getting her own way with many of the tantis, but Jean was different. She refused to bend to Rodica's whims, and yet Rodica dearly loved and respected her. Rodica began to blossom into a respectable twelve-year-old under Jean's constant direction.

"Tata Johnny," called Mihaela from the orphanage kitchen doorway, "some visitors are here."

"Where are they?" I asked.

"They have just now come, and they are in front of the orphanage. And Tata Johnny," she exclaimed excitedly, "they are from Japan!"

We had received visitors from many countries, but this was the first time I could recall having visitors from Japan. This was noteworthy!

I hurried toward the front of the orphanage and rounded the corner just as the last of our guests emerged from their car. There were six in all, and one was a tall, handsome black man in his mid-twenties. *He's probably from Nigeria,* I thought, recalling that during the communist era many African students had studied in Bucureşti. Children flocked about me as I welcomed our visitors.

"Welcome," I said in English, as I spread my hands wide in a gesture of friendly invitation, conscious that they might not understand English.

"Thank yah," responded the tall black man with a beautiful smile. His accent was decidedly American South, and it reminded me of my boyhood days in Virginia.

I quickly reverted to the accent I had learned in my youth and responded, "Why, I think I hyear a little Narth Carolina in dat."

His grin spread even wider as he recognized that homey, Southern accent. He responded, "Yah sho do, man! I'm from Charlotte, Narth Carolina."

"What wouldn't I give fo' some colla't greens and co'n bread!" I added to our dialogue.

"Yeah, man, and some okra!" responded our guest good-naturedly.

By this time our unusual guest had come closer and, stretching his hand over the heads of the curious children, clasped my hand and said in a booming voice, "I'm pleased to meet yah!"

I greeted our Japanese visitors and welcomed them all. I soon learned that the young man from North Carolina was a born-again Christian and had married a young lady from Japan. He was traveling with his wife and her family as they visited Europe. Somewhere in their travels they had heard of the Nathaniel Christian Orphanage and wanted to see it for themselves.

While the introductions were being carried out, news spread that visitors had come from Japan. The children thronged me as I tried to speak with our guests. Our visitors were asking questions faster than I could answer them.

"When did this work begin? Were you here from the beginning? How many children live here? Are they all orphans? How did you find the children who needed the most help? Are they being adopted into families? How do you find funding for so many children?"

While I answered these questions, the children turned to me with questions of their own, which of course they asked in Romanian.

"Tata Johnny," asked Mihaela soberly, "why is that man black?"

"Yes, yes, Tata Johnny," chorused several children, "tell us why he's black."

It dawned on me that this was the very first person of African descent the Nathaniel children had ever seen, and they were amazed.

Our gracious visitor sensed that the children were badgering me with questions about him, and he gave me a reassuring smile.

"They want to know why you are black," I translated cautiously.

His friendly smile dispelled my fears. "You tell 'em it's 'cause the Good Lawd made me that way."

So I turned and explained this simple truth to the children.

"But . . . but . . ." sputtered Beti, "then why are the palms of his hands so white?"

I looked imploringly to our guest, and he nodded toward Beti, as if to say, "What is she asking?"

I was becoming uncomfortable with all the questions. What would they ask next?

"Beti noticed that the palms of your hands are much lighter and wants to know why."

"You just tell her that the Good Lawd made 'em that way too." He smiled affectionately down at her.

I turned my attention momentarily to the children and began explaining that God made people with differing hues, that our guest was a believer, and that God had made him just as he was. To my horror, while I was explaining, Beti reached up and grasped our visitor's hand. Then, with her outstretched forefinger, she vigorously rubbed the back of his hand. She turned it over and examined her finger, obviously expecting that some of his color would have rubbed off. I was mortified! Thankfully, our Southern gentleman took it all with good grace.

I told the children to go in and get ready for supper while I gave our guests a tour of the orphanage and farm. Reluctantly, they obeyed, sauntering off and talking excitedly about the black man God had made.

I guided our visitors to points of interest around the farm. We visited the little animal barn where the boys kept their assortment of bunnies and pigeons. They were impressed with our mare Stella and wanted to know if the children had learned to ride.

"Most of the children enjoy horseback riding," I answered, "but we don't want them to get hurt, so we do monitor their riding pretty closely."

"And the sheep?" they asked. "Do you raise the sheep for their wool?"

"No," I explained, "these are known as fat-tailed sheep. Notice the unusual size of the top portion of their tails."

"I have never seen sheep like this before. What makes them that way?" asked one of the Japanese ladies.

"This is a special breed that was developed in Russia, and the fat upper section of the tail is considered a rare delicacy."

Our guest made a wry face.

"The big Russian ram was given to us, but was lonely, so another farmer gave us a ewe, and we are hoping she will bear young in the spring," I explained.

"Is the ram aggressive?"

"Not unless our boys tease him," I answered. "Our farm director, Alvin, once heard a commotion in here and came to investigate. He walked in quietly and found a group of boys taunting the ram. He observed as several boys jumped into the pen and dashed about in different directions. First the ram charged one boy, then switched and chased after another. Finally the ram became infuriated and chased the boys wildly about, intent on butting them into the ground. At that point three boys scrambled up onto a big, round bale of hay, while others got out of harm's way by climbing over the gate. They howled with glee at the ram's frustration!

"This was more than Alvin could take. 'Boys!' Alvin called out, and their laughter died. 'What are you doing? That's no way to treat an animal!' Alvin opened the gate and entered to confront the boys face to face. 'You boys know better than this! I am really disappointed in you!' he told them.

"The boys hung their heads guiltily. They hadn't known Alvin was around.

"Meanwhile, the ram had finally spotted a target he could hit, and he proceeded to do so with all the power and speed he could muster. The ram hit Alvin squarely from behind. Alvin made a hasty retreat to a safer position, where he explained with newly acquired appreciation why it is never wise to tease an animal.

"So, you ask if he is aggressive," I concluded. "I wouldn't want to turn my back on him!"

My Southern friend smiled appreciatively.

We visited the new school building, where I explained our vision for a Christian education. I showed them the classrooms and explained that we were hoping to occupy the building soon.

"What will you do with the present school building?" they wanted to know.

"We plan to remodel it for use as a girls' dorm. Right now we are cramped for space, with four children in each bedroom. As our children grow older, they need more room. Right now the girls and boys are separated by a central room and a double set of doors. We feel that as the children become older, it would be more appropriate and provide more privacy for the boys and girls to be housed in separate buildings."

"We can see that you really do care for these children, and I am impressed with your desire to teach them godly principles," said the elder Japanese man in the group.

"Thank yah so much for showin' us around, and may God bless yah as yah continue guidin' these young souls," said my North Carolina friend. "We'll be prayin' for your work hyere."

"Thank you for both your visit and your prayers. We need them!" I said.

There was a warm feeling in my heart as we waved goodbye. Their visit had been encouraging indeed.

It was late evening as Alvin glanced about. Most of the forty-four milk cows were lying in their stanchions, contentedly chewing their cud. The milking and chores had been done, and another beautiful autumn day was drawing to a close. Sunset painted its colorful glow, silhouetting his two-story house and the orphanage beyond. His heart thrilled again at the beauty of God's creation.

As he walked up the lane toward home and the fine supper he was sure Lil was preparing, Alvin glanced through the chain-link fence into the horse pasture. Its beauty was marred by several broken cinder blocks and some large sticks which the orphanage boys had left lying about. Alvin shook his head and thought, *I wish I could be more successful in teaching these boys to pick things up when they see them.* Then, glancing at his watch, he saw that he could clear those items from the horse pasture and still be in time for supper.

Alvin closed the gate behind him and glanced toward the young bull grazing contentedly at the far end of the pasture. Heading directly for the large stick he had seen, Alvin picked it up and proceeded to where the pieces of cinder block lay scattered about. *I must have a meeting with the boys about this,* he thought as he threw another glance in the bull's direction.

Alvin gave a start, for the bull was running toward him. Alvin waved his stick to shoo the bull away. The bull paused a scant several yards from him to look the intruder over. Alvin took a tentative step in the bull's direction, sure it would now back off. But the bull dropped its head and eyed him menacingly. Alvin knew he was going to have to teach this young bull a good lesson. Taking a firm grip on his stout stick, he carefully measured the distance between himself and the bull's tender nose. He took a long, quick step in the bull's direction like a batter stepping into a home-run swing. With strength born from the adrenaline pounding through his veins, Alvin swung at the bull's nose with all his might—and missed. The bull hit him before he knew what had happened and sent him sprawling. He scrambled onto his knees, thinking, *I've got to get to the barn before that bull hits me again!*

Wham! The bull hit Alvin with such force that he saw stars. His body spun across the pasture. He lay on his back, stunned. Dull pain engulfed him.

Down near the farm Franklin stood talking with two of the workers. As they chatted, Franklin glanced through the fence and saw the young bull acting strangely, running about excitedly and butting something on the ground. *Probably just a piece of trash,* thought Franklin. Then he recognized the blue shirt as Alvin attempted to rise.

"Hey, that bull is after Alvin! Come on!" Franklin shouted wildly as he vaulted over the fence.

Through his daze Alvin saw the bull looming over him and thought, *This is serious! This bull could kill me! I've got to get out of here!* In desperation Alvin's hand sought for and found the bull's nose. He rammed his thumb and fingers into its slimy nostrils, hoping his grip would not slip! His other hand groped blindly and felt the bulge just above the bull's eye. With force born out of a desperate desire to live, Alvin thrust and twisted with all of his might. The bull's massive head lifted, twisted, and Alvin heard his heavy body colliding with the solid earth. The bull was on its back. Alvin rolled onto his knees and scrambled unsteadily to his feet. His body protested. He hurt everywhere! But hurt or not, he had to make it to the safety of the little animal barn before the bull got him again. Crouching from the pain, Alvin ran for his life. Behind him the bull righted himself and lunged to his feet. He saw the object of his anger already halfway to the barn and immediately sprang after him.

Alvin was spurred onward by the sound of pounding hooves. Directly before him was the boys' large, unused rabbit hutch. It was only two feet high as it lay on its back with its chicken-wire netting facing upward. It offered little in the way of protection against an angry bull, but Alvin was desperate. He scrambled across it as best he could, stepping on its thin partitions. He made it to the far side and clung to the fence, trying to catch his breath. He was hurt too badly to climb over the five-foot fence. He watched in horror as the racing bull skidded to a stop and placed its forefoot on the rabbit hutch. But when the bull felt the chicken wire give under his weight, he sidestepped and tried again at another spot. Again and again he tried, but the unsure footing of the chicken wire confused him. Head lowered, ears erect, and nostrils flared, the bull wasn't about to give up so easily.

Alvin heard someone hollering and looked up in time to see Franklin racing across the pasture toward him and the angry bull. "No, Franklin, no!" Alvin shouted at the top of his lungs. "Go back! Go back! This bull is dangerous! Go get the dogs!"

Franklin needed no second invitation, and was back over the fence in a flash, running to bring the dogs. In seconds the dogs were raising a terrific din just across the fence, and the bull transferred his attention to them. This was the break Alvin needed. He sprinted out from behind the fallen rabbit hutch and lifted the latch on the gate leading to the fenced-in alley between the little barn and the pasture. He slipped through the gate and firmly latched it behind him. Pain wracked his body as he turned and made his way falteringly forward. Just then a shadowy form entered the narrow alleyway ahead of him. It was the big Russian ram, standing his ground and guarding his alley. He arched his neck and ducked his head at the intruder. Alvin saw his massive curled horns and decided he'd already endured enough pounding for one night. When he drew within arm's length of the ram, Alvin's hand shot out and poked the ram right in the eye. This unexpected turn of events took the ram completely by surprise. Blinking and shaking his head, he backed off just enough to allow Alvin to pass by without further incident.

Alvin was laid up for several days with what appeared to be broken ribs. The bull was loaded up and carted away, his aggression having demoted him from the list of potential breeding stock to that of immediate hamburger.

Going and Coming

"Hurry, Ruth! Do hurry! The train leaves in twenty-five minutes, and we have to get going!"

I felt all jittery inside, as I usually did when it was time to leave. "Is that it?" I shouted up the stairs.

"No, I still have my carry-on up here," Ida Jane called back. I dashed up the steps to where our daughter Ida was struggling to cram the last of her belongings into an overloaded carry-on. I helped her get the zipper closed and rushed with it to the waiting Suburban.

"All aboard!" I hollered.

Ruth climbed in, followed by Franklin, Caroline, and Ida Jane. I nodded to Alvin, who was driving, and we were off.

Ruth gave me her encouraging smile as we started up the drive. "You always get into such a tizzy when we are getting ready to leave," she reminded me.

"Yes," I sputtered, "but trains don't wait."

"Have you ever missed one?" she asked.

Her calmness irked me! "No," I responded, "and I certainly don't want to miss this one either!"

"Oh, look at that!" Ruth said as we rounded the corner of the orphanage school building.

I looked up ahead and my heart lurched. There in the gate opening stood at least fifty orphanage children! They formed a human barricade. I couldn't believe this. Only fifteen minutes until train time, and the orphanage children were blocking our way! I felt my wife's gentle hand on my arm. Her warning glance helped curb my urge to shout for the children to get out of our way.

"Just look at those children," Ruth chuckled. "They are pretending they could keep us here and not let us leave for our furlough. They really do hate to see us go."

I rolled down the window and poked my head out, only to hear the children chanting, "No, no, you can't go! No, no, you can't go!" Ionela was shouting louder than the others. All the children were grinning mischievously, but Ionela's smile was the biggest of all.

Several workers rushed up to tell us goodbye. Then slowly, reluctantly, the children began to separate to either side of the gate, giving us room to pass between them. Amid waves and shouts of goodbyes, we eased through the children and onto the road. I looked back and saw the gate choked with children once more. A few were still waving, but their smiles had faded. We would be separated for a whole month. I, too, experienced a pang of sadness at the thought.

CAM's open house in Pennsylvania was a delightful experience. We met with child sponsors who asked about the orphanage, showed them recent snapshots of the children, and explained about each child's struggles as well as his areas of progress. This gave the sponsors a fresh glimpse into the heart of the child for whom they had sacrificed and prayed.

I spoke with Gabi's sponsor and encouraged him to bring his family to visit. "Our children often feel that even though their basic needs are being met, they do not actually belong. They continually thank God for their sponsors, who hold a special place in their hearts. But when sponsors visit their children, it helps the children feel connected, as though they have found a family to whom they belong. And they can claim the sponsors as their very own."

Gabi's sponsor was receptive to the idea. "We have considered a visit to Romania," he told me.

I couldn't wait to see Gabi's face when he heard the news. As an abandoned child, Gabi had frequently slept with the village cows in order to keep warm during the cold winter nights. Now his sponsors were planning to travel all the way from America to visit him. Gabi would be thrilled!

Ben and Lois Friesen wanted to know how Ovidiu was doing. I explained that he had to put forth a lot of effort to make good grades in school due to having missed two years of schooling before he came to us. "But he is catching up," I assured them. "Have you considered coming to Romania to visit Ovidiu?"

"Oh, now, that's an idea. We'll have to see about that," Ben responded as he looked questioningly to his wife.

"It would mean so much to Ovidiu if his sponsors would come visit him," I explained. "Pray about it."

"There is one thing I would like to do," Ben added. "I would like to ship a stainless steel sliding board to Romania for the children to play on. Do you think the children would like that?"

"Oh, I know they would! They do not have a sliding board, and they would be delighted!" I said. I could already envision a long line of excited children awaiting their very first sliding board experience!

"If I send the slide portion, could you build the frame and steps over there?" he wanted to know.

"We have a metal shop and an experienced welder. I am sure we could build a proper frame," I assured him.

Ruth was kept busy answering questions about the children, their development, their schooling, and their futures. "We are trying to make the Nathaniel Christian Orphanage as warm and as homey as possible," she explained to several ladies who had gathered about her.

"But how can you do that with so many children?" asked a concerned mother.

"We live right there on the compound, and girls come to my house every day. I give them little jobs to do so they learn how to work."

"What kind of jobs?" asked a mother holding a little girl.

"I have taught some of the older girls to iron shirts. Others have learned how to use the washing machine, and all of them like to try their hand at baking. Several girls have learned to follow a recipe and bake a simple cake, and Loredana has perfected the art of baking angel food cake. But usually the privilege of baking a cake comes as a reward for having done a good job cleaning, ironing, or washing windows."

"Don't the girls feel like you are using them?" asked a young mother.

"Oh, no," Ruth replied. "They love to come to our house, and I am careful to treat them just as I do my own girls. When the work is done, they often stay and read, or we just sit in our living room and talk. Sometimes after an especially hard task I invite the girls to stay and have supper with our family. It helps them feel like they really are a part of us when we share our lives together. It is such a devastating experience for a child to feel unwanted, and this helps them feel like they belong."

We were encouraged by supporters who assured us of their prayers. More and more we realized the importance of the prayers offered for our Nathaniel children.

CAM's open house and our furlough flashed by amid travels, meetings, and family visits. We were soon packing up to head back to Romania. What should we take with us? What must we leave behind?

My dear wife had one request—that I would haul two frozen turkeys back to Romania for Thanksgiving. The orphanage children had never tasted turkey and had asked many questions about our American Thanksgiving traditions.

In the end I conceded. I bought the turkeys and a cooler. On the day of our departure I swallowed my pride, wrapped our frozen turkeys in many layers of newspaper, and loaded them into the cooler. I securely taped it shut, tied a rope harness about it, and prayed that the customs officials would either be blind or very gracious.

We landed in București on Thanksgiving Eve in the midst of the heaviest snowfall of the season. As we passed unchallenged through customs with our conspicuous blue and white cooler intact, Ruth looked up at me with a knowing grin. She nodded as if to say, *I told you so*, but thankfully did not rub it in.

The snow had snarled București traffic to a virtual crawl, and it took us an additional three hours to drive from the airport to the train station. Our scheduled train to Suceava had departed several hours earlier, and we had to wait for a later one. Having already traveled for seventeen hours and having lost seven hours crossing time zones, we were too tired to care. We slept fitfully in our overloaded compartment during the seven-hour train ride north toward our big Nathaniel family and home.

Conductors roused us to check our tickets. Beggars woke us numerous times when we stopped at stations along the way, pushing the door open to beg for food and money. Fearing lest thieves would clean us out while we slept, Franklin positioned himself with his feet securely propped against the door.

Screeching brakes and the bustle of passengers roused us from our stupors. Wiping the fog from the train window, I peered through the falling snow to discover that we were indeed rolling into the Suceava station. I wondered if the message had gotten through that we would be on a much later train. *What if no one is there to meet us?* I wondered. *How will we ever handle all this baggage?*

I struggled down the long, narrow aisle toward the door, pushing a large suitcase ahead and dragging another one behind. Suddenly I heard Ida Jane squeal, "Look, Dad!"

I could hardly believe my eyes. There on the platform stood twenty of our faithful staff who had come to welcome us home—at 3:45 in the morning! What wonderful people! Their joyous greetings and heartfelt welcomes warmed our hearts. I could hardly tell which was the largest, the smile on my face or the lump in my throat!

After unloading the baggage at our little gray house, we bid our friends goodnight and fell into bed, giving ourselves over to our utter exhaustion.

After what seemed like only minutes, faraway voices came to us, as if in a dream. Sitting up in bed and looking about, it took a moment to realize where we were. The clock said 7:40, and from somewhere voices were chanting, "Tata Johnny, Mama Ruth! Tata Johnny, Mama Ruth!"

We scrambled out of bed, dressed, and rushed to the door. On the porch stood a large group of smiling children. They had been on their way to school, but just had to come welcome us. What a happy, energetic bunch! It was so good to see them again! Amid the hellos and hugs, Davucu wanted to know what we had brought him from America.

"Wait a minute," I teased. "First of all, I must see if you were good."

"He really was good," his sister Lavinia soberly assured me.

"You children must hurry to school so you won't be late," Ruth said. "After we have unpacked our things, we will have a little something for each of you."

"Oh, goody!" shouted Ionela. "Come on, let's go!" And off she dashed through the snow with the whole pack following. Ruth and I stepped back inside and closed the door against the November chill. I stood close to Ruth with my arm about her waist while we watched from the window as the last of the children bustled into the school building. How privileged we felt that God should give us the opportunity to work with these loving children!

Two days later Ruth helped the cooks fix turkey and dressing for our Thanksgiving dinner. The children could hardly wait to taste it. Following the meal I related the story of the Pilgrims and the American Indians. I explained how hardship and death had visited many of those first settlers during the harsh winter of 1620. The Nathaniel children listened with rapt attention as they heard for the first time how Squanto, the friendly Indian, taught these European settlers how to fertilize each hill of corn by burying a fish in the soil. The bountiful harvest the following fall had led the Pilgrims to hold a day of thanksgiving to God for His bountiful blessings. They invited the Indians to share. I explained that the Indians were happy to join in this feast and no doubt brought deer and wild turkey as contributions. This was how turkey became a part of the American Thanksgiving tradition.

Following this special meal we invited a child from each of the six dining room tables to lead in prayer as we stood. My heart was moved as I heard child after child praying, "Dear Lord, we thank you for our sponsors. Bless them for all they have done for us!"

Thousands of abandoned children all over Romania had no mother or father to really care about them. Neither did they have sponsors who loved them, gave for their benefit, or prayed daily for their salvation. Indeed, the Nathaniel children had much for which to thank God!

Several weeks later Ruth and I drove to a village some distance away to pick up two of our little girls who had spent the day with their relatives. Tina and Larisa were glad to see us, and they chattered away as we drove home. Tina overheard me saying that I was tired and proceeded to give me a neck rub as she stood behind the driver's seat. After rubbing my neck for a bit, she ran her little fingers over a recently shaved area of my throat and exclaimed with obvious delight, "Oh, it's just like pigskin!" I burst out laughing, immediately understanding her comparison.

In a Romanian village when a pig is butchered, they customarily pile straw over the hog and light it as soon as the pig has been properly bled. When the fire has died down, the charred hair is scraped away with knives. Children appear as if by magic, waiting for the treat they know will be forthcoming. Each fortunate child is given a four-inch square of chewy, rubbery pigskin, which they love to salt and eat. The scraped stumps of the bristles can still be felt, which helped Tina make the comparison between my throat and the pig-skin she so loved. Her comment could only be appreciated with an understanding of her culture.

Our groundskeeper, Aurel, was in charge of butchering our or-phanage-raised hogs. Instead of burning the hair with straw, he used a large gas-powered torch. It accomplished the same thing, but with less mess. The mess came after fifteen or twenty children had been given their square of pigskin to chew. On one such butchering day I wanted to enter the orphanage, but found that I had to use two hands in order to turn the doorknob, which had been slathered with grease from the hands of our pigskin-loving Nathaniel children!

"Tata Johnny," pleaded Dorica, our bakery worker, "I have a cousin who is in the hospital with heart trouble, and I would like to go visit her. Would you like to go along?" Dorica was a dedicated Christian with a servant's heart. She had helped us much in organizing our bakery.

"Yes," I said, "I will take you this evening after work."

"Is it okay if several other workers go along?" she wanted to know.

"Of course," I responded. "I'll drive the Honda."

That evening three of our workers crammed into the narrow back seat of our Honda, and Dorica sat in the front passenger's seat as we started off for the Suceava hospital. A guard stood beside the closed gate, blocking our way into the hospital compound. He interrogated every driver before opening the gate and allowing entrance. His obvi-ous expectation of a tip was a bit overbearing, to my way of thinking. However, my Romanian friends thought nothing of it, and one of them slipped a small bill into his waiting hand. *Another one of those cultural differences,* I thought. This was an expected courtesy for them just as leaving a tip for a good waitress was for me.

We parked and Dorica led the way through a confusing array of dimly lit corridors and staircases to the third floor. There she showed us into a meagerly furnished, six-bed women's ward. Every bed was filled.

It had been a long week for Dorica's cousin, and she was happy for visitors. Following several minutes of discussion concerning the patient's heart ailment and its treatment, Dorica announced that we visitors had a song we would like to sing. Her prominent soprano voice carried well beyond the ward we were visiting, and I was fearful of disturbing other patients. Our bakery workers had no such thoughts, but seemingly nourished a fervent hope that these blessings would float as far down the hallway as possible. I was actually relieved when the hymn finally ended and no nurses had come to chase us out. The second and third hymns were sung with the same sincere fervor.

Dorica shared a poem. I glanced about, worried that the non-Christian patients would take offence at the spiritual warnings voiced through its eleven stanzas. But to my amazement they seemed to be listening with interest. One of the patients asked a question about the Bible, and a spontaneous spiritual discussion began. *Why,* I thought, *these non-Christian Romanians are more open about their spiritual lives than many American Christians!*

After some time I suggested we close with prayer. Standing, I began to pray in English. Imagine my surprise and embarrassment when not only each of our workers fell to their knees and began praying aloud, but four of the patients also climbed from their beds and knelt, lifting their voices in prayer! I quickly knelt and joined them.

We arose from our knees to find one of the non-believers in tears. Dorica immediately went to her aid and, kneeling beside her bed, gave her personal counsel from the Word of God.

Afterward as I walked toward the little gray Honda, I thought within myself, *That was more like a revival service than a hospital visit!*

Perhaps our American culture had taught us to be loud and assertive in secular matters, but overly timid on spiritual issues. I was humbled. The night had certainly been a learning experience for me!

Excitement was in the air; Christmas was just around the corner! Festivities and programs were being planned. In addition to this, the Marvin Miller family was moving to Romania to assist us with the work. Eight months earlier they had visited us for several weeks and set up our bakery equipment. The children had learned to know them and made friends with the Miller children during that visit. Now they were returning to live and work among us, and the Nathaniel children were begging to go along to the train station to welcome them.

Marvin and Ruth were from our home community of Minerva, Ohio, and were bringing their entire family with them. Titus, their oldest, was seventeen, and Esther, their youngest, was only one year old. Their nine children would surely be a blessing.

Friday evening finally arrived, and we made plans to head for the train station. A number of the orphanage children begged to go along and meet the 10:30 p.m. train from București. Due to the lateness of the hour, only the oldest children were allowed to accompany us. After promising the younger children that they would be able to go along another time, we had the tantis tuck them into their beds as we loaded the older ones into vans and headed for the station.

We huddled close together on the canopy-covered platform of the train station and talked excitedly as we waited for the train. Our breath hung in the air as we discussed the Marvin Miller family and the addition they would make to our great family.

"Where are they going to live?" asked Elena.

"Well, the only house we have available is the white house right beside the store," I answered.

"You mean *that* old house?" Loredana wanted to know.

"It's not so bad, now that we have cleaned up around the outside and added an indoor bathroom," replied Ionuț.

"What kind of work are they going to do?" asked Manu.

"Their three oldest sons are good carpenters, and I hope they will help us finish the inside of the school so we can move into the new building during our spring break," I replied. "I would also like for Marvin to take over our bakery responsibilities since he has had experience in running his own bakery back in America. But Marvin's family will need some time to adjust, and they will also need time to study the Romanian language."

"Here comes the train!" shouted Franklin as he peered through the darkness.

The thunder of the approaching locomotive rendered further conversation all but impossible. It roared by, slowing the string of coaches with screeching brakes until it finally came to a stop. The boys took off running down the long platform as the train slowed, and they peered expectantly into each car as it passed. "Here they are!" the boys shouted, waving for us to follow.

We hurried to where the older Miller boys were helping with the baggage, arriving just as the younger children clambered down the high steps of the train with their mother. Finally, Marvin himself emerged, and they were all welcomed enthusiastically. The orphanage children all wanted to help, and their small hands grasped the handles of the suitcases to assist the adults who were straining to get them into the waiting vehicles.

Laura walked along beside Marvin and wanted to help with his carry-on and briefcase.

"I am so glad your family is going to live here!" she gushed. "How long are you going to stay in Romania?"

"Well, we would like to live here at least ten years," replied Marvin, smiling at her straightforwardness.

"Oh, but Americans don't stay that long," stated Laura knowingly. "They move back to America after a couple of years."

Marvin was struck by her words. How difficult it must be to touch hearts for God when one's view was clouded with a short-term vision!

Marvin's family was ushered into the old white house beside the store. There a tasty, late-night supper awaited them. Their first night in Romania was filled with mixed feelings of anticipation and apprehension, excitement and fatigue. What experiences did God have in store for them? How would He use them in this portion of His kingdom? One thing was sure: God had called them, and He would lead them.

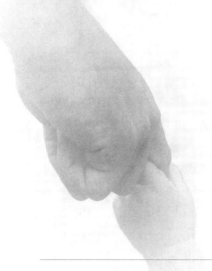

Chapter 21

The Sponsors

Weeks passed and the new school building was nearing completion. The first Saturday in March dawned bright and clear. Nicu yawned as he stretched. He looked out the window to the new Nathaniel School building just beyond the greenhouse and church. Today they would move into the new school. Marvin Miller's sons were still busily putting the finishing touches to a few of the classrooms, but Nenea Ionică had said that today would be moving day!

"Come on, Ionuț," Nicu called as he gently shook his twin brother's bottom bunk. "Today's the big day!" In the next room he heard Iliuță and Marius talking excitedly. Down the hall Nenea Geo was waking the boys in yet another room.

"Yes, yes," he heard Nenea Geo saying, "we will move all the desks and maps and books and papers and pencils—everything gets moved today! My own children are excited about this too. They can hardly wait for spring break to be finished so they can begin attending the new school. So come on, boys, up and at 'em!" he shouted good-naturedly.

"Are they going to move the glass chalkboards too?" asked Marian.

"Didn't you hear?" asked Nenea Geo. "Christians in Ohio have donated money for new, modern chalkboards for all our new classrooms. They have been shipped from America and are being installed. You'll never believe how well you can write on them. But listen, I stopped by the kitchen and Roza has a huge stack of hot pancakes all ready for your breakfast. After breakfast we will work together to carry supplies from the old school to our new one. So get up! Let's beat the girls to the dining room this morning!"

Nicu smiled as he quickly buttoned his shirt. He heard the thump of feet hitting the floor as boys jumped from their top bunks. Nenea Geo had a way of making everything sound so exciting! The boys dressed quickly and rushed pell-mell down the stairs, but to their dismay they found three girls already standing in the hallway ahead of them, talking excitedly about the new school.

After prayer the boys hurriedly spread a liberal coating of peanut butter on their pancakes and poured the hot syrup lightly over them. They were delicious! But today the children wanted to get breakfast over with as soon as possible. Nicu found his attention wandering during the devotional. His mind kept straying to the new school building as if pulled by some magnetic force.

The children were soon dismissed from their tables and hurried to find their coats. Ionică was in the new school to tell them where to put everything. The boys pulled their wagons loaded with cardboard boxes of school supplies down to the new school. Once there, they asked Nenea Ionică which classroom was going to be theirs. Patiently he showed the children the brightly lit classrooms with their large windows, native wood wainscoting, and new, green chalkboards.

School desks were loaded onto vans and delivered to the door of the new school, where the older boys carried them into their proper classrooms according to their sizes. The teachers were on vacation during spring break but came to help organize their classrooms. By evening the transition was complete.

Spring break came to an end, and the Nathaniel Christian School officially took up residency in the new building. All too soon the inspectors arrived. They were impressed with our new building, but said it wasn't legal for us to have the classrooms carpeted. When asked why, they replied that carpet fibers provided places where vermin could hide. When we explained that our central vacuum system should be more than adequate to keep any mites from thriving in our classroom carpet, they relented and allowed us to keep the carpet. We were grateful.

Sam and Danielle Wray traveled all the way from Ellensburg, Washington, their hearts filled with a burning desire to know the child they had been sponsoring for nearly five years. They had seen photos of Elena Biţica and had imagined what kind of girl she must be. But now they were actually going to meet the girl they had so diligently prayed for. Five of the six Wray children accompanied them on this trip, and they were filled with anticipation. Would Elena be outgoing or shy? Would she know enough English to communicate freely? Would she accept them or hold them at arm's length? These questions tumbled about in their thoughts as the plane banked steeply left and lined up for landing at the Bucureşti airport. Sam wondered if anyone would be there to meet them since their flight from London had been delayed by over an hour. If they missed their connections, how would they be able to communicate since they couldn't speak Romanian? They couldn't even make a phone call!

After passing through immigration, they collected their luggage. With feelings of apprehension, they began walking past the customs examining tables. Others were forced to undergo thorough baggage searches. The uniformed officer stood at attention watching them, but only nodded soberly as they passed. The Wray family exited into a large lobby milling with hundreds of people. How could they know if anyone was there to meet them? Sam found himself glancing from face to face among the hundreds of people, but there was not one glimmer of recognition. Other passengers were greeting family members with hugs and kisses, but their speech was completely unintelligible to the Wrays, who felt very much alone in the midst of this huge crowd.

A clean-cut young man approached Sam and spoke in broken English. "I work for Christian Aid, and I come for you, yes?"

Was he really a CAM worker? How could they be sure? Could they trust this man?

"Your plane is come late, and now is not possible to go on first train to Suceava."

"Yes, we understand," said Sam, "but can we catch a later train this evening?"

"Yes. Come, I take you now to the train station."

Their ride across the huge, sprawling city of Bucureşti was filled with interesting sights. The sidewalks were teaming with pedestrians. Trolleys and buses reminded the children of huge bugs with antennae, but these antennae connected them to overhead electric lines from which they received their power to operate. The trolleys were jammed with laborers returning from their jobs to the tall apartment buildings which seemed to line every major street. Multitudes of glass-sided shops and tiny sales booths beckoned people to stop and buy. People were everywhere. This was Romania!

"What is this?" asked Sam as they reached a huge traffic circle. Its center was dominated by a massive stone arch several stories high which was lit by powerful beams of light.

"This," explained their driver, "is like the Arch of Triumph in Paris. It is a memorial to victory."

"I see," said Danielle. "Thank you for explaining."

The Romans had conquered large portions of Romania early in the second century, giving Romania its name and leaving Rome's cultural stamp upon its people. This arch commemorates that historical victory.

CAM's worker bought the train tickets and led the Wrays through the confusion of Bucureşti's central station. A number of the twelve sidings had trains sitting on them, but CAM's worker kindly showed the Wrays into the proper compartment of the Suceava-bound train and helped them stow their luggage on the overhead racks, which were decidedly too small. "Be sure and get off at the Burdujeni Station," he cautioned as he shook hands and wished them God's blessing. Then he waved and left. They were all alone in a strange land among a people with a strange language. Yet God had brought them thus far and God would see them through.

The train looked old and rickety and the fetid odor of its nearby lavatory assailed their senses. But they were together, and they would soon be headed for Suceava. They had so much to be thankful for!

With hardly any warning, the train creaked and groaned to life as it began creeping out of the station. It lurched and shuddered as it picked up speed and clattered through the many switches. It would be a long night, but Lord willing, they would arrive in Suceava early in the morning. After a time, one sort of got used to the rocking motion of the train and the hum of its wheels. One by one their children began to doze off. The ten time zones between their home and Romania wreaked havoc on their inner clocks, and though they felt excited, they were also quite exhausted.

About thirty minutes into the trip the conductor asked for their tickets, which he punched and handed back to them. He tipped his hat politely and continued up the narrow aisle toward the next compartment. Soon, however, a beggar pushed the door open and entered. He made motions to his stomach and then to his mouth, speaking Romanian all the while in a sing-song professional beggar's voice. Sam remembered the warnings he had heard from those familiar with life in Romania. Most veterans do not give money to the numerous beggars that sneak onto the train unless there is some observable handicap like the loss of an arm or a leg. They have learned that far too many of these beggars are excellent actors playing on the sympathies of tender-hearted people. Far too often these gifts of charity are used to purchase alcohol, cigarettes, and drugs.

Time dragged by and finally the train pulled into a station. A black-robed Orthodox priest passed through the train, calling out for donations. Soon they were on their way once more, and a vendor with a sack of magazines passed through their car, calling over and over again in a loud, raspy voice.

Danielle looked at her watch. Four more hours to go! She was beginning to feel numb from lack of sleep. However, she had a subconscious fear that if they slept soundly, they might miss the station where they were to get off. They dozed fitfully, waking each time the train crossed the metal bridges or pulled into a station.

Sam thought they must be nearing Suceava. Would someone be there to meet them? Once again the train slowed as it pulled into a station. It screeched to a stop. Sam opened the compartment door, pointed to the station, and asked, "Burdujeni?"

"*Da* (yes), Burdujeni," a lady in the crowded aisle nodded.

"Look!" cried Danielle as she roused her children. "Those must be the people who have come to meet us. And that must be Elena!"

Elena stood on the station platform with the others who had come to meet her sponsors. "Oh, look, Tata Johnny," she squealed, "they're here. They're really here! Oh, I can't believe it!" How she had looked forward to this moment! Her dreams had finally come true!

When Danielle hopped down from the train's steps and turned to face the waiting crowd, Elena could contain herself no longer. She ran to Danielle, threw her arms about her in a loving embrace, and in her best English said, "I'm so glad you have come!" She had lived for this moment. Her own dear sponsors had come all the way from America to see her! Oh, how she loved them! If only she could be theirs and belong to them forever.

Danielle gazed for a long moment into Elena's dark eyes and knew in her heart that God in heaven had brought them together. Elena met Sam and each of the children with the same joyful openness. She knew they would soon leave to go with their hosts to the guesthouse where they would be staying, and she would have to go back to her bed in the orphanage, but she was sure that she wouldn't be able to sleep a wink. She was just too excited!

"Tata Johnny," Elena begged as I turned in at the orphanage gate, "may I go stay overnight with my sponsors at the guesthouse some nights? Aren't they a wonderful family? Don't you just love their children?" she asked all in one breath.

"I think you may stay with them some of the time," I answered, "but you know how important it is that you keep up with your schoolwork. You don't want to get behind."

I stopped to let Elena off at the orphanage. "Thank you, Tata Johnny, for taking me along to the train station. That was so wonderful! I just love them!" she exclaimed as she turned to go.

The next day the Wray family came to tour the newly completed Teaching Ministries Program building. Willis Bontrager showed them around as he explained the work.

"We distribute CAM's monthly *Seed of Truth* magazine through this department. It is given free to churches throughout Romania, and we have a current circulation of 80,000. A search is made for appropriate articles in American periodicals. Those articles are then translated and published," he explained.

"Another encouraging work is supplying Romanian study Bibles and newly translated, spiritually challenging books. Under communism these items were severely suppressed, and there is a tremendous hunger for them now. This is an open door through which we can help encourage Christians. Right now we are in the process of setting up a correspondence Bible study course."

"Will that also have to be translated, graded, and responded to, all in Romanian?" asked Sam.

"That's right," said Willis. "It's a big job. We also organize and hold several Bible seminars each year, both here in Romania and in the neighboring country of Moldova. Attendance varies anywhere from 150 to 500, depending where it is held."

Downstairs the visitors were pleasantly surprised to find several girls from the orphanage busily engaged in counting out bundles of *Seed of Truth* magazines and readying them for shipment to their respective churches. And there sat Elena hard at work!

Right then their guide announced that they needed to leave since they had several more stops to make.

"Mom," said three-year-old Janae, "I want to stay with Elena. May I, Mom?"

"Oh, do let her stay," said Elena. "I'll watch out for her, and she can go back to the orphanage with me when we are finished here."

"Are you sure you don't want to go with Mom and Dad?" Danielle asked her daughter. "We are going to see castle ruins and then go to the market. Don't you want to go with us?"

By now Janae was standing close to Elena. "No, I want to stay with Elena."

Danielle was amazed. This was only the second time Janae had seen Elena, but already they were bonding. "Well, okay, you may stay, but you be good and listen to Elena while Mama is gone. We'll come back to pick you up at the orphanage when we come from town."

The hosts from the guesthouse took the Wrays to see the castle ruins in Suceava. This castle was reportedly built by Stephen the Great late in the fifteenth century. He was a ruler who subdued many warlords and did much to unify Romania. Legend has it that whenever he won a battle, he decreed that a church be built on the spot to commemorate his victory. Many churches from that era still stand throughout Romania.

After stepping back in time to witness this bit of history, the Wrays experienced present-day Romania at the local bazaar. The parking lot was full, and they had to park some distance away. So many people were pressing in through the bazaar gate that they had to wait their turn to pay the ticket agent and enter. Once inside, they made their way through the jostling crowds toward the section where merchants' booths were packed with bolts of fabric. This never ceased to impress lady visitors, and the Wrays were no different.

They passed stands where vendors were preparing sausages. The heavy aromas wafted on the air, accompanied by pounding music from a nearby tape vendor. A lady whose arms were draped with men's socks blocked their guide's path, trying to interest him in men's footwear, but he deftly dodged around her and motioned for the group to follow. Hundreds of watches were displayed at yet another booth. Water pumps, bicycle parts, electric drills, dishes, sweaters, dresses, jackets, light bulbs, tools, flashlight batteries, and fishing tackle abounded in every direction. No prices were marked. Each vendor had a mental list of prices for every item in his booth.

They wound their way past a display of light fixtures and another of floor coverings. Then, deep in the heart of the bazaar, they finally came upon the section where material was sold. There were no less than four booths with great stacks of fabrics on display: bolts of heavy drapery material, suit material, and dress material of all colors and patterns. The prices were very reasonable, and the ladies were in their glory.

That evening the Wray family joined the orphanage children for supper, and a special table was prepared for them. Elena was allowed to join them instead of sitting at her assigned seat. Right after prayer Elena came to my table and asked, "Tata Johnny, may Vasilica come sit with us too? I want my sister to know my sponsors. May she?"

The usual noise and chatter filled the dining room as I glanced about, considering Elena's request. Suddenly Vasilica's sweet smile caught my eye. She was looking at me as she tilted her head imploringly and mouthed the words, "May I, Tata Johnny?" I knew I was bending the rules, but I smiled back and nodded. Vasilica scooped up her plate and utensils and happily joined Elena at her sponsors' table.

Following the meal, Elena went to her room to study, and I gave the Wray family a tour of the orphanage and farm. I explained that in an orphanage with fifty-three children we were forced to have rules that might seem a bit out of place in a normal home setting.

"Like what?" asked Danielle.

"Well, there are the normal rules like no jumping on the furniture, make your own bed, brush your teeth, wash dishes when it is your turn, and ask permission before going somewhere. However, we have to keep a more rigorous schedule than most homes would. Mealtimes are set, and delays cannot be tolerated. And we use a bell to help keep order with so many children.

"We also had to make the rule that girls are not allowed to trade dresses without permission."

"Oh, really? Why is that?"

"Well, it's like this. When one girl gets a new dress, others *oooh* and *aaah* over it and ask if they may wear it. So it gets passed from one girl to another to another. Often the borrowers are not quite so careful and soon the dress is no longer new."

"But why can't the girl just say no and not lend her dress to the others?"

"In Romanian culture, if you have something and a friend asks to borrow it, you cannot refuse him, because he is your friend. This compulsion is very strong. They are a very generous people."

The Sam Wray family with Elena and her sisters.

"By the way," said Danielle, "we made matching dresses for the girls in our family, and I made one for Elena as well. Do you think she will like that?"

"Oh, I'm sure she will! It will make her feel like she is part of your family. That was very thoughtful of you. Be sure and let me know when you are going to wear them. I want to see this."

As we entered the old school building, I pointed out the remodeling process already under way. "We have removed the old glass chalkboards, closed up a number of windows, moved walls, and cut in new doors. We are making room for all the girls to live here. This is to be the new bathroom with a shower, a bathtub, three sinks, and three toilets. There is another bath like this one on the first floor. But can you imagine twenty-eight girls all crowding into these two bathrooms, trying to get ready for church on time? So we are proposing that a vanity, sink, and mirror be installed in each bedroom to relieve the congestion and make life easier for everyone."

"When do we start?" asked Sam.

"Well, we really don't like to put our visitors to work right away. We thought it would be nice to allow you several days to unwind and get rested from your trip. But there is plumbing to be done in the girls' dorm. We thought it might be a project you'd enjoy helping with."

"We came to help, and the sooner we get started, the sooner we can finish," said Sam as his practiced eye surveyed all the work to be done.

"By Monday," I said, "you will have had time to look over the plans, and we will have the materials ready for you."

"Sounds good to me," he replied.

That evening I ambled into the orphanage's spacious living room. Elena was seated on the sofa beside her beloved sponsors. Danielle and her daughters were clustered about her. They were totally absorbed in Elena's photo album.

"And this," Elena continued, "is the house where I lived until I was six years old. This is where we lived when my father killed my mother, and then we came to live here in the orphanage. I can take you to see it if you want. It really isn't far away. It only takes fifteen minutes to get there. And would you like to visit my father in prison? He's a Christian now, and we want to go visit him."

"Okay," Danielle replied thoughtfully, "when Sam has completed the plumbing on your new dorm, we will travel and do some sightseeing. And we would also like to visit your father in prison."

Sunday morning found Danielle sitting in the Nathaniel Church, deeply moved as the rich singing swelled heavenward. Although she could not understand the words, she could feel in her heart that they were reaching heaven's throne. She glanced across the aisle to where her husband sat straight and tall between their two sons and wondered if they were experiencing the same feelings. She glanced to where her daughters were sitting with Elena, and her heart rejoiced that God had granted them the privilege of coming to Romania to meet her and worship with her people in this place.

Sunday school was soon over and a group of twelve children gave a short program. Danielle sat forward and watched intently as they sang, their angelic voices matching their faces. Tears in her own eyes caused their faces to swim as she realized that they had all suffered the loss of their homes through death, abuse, or abandonment. Oh, how her heart ached for them! How she wished there was some way she could help each one of them! Then she remembered Elena. She could make a difference for her.

Chapter 22

The Shell

"Tata Johnny," said Beti as she and Oana burst into my office, "guess what. They say there's a truck here that brought a shipment from Pătrăuţi, and it has a slide on it!"

"A slide?" I asked. "What kind of slide?"

"I don't know," responded Beti, "but it's a slide, and it's for us."

"How do you know it's for us?" I teased.

"Because," she faltered, "because slides are for children, so it has to be for us."

"I believe I know what it is. When I was in America, I met with Ovidiu's sponsors—"

"You mean his new ones?" interjected Beti.

"Yes, his new sponsors, Ben and Lois Friesen," I continued patiently. "They promised they would send you children a stainless steel sliding board, but only the part that you slide on. We will have to make the frame and steps down at the welding shop, and then you children will have a wonderful time playing on your new sliding board."

"Wonderful! Come on, Oana," Beti said as she jumped off her chair and dashed out the door, no doubt intent on finding someone else with whom to share the good news. I shook my head. Beti had been abandoned at such an early age that she couldn't remember her own mother. She had no idea who her father was. I was sure there lived a princess inside her tough outer shell. I prayed that she would allow God to break through that shell and release the princess within.

We gathered in the orphanage living room for Jean Mullet's farewell. She had worked with us only one year and was terminating her service to return to her home in Ohio. We deeply appreciated her dedicated assistance, but now she was leaving, and the children were sad. This was to be her last evening with them. By the next morning when they woke up, Jean would be gone.

With the sober children nestled about the room and listening intently, different staff members rose to their feet and addressed the group. Ida Jane spoke of how she appreciated Jean and treasured pleasant memories of working with her. Several of the tantis spoke of their love and appreciation as well. Finally it was Jean's turn, and she rose to face the staff and children.

"Tonight," she began, "I want to thank every one of you for making my stay here in Romania a precious experience. God has blessed my life in being able to spend this year with you. But now it is time to say goodbye. By this time tomorrow I will be on my way back to America. I don't know if I will ever have the opportunity to come back to Romania or not, but one thing I know, I will always remember you and the wonderful times we have had here together." Jean wiped her tears as she continued, "I know I will miss you terribly."

Sniffles could be heard from the children. Larisa sat on the floor with her head on her knees, wiping away her tears. Tina got up and rushed from the room. Jean struggled to finish saying what was on her heart. "If my being here has made a difference in one child's life, it has been worth it all. Each one of you holds a special place in my heart. I can never forget you!"

I glanced over to where Beti had been sitting stoically on the floor among several of her friends. I was surprised to see that she was crying softly. Beti seldom cried about anything. She had acquired that tough demeanor roaming the streets as an abandoned little girl. As

I watched in amazement, Beti began to cry aloud, tears streaming down her face. Somehow I had missed the closeness that she and Jean must have shared.

"I am not going home to America," concluded Jean brokenly. "I'm only stopping there on the way to my heavenly home. I want each of you to come also so that we can be together up there. God bless you until we meet again." Jean resumed her seat.

We prayed together and dismissed the children. Several boys shuffled self-consciously, not quite knowing how to express themselves. A group of girls and staff surged around Jean to tell her goodbye. Many were talking at once. Hearing hoarse sobs, I glanced about. My heart nearly broke when I saw tough little Beti on her knees with her face buried in her hands. Her forehead rested upon the carpet and great, uncontrollable sobs shook her small frame. I wanted to go to her and comfort her in her grief, but I thought better of it, realizing that at this moment she would rather cry out her heartache alone. But the scene of that lonely little girl huddled forlornly on the living room floor, sobbing out her grief at yet another forced parting from one whom she had come to love was more than I could bear. I had to look away and steel myself to gain control of my own emotions. Beti's raw pain became indelibly etched in my mind.

A few days later at lunchtime I entered the dining room. I tried to bring order so that we could begin our meal, but to no avail. Outside, workers were placing the legs and braces of the new sliding board into freshly poured cement, and the windows and doors were crowded with excited children watching the men at work. Some had ventured outside in order to see better.

"Come, children," I called. "I have an announcement to make about the new sliding board. Come take your places at the table, and I will tell you all about it."

"Can we go sliding this afternoon?" asked Gheorghe on the way to his table.

"Children, please listen." I was having a hard time making myself heard. "This sliding board is a gift from Ovidiu's sponsors, and they are giving it to all of us. However, you must remember two things. If we use it before the cement is properly hardened, the legs will break loose from the cement and we will have to repair it before we can use it again. They are tying a yellow plastic ribbon around the sliding board, and I don't want anyone crossing that ribbon. Does everyone understand? I will tell you when the sliding board can be used.

"The second thing is that Ovidiu's sponsors have requested that he be allowed to go down the sliding board first." I glanced at Ovidiu, who was smiling self-consciously. "We are thankful for their gift and want to honor their request." All heads turned in Ovidiu's direction with new looks of respect.

Two days later the children could hardly contain their excitement as they gathered near the new sliding board. "Come on, Ovidiu!" the children shouted as they waved him to the front of the line.

Enjoying the new slide.

"Sure, go ahead," I encouraged as Ovidiu reluctantly made his way forward, embarrassed by all the attention. Slowly he climbed the steps. Behind him was a long line of children jumping up and down with excitement. As Ovidiu reached the top, he sat down for a long moment. Then he let go. *Swish,* down the shiny new sliding board he flew.

"My turn! Now it's my turn!" clamored several others in unison. Soon there was a long line of happy children whizzing down the new sliding board and then rushing around to get in line for another turn.

"Tata Johnny, you go! It's your turn! Come!" shouted several children, making room for me at the head of the line.

"You'll just love it!" added Tina, her eyes shining as I climbed the steps. I paused at the top to look down at the excited children. I grabbed the guardrails and trembled, acting as if I were afraid to let go.

"Go! Go! Tata Johnny!" shouted the children. "Don't be afraid! It's all right!"

I launched away and slid to the bottom amid gales of laughter from the children.

"Do it again, Tata Johnny! Do it again!" they begged.

I looked up from my Saturday morning work and saw Beti passing by my office. An idea popped into my mind. "Say, Betz," I called. Beti stopped and walked in. "I am going to the market. Would you like to go along? Mama Ruth has a list of things she needs, and I could use your help."

"Sure," came her ready response, "I'll go."

"Who is your tanti today?" I asked.

"Lenuța."

"Okay, you run and tell Tanti Lenuța that you have permission to go to the market with Tata Johnny, and I'll be ready to leave in about five minutes."

"All right!" cried Beti, and off she rushed to find Tanti Lenuța.

The market was teaming with people, and Beti stuck close to me as I made my way from stall to stall. I bought two bunches of carrots, several pounds of tomatoes, and the bell peppers Ruth had requested. Then I made my way to the stall where a pleasant-looking man was selling crates of oranges and inquired the price. Five dollars per crate didn't sound too bad.

"Are they sweet?" I asked.

"Try one." He handed me an orange. "These are imported from Greece, and Greece produces the finest oranges," he announced as I set my bags down and peeled the orange.

I handed a section to Beti and tried one myself. They were juicy and sweet.

"What do you think?" I asked.

Beti's eyes gleamed with delight as she nodded enthusiastically.

"I'll take two crates," I told the vendor as I counted out the money.

"Okay, Beti, can you handle the bags if I carry the oranges?"

"Sure," she responded as she grabbed the bags with an air of importance and followed me toward the gray Honda.

"What's that?" Beti asked as we passed a restaurant. She looked through the large plate-glass windows as a waitress brought food to a couple seated at one of the many tables.

"That's a restaurant where people buy food and eat," I explained, suddenly realizing that Beti had never been inside a restaurant.

"Are you hungry?" I asked.

Beti shrugged.

"Come," I said, "let's go get ourselves a hamburger."

We entered and I chose a small table right by the large window overlooking the busy street. We could see people streaming in and out of the market. Beti's big brown eyes missed nothing. Her little head was kept busy swiveling about trying hard not to miss any interesting scenes inside or outside the restaurant. I tried to explain the items on the menu, but I had a hard time holding her attention.

There was just too much to see!

I suggested that we order hamburgers and fries and she agreed. We talked as we waited for our food.

Beti was full of questions. "Where do they get the food? Who cooks it? Do we have to pay for it?"

When our plates came, I said, "Let's pray." I knew that if I prayed in English, Beti would hardly understand. *Well,* I thought, *what better time to begin praying in Romanian?*

Halfway through my prayer I heard a snicker. Next came suppressed giggles. I cut my prayer short and hurried to an "amen." Instantly Beti burst forth in uncontrollable laughter. "Tata Johnny," she said when she could talk, "you sound so funny when you pray in Romanian!"

Beti took a tentative bite of her first hamburger and made a wry face.

"Here, let me help you," I suggested. After adding ketchup and mayonnaise, she gave her hamburger another try. Much better! Even so, Beti could only down half of her first hamburger. It was just too new an experience.

"Beti, I am going to the bazaar. Were you ever there?" I asked.

Beti slowly shook her head. She had lived most of her nine years within five miles of Suceava's huge bazaar, yet had never been there. Today we would change that.

We soon arrived at the bazaar, but had to park several hundred yards away because the parking area was crammed. Beti was full of questions as we walked toward the gate. "Remember to stay right by me. If you would get lost in this place, I'd never find you," I warned her.

As we crossed the busy street, my attention was arrested by a teenaged girl sitting on the ground with her back against an electric pole. Her olive skin and black hair were squeaky clean. She was dressed neatly. Her entire bearing screamed, *I do not belong here!* People streamed around her, unheeding. The scarred stubs of her footless ankles stood out in stark contrast to her pleasant face and the delicate hands she raised imploringly to the passing crowd. She was a beggar.

Her eyes were intelligent, but I also saw intense pain in them. It wrenched my heart to see her there. I quickly looked away, making a mental note to have a little money ready and speak with her when I returned.

I paid the gatekeeper and glanced around to make sure Beti was close by, but I needn't have worried. She was within six inches of me. People were rude, to my way of thinking, and cut in right in front of us. Several times they even pushed between Beti and me, separating us and causing me to stop and wait until Beti could make her way through the flowing crowd to catch up with me. One had to be on a sharp lookout every moment because of the expert pickpockets whose business thrived here.

I stopped in pity when I saw a beggar with only one leg sitting in the dirt. I was being pushed and bumped on every side when I felt a sly hand reach into my hip pocket. I jerked my hand toward the pocket where I kept my wallet. My elbow jabbed into someone's soft midriff rather sharply, and I heard a heavy grunt, but I turned to find only empty space behind me. Thankfully I still had my wallet.

I had to think of Lil who had been shopping in this very bazaar not long ago. It hadn't gone as well for her. She had bought a large plastic bucket and used it to carry her smaller purchases. Then she had spied another article she needed, but when she went to pay for it she found that her purse had been opened and her wallet was gone. Money, driver's license, and credit cards were all lost. In utter disgust, she had made her way to the gate and left. Why were there such people in the world?

At home she had poured out her discouraging story to her sympathetic family. As she had emptied the items from her new plastic bucket, there lay her driver's license and credit cards, just as pretty as you please! Some well-meaning thief had stolen her wallet; then, realizing that Lil hadn't even found it out, he had slyly worked his way close enough to drop her driver's license and credit cards into her bucket!

As Beti and I kept walking, I located an umbrella I wanted and asked the price. "Three twenty-five," responded the attendant. I thanked her and said I wanted to check around a bit. I moved on to another stall and asked the price of this lady's umbrellas, and then on to yet another. "Three twenty-five" came the ready answer at each place. The same-style umbrella was exactly the same price regardless of which vendor was selling it. How the vendors kept all their prices straight by memory was beyond me.

"Tata Johnny," Beti called, bringing me back to the present, "look

Beti holds her prized red rose.

at those beautiful flowers." Beti had stopped before a display of colorful plastic flowers. They were too large and gaudy to suit my taste, but they were beautiful to Beti.

"Which one do you like best?" I asked. She chose a huge imitation flower nearly as tall as she was, with large, blood-red petals. The look on her face as she walked through the bazaar crowd waving her flower was well worth the fifty cents it had cost me.

Soon it was time to head back to the orphanage. As we exited through the bazaar's gate, I remembered the beggar girl. She was still seated on her woven mat by the electric pole. *"Pace,"* (peace) I greeted her with the Romanian Christian greeting. I extended my hand and dropped a bill into hers.

Our eyes met as she said, "Thank you," and then she lowered her gaze as if deeply ashamed.

"Are you here by the bazaar often?" I asked.

"Yes, but I move around a bit also," she explained.

"How do you come?" I asked in my best Romanian.

A wistful smile played across her face, and she said with hardly an accent, "I can speak English."

Relieved, I reverted to English. "So, do you live close by? How do you come here?"

"I live in Suceava. Someone brings me and returns in the afternoon to pick me up."

I was beginning to get the picture. There are unscrupulous operators who work several beggars at a time. The beggars are given a place to stay and are forced to beg, but the operator collects most of the money for himself.

"How did you lose your feet?" I asked gently, having heard that small, healthy children are sometimes bought and then mutilated in order to make life-long beggars out of them. I would probably never know, but this girl looked as though this could very well have been her lot in life.

A faraway look crept into her eyes before she dropped her gaze and murmured, "I lost them in a train accident when I was little."

I sincerely doubted that was the case, but I said nothing more about her missing feet. "Do you attend church?" I asked.

"Sometimes," was her non-committal answer as she glanced away.

"I am a believer, and I help pastor the Nathaniel Church in Iţcani. We'd love to have you visit us. The children from our orphanage attend there, and I think you would really enjoy it. In fact, we could arrange to pick you up, if you would like."

She shook her head slightly. Apprehension and fear clouded her eyes, and I wondered if her "boss" didn't want her to develop friendships outside of his control.

I reached out my hand, and she shyly grasped it. "Goodbye," I said, "and God bless you!"

"Thank you, and God bless you too," she replied softly as I turned to find Beti's hand. We crossed the busy street and made our way to the waiting Honda. Oh, how my heart bled for that poor girl! I longed to somehow help her. I made a personal commitment to pray for her and talk with her each time I visited the bazaar.

"Tata Johnny, what were you saying to that girl?" asked Beti. "I feel so sorry for her! Did you see that she doesn't have any feet at all? And she is so pretty."

As best I could, I explained to Beti my conversation with the beggar girl who had no feet.

Our morning together had certainly been wonderful. I had enjoyed having Beti with me, and I hoped that we were building a bridge of communication. My prayer was that one day soon God would show us the princess who lived behind Beti's heavy, protective shell.

Chapter 23

A Heart to Belong

Sam Wray and his fifteen-year-old son Jamin were making wonderful progress on the plumbing in the girls' dorm. The new laundry was hooked up. Both of the bathroom rough-ins were completed, and they were running the piping for the vanities to be installed in each of the girls' bedrooms. I was impressed!

Elena took it upon herself to deliver a snack to the working men each afternoon. She delighted in fixing hot chocolate and cookies. The cooks noticed that she took extra pains to have that plate of cookies artistically arranged. She wasn't satisfied unless it was fixed just right. This was her sponsor and he deserved the best!

Manu and Ionuț were fascinated as they watched father and son measure, cut, and install the plumbing pipes. If Jamin could help, why couldn't they? Every chance they had when not in school or doing their homework, they made their way to the old school building. Sam soon had them running errands for him, handing him pipes, fittings, and tools. They loved working with Sam and Jamin. But what they liked best was to hear Sam trying to speak Romanian.

"*Bună seara,*" they said as they dropped in one evening after their schoolwork was complete.

"*Bonă sarah,*" Sam greeted them in return, certain he had gotten the accent right this time. But to his dismay he heard the boys chuckling good-naturedly once again.

"I'm sorry to laugh, but you sound so funny when you talk Romanian!"

"I'll get it right if I keep practicing," responded Sam with a grin.

"Manu, could you hand me that elbow?" Sam asked.

"Sure," said Manu as he stretched to place it on the stepladder where Sam was working.

"*Mutamess,*" said Sam in an attempt to say thank you. Manu burst out laughing again.

"All right," Sam said, grinning, "just how do you say thank you?"

Still chuckling, Manu said, " It's *mul-ţu-mesc.* You have to put that *k* sound on the end of it." The boys delighted in teaching him, and Sam never got tired of learning. And they loved him for trying!

Following supper, Sam called the children into the orphanage living room. After talking with the children a bit, he explained that they had brought small gifts for each of them. There were red and yellow jars of liquid bubbles and hand cream for each of the girls. Within minutes children were running delightedly about the living room, chasing bubbles.

"Look, Danielle! Look at Tina's huge bubble!" shouted Roxana excitedly.

Sam began passing out yo-yos to the boys. The bigger boys tried time and again to learn just when to pull in order to coax their yo-yos to climb back up their strings. Sam demonstrated over and over, first with one boy and then with another. Finally he took hold of their hands and made them wait to pull until just the right moment, and up came the faithful yo-yo. Smaller boys were soon standing on chairs because their yo-yos kept hitting the floor. There they stood, waving their arms up and down while the girls chased bubbles around them. It was the first time the boys had ever seen a yo-yo. Sam and I were kept busy untying knots, untangling strings, and giving lessons.

Little Marinel stood on a chair with a group of children gathered around him. His arm waved up and down, and his red and blue yo-yo dutifully ran up and down the length of its string at his bidding. His friends' heads bobbed up and down, keeping track of his yo-yo as they counted aloud, "197, 198, 199, 200! Keep on, Marinel! Keep on!" they shouted. Marinel's arm was getting tired and shaky, but he wouldn't give up. More and more children gathered around him as he continued. His contest had become their contest, and they cheered him on.

"Look, Sam," cried Iliuță, "Marinel did his yo-yo two hundred times."

"Nope!" corrected Marian. "It's 216, now 217."

We watched as Marinel continued. "Do three hundred, Marinel, do three hundred!" shouted Marius.

Heads bobbed, and excitement mounted as the yo-yo continued to roll.

"Look, Sam," said Iliuță, jumping up and down with excitement. "293, 294." Marinel was nearly exhausted now. "295, 296, 297 . . ." And the yo-yo refused to climb the string one more time. It twirled to a stop at the bottom of the string. Marinel's arm dropped for a much-deserved rest, and he grinned as the children applauded enthusiastically.

The girls were discovering the delight of hand cream. "Smell mine, Tata Johnny," said Ramona as she raised her hand. I sniffed as she pressed her hand against my nose.

"Mmm, yes, that does smell very good," I said, resisting the urge to rub the excess hand cream from my nose until she had turned and dashed off to find Ruth.

It was wonderful to watch the children so delighted with their gifts, though it was hard to tell who was the most pleased, the orphanage boys and girls or Sam and Danielle Wray.

Elena joined her sponsors nearly every evening as families from the church and community invited them for supper. She felt just like one of the Wray girls, especially when she wore her matching dress. She dreaded the day when she would have to tell the Wrays goodbye, when her dear sponsors would go back to their home far away in

America. Oh, how she wished she could really be a part of their family! Perhaps someday she could go live with them.

On Saturday there was no school and Elena was excited. Quickly she made her bed and tidied her room. Her sponsors were going on a trip to the mountains. Oh, she hoped she would be allowed to go!

Tap, tap. "May I come in?" asked Elena.

"Of course you may. You are always welcome!" I invited her into my office.

"Tata Johnny, you know my sponsors are going to be here for only one more week. Well, they are going sightseeing today, and I was wondering if you would let me go with them. Please?"

"Well, I don't know. Let me see, what are your qualifications?" I made a show of studying the chart containing each child's behavior records, knowing full well that I could count on Elena to have good behavior. "You really have been going away a lot lately," I reminded her, "and I'm not sure if this would be fair to the other children." I acted as if I were carefully weighing all the pros and cons.

"But Tata Johnny," Elena said in exasperation, "they are *my* sponsors!"

"I know, I know. Sam has already asked if they may take you along. Besides, they might need you for an interpreter," I grinned.

"Oh, you are so bad!" said Elena when she realized I had only been teasing. "Then you really will let me go?"

"Of course you may go. We want you to have as much time together as possible."

"Oh, thank you!" She paused at the doorway. "I'll run get ready!" she announced, and then she was gone.

Several days later Sam and Danielle made arrangements to take Elena, her sisters, and her brother to visit their old home in Mitoc. Our cook, Lăcri, who had grown up in Mitoc, offered to show the way.

"Turn here," Lăcri instructed, and Sam turned the van off the pavement and onto a rutted dirt road. In the back seat Ştefania was silent, but Vasilica chatted away merrily with Julie Wray. Marian was pensive, and Sam wondered if painful memories were troubling him. How would their tender hearts respond to this visit to their old home? Would reminders of their last night here upset them? Would this re-open those deep wounds?

"It's right around this corner," announced Elena. She sat forward and pointed eagerly. "There it is. That's our old house! Come on, let's get out and see it!"

Sam and Danielle exchanged a glance. The house was so small. The sadness of the place seemed to seep into their souls as they walked around the tiny, overgrown yard, talking in subdued tones.

Sam turned and found Elena with her hands cupped about her face, peering through one of the windows. Others soon joined her. The inside was chaotic. Things were just as they had been six years earlier. The crime had so shocked the community that people shied away from the property.

From the house they proceeded to the village cemetery, where Lăcri led the group through a maze of paths among the hundreds of graves. Finally they came to the grave of Nicoleta Bițica. Danielle looked at the marker at the head of Elena's mother's grave and thought, *We were nearly the same age, but oh, how different our lives have been! If only she had known the Lord!*

Dawn was lighting the eastern sky when we stopped the big van by Silvia's apartment.

"Good morning, everyone," Silvia greeted us cheerily as she climbed in and joined us. We prayed and were off.

"So you are going to see Daddy today!" Silvia smiled as she addressed the Bițica children. "This is great!" she said, turning to Elena. "Isn't it wonderful that your daddy will get to meet your sponsors?

"Sam and Danielle," continued Silvia, "I'm sure this visit will be very special to Elena's father. And you have your children along too! I'm sure seeing your family together will be an added blessing for Nelu."

It wasn't fully daylight, and I had to keep a sharp lookout for horse-drawn wagons headed to family plots outside of town. Farming families would work all day in their fields and return late at night.

We were headed for the city of Bacău and the prison where Nelu Bițica was serving his sentence. There was joy even in prison since Nelu had repented from his life of sin and given his heart to the Saviour. We rejoiced with him.

After passports and securities were thoroughly checked, we were ushered by a prison official through the courtyard and into the prison's dining room, where we were told to wait.

"Excuse me, sir," I told the guard, "but I brought enough cookies from our orphanage bakery for the prisoners' lunches. And," I said as I offered the bag, "there should be enough for the staff also." He thanked me and took the bag to the prison kitchen.

The minutes ticked slowly by as we waited. The children fidgeted. Elena kept watching the courtyard through the window. Finally she announced, "Here he comes!" Then she suddenly turned shy and moved to the back of our group. A guard ushered Mr. Bițica in to us, and it was moving for us to observe the smiles, hugs, and kisses that spilled out of the pent-up emotions from months of separation. This was only the third time the children had seen their father in the six years since he had been taken to prison.

Silvia rapidly explained to Mr. Bițica that we had brought Elena's sponsors, the Wray family. She told how they had come from America to meet Elena, and now they wanted to meet him also.

Silvia interpreted for us and helped us communicate while the guards hovered nearby. We talked about developments in the orphanage, and the Bițica children warmed up as they began telling their father about the new school and the new dorm. Marian told his father about Sam and Jamin's work on the plumbing and how the older orphanage boys had helped too.

Through all of this rich interchange, I caught Nelu gazing at his children like a man in a dream. It was the gaze of a starving soul that had finally been given a morsel. It was so satisfying and yet so meager. Nelu's fatherly hand strayed occasionally to caress Elena's shoulder and then moved again to brush Ștefania's unruly hair from her forehead. At one point he impulsively leaned over and planted a kiss upon his son's cheek. Another time he gave Vasilica a squeeze. He listened to all that was being said, but his heart was all the while feasting on the nearness of his dear children. He knew that all too soon it must come to an end.

"Please," asked Nelu, "could you sing 'Taria Mea' (My Strength)? I heard the song on a recording of the orphanage children, and it has been a great comfort to me."

"Sure," said Silvia. She opened a hymnal she had brought and found the page. Her clear, rich soprano led and those around the table joined in.

"O my heavenly Father, you are strength of my strength, and through my darkest trials, with you, I shall go forward." The message of this song, coupled with the plaintive notes of the melody, spoke to something deep within each of us. Nelu sang along, but was soon overcome with emotion. His voice broke. He could no longer sing. A tear trickled down his cheek. Again he tried to sing, but the tears won.

Silvia never wavered but began the second verse. Even the guards fell silent and listened.

"O Jesus, you are strength of my strength, and when my heart is sorely bruised, you give unexplainable power." Elena's voice cracked. Her face was wet with tears, but bravely she struggled on. "O Holy Spirit, you are strength of my strength. Through you I receive and hold a marvelous victory!" Elena couldn't go on. She buried her face in her arms and wept.

I gave up trying to sing around the great lump that threatened to choke me. Vasilica's alto continued unfalteringly in spite of her tear-filled eyes.

Elena's face becomes tear-stained as the group sings for the Bițica children's father.

"O strength of my strength, I magnify and give you glory, and will praise you, both now and forevermore!" The song limped to its conclusion, leaving us feeling as though we had just glimpsed into the depth of a shattered soul—a soul wounded by sin, yet marvelously delivered by God's amazing grace!

Our conversation continued. Nelu had many questions about his children's schooling, their progress, the orphanage, and the farm. But all too soon a guard interrupted and gently announced that our time of visitation was nearly over. After asking permission, we took several photos. Nelu had humble words of thankfulness and deep appreciation for Sam and Danielle for the help they had been in sponsoring Elena. With tears close to the surface once again, he bid us goodbye, and we made our way through the prison gate.

I glanced back as we were leaving. The guard who had ushered us to our van paused as he took a large cookie from his pocket. He took a huge bite and nodded appreciatively as he headed back toward the prison.

On our way home the children in the back were quite talkative.

Their tension had been relieved, and now they seemed relaxed.

"How many more years will Mr. Bițica have to serve?" Sam asked.

"He would still have twelve more years without time off for good behavior. However, I understand that for each month he works in the woodshop, his sentence is reduced by three days. Also for each month that there is no offence, an additional week is subtracted. So his sentence could be reduced by several years."

The excellent record of this particular prison had come to the attention of the officials in București. Other prisons had reported fighting, riots, and even murders. But this prison had a very clean record. So the officials had wanted to know what made the difference. When they found out that the good record was due to the evangelists who were working in this prison, the evangelists were called to București for an interview and were questioned about what they had been teaching these inmates. For two hours the evangelists had the officials' full attention as they explained the way of salvation and the Christian life. In the end they were told to go back to Bacău and continue their work.

"I am so glad you took us to see Elena's father," said Sam. "This will no doubt be a major highlight of our trip to Romania."

"And I'm so glad you came. This has been a valuable experience for all of us," I said.

On the last Sunday evening before the Wray family left to go back to America, they chose not to accept any supper invitations. Instead, they just wanted to be with the Nathaniel children. It was so sweet to see the way their eight-year-old Josh and Liviu played together. Josh was big for his age, while Liviu was very small for his age. Yet they bonded like long-lost brothers. Ionică, who had no boys of his own, was especially drawn to Josh and bantered with him whenever they met.

Sam soon found himself pushing Beti on the swing. "Higher!" she giggled "Higher!" But her giggle turned nervous and she curled her legs back under the seat as though she wasn't sure she really wanted to go much higher.

"Over here, Sam. Push me, push me!" cried Cristina, not wanting to miss out on the fun. She was soaking up her time with a father figure her soul so desperately craved.

The entire Wray family played with the orphanage children until nearly bedtime, making memories that would be theirs for years to come and that would most certainly be locked away in the hearts of the Nathaniel children for a lifetime.

Dawn was just beginning to brighten the Burdujeni train station as a sober group assembled there to see the Wray family off.

"Sam, thanks for all you have done for us!" I said as we embraced. "I don't think you can fully know what this has meant to Elena and her family. God bless you and be with you!"

I turned to say goodbye to Danielle. She and Elena were standing close together, and Danielle was speaking with her like a mother to a daughter. Both were crying. They embraced for a long moment, reluctant to part. When they released, Danielle squeezed Elena's hand before turning toward the waiting train.

All too soon the train began to move south, slowly at first. We fastened our eyes on the departing figures waving from the train window. With tears streaming down her face, Elena returned the wave. It was a wave of hope—hope that someday she, too, would belong.

GLOSSARY

Adi	AH dee
Andi	AHN dee
Anişoara	ah nee SHWAH rah
Arbore	AHR boh reh
Aurel	ah WOO rehl
Bacău	bah KOH
Bădiliţă	buh deh LEE tsuh
Beni	BEH nee
Beti	BEH tee
Biţica	bee TSEE kuh
Bogdan	bohg DAHN
Botoşani	boh toh SHAHN ee
Bucureşti	boo koo REHSHT
bună seara	BOO nuh see AH rah
Burdujeni	boor doo JEHN ee
Caterina	kah teh REE nah
Ciocan	choh KAHN
Costel	koh STEHL
Costică	koh STEE kuh
Cotleţ	koht LEHTS
Cristi	KREES tee
Cristina	krees TEE nah
Daniela	dah nee EH lah
Davucu	dah VOO koo

Dorica	doh REE kah
Dumitru	doo MEE troo
Elisabeta	eh lees ah BEH tah
Florentina	floh rehn TEE nah
Florica	floh REE kah
Gabi	GAH bee
Geo	JEH oh
Gheorghe	GE ohr gay
Gheorgheş	GYOHR gehsh
Gigi	JEE jee
Hreaţca	HRETS kah
Huţuţui	hoo TSOO tsooee
Ica	EE kah
Ileana	ee lee AH nah
Iliuţă	ee lee OO tsuh
Ioana	ee WAH nah
Ionela	yoh NEH lah
Ionese	yoh NEH seh
Ionică	yoh NEE kuh
Ionuţ	yoh NOOTS
Iosif	YOH seef
Iţcani	ehts KAHN
judeţ	JOO dehts
Lăcri	LUH kree
Larisa	lah REE sah
Lavinia	lah VEE neeah
Lenuţa	leh NOOTS ah
Leonte	leh WOHN teh
Liviu	LEE veeoo
logodna	loh GOHD nah
Loredana	loh reh DAH nah
Manu	MAH noo

Marian	mah ree AHN
Mariana	mah ree AH nah
Marinel	mah ree NEHL
Marius	MAH ree oos
Marta	MAHR tah
maskcats	mahs KAHTS
Mihaela	mee hah EH lah
Mihai	mee HI
Mitoc	mee TOHK
Mocanu	moh KAH noo
Monica	moh NEE kah
mul-ţu-mesc	muhl TSOO mehsk
Neli	NEH lee
Nelu	NEH loo
nenea	NEHN yah
Nicolae	nee koh LAH yeh
Nicoleta	nee koh LAH tah
Nicu	NEE koo
Oana	WAH nah
Ovidiu	oh VEE deeoo
pace	PAH cheh
papagal	pah pah GAHL
Parnica	pahr NEE kah
Pătrăuţi	puh truh OOTS
Pavel	PAH vehl
Petrică	peh TREE kuh
pocăit	POH kuh eet
Rădăuţi	ruh duh OOTS
Rodica	roh DEE kah
Roxana	ruhks AH nah
Sami	SAH mee
Sandu	SAHN doo

sarmale	sahr ah MAH leh
Silviu	SEEL veeoo
slănină	sluh NEE nuh
sora	SOH rah
Ştefania	shteh fah NEE ah
Ştefi	SHTEH fee
Stela	STEH lah
Steluţa	steh LOO tsah
Straja	STRAH zhah
Suceava	soo CHAH vah
Sveduneac	shveh doo NYAHK
tanti	TAHN tee
Tărniceriu	tuhr nee CHEHR yoo
Tatiana	tah tee AH nah
Valentina	vah lehn TEE nah
Vali	VAH lee
Vasilica	vah see LEE kah
Vaslui	vahs LOOEE
Veronica	veh roh NEE kah
Vicov	VEE kohv
Viorica	vee oh REE kah

ROMANIA

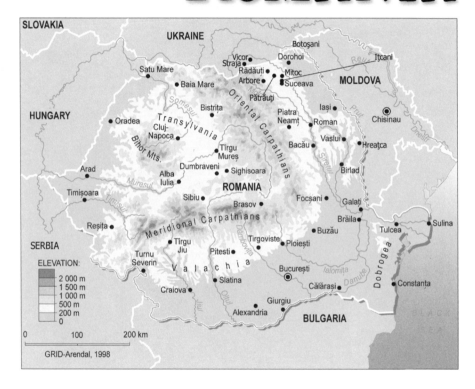

SLOVAKIA

UKRAINE

Botoşani

Vicor
Straja
Dorohoi
Iţcani

Satu Mare
Rădăuţi
Mitoc

Arbore
Suceava

MOLDOVA

Baia Mare

Pătrăuţi

HUNGARY

Bistriţa

Oradea

Transylvania

Piatra
Neamţ

Iaşi

Chisinau

Cluj-
Napoca

Tîrgu
Mures

Roman

Bacău

Vaslui

Hreaţca

Bihor Mts.

Dumbraveni

Sighisoara

Birlad

Arad

Alba
Iulia

Muresul

ROMANIA

Focsani

Galaţi

Timisoara

Sibiu

Brasov

Bräila

Reşiţa

Meridional Carpathians

Tîrgoviste

Buzău

Tulcea

Sulina

SERBIA

Turnu
Severin

Tîrgu
Jiu

Pitesti

Ploiesti

Dobrogea

ELEVATION:

Valachia

Bucuresti

2 000 m
1 500 m
1 000 m
500 m
200 m
0

Slatina

Craiova

Giurgiu

Călăraşi

Constanţa

Alexandria

BULGARIA

0   100   200 km

GRID-Arendal, 1998

About the author

Johnny and Ruth have lived in Minerva, Ohio, since they moved back from Romania in 2007. Though they live far from Romania, their hearts are still with the Nathaniel children and they pray for them often. They keep in touch by phone and email.

Johnny ministers at Christian Fellowship Church in Minerva. He spends much of his time writing for CAM. He also enjoys being a tele-counselor for CAM's Billboard Evangelism program as well as teaching at their annual Teacher's Training Retreat in Haiti. Johnny occasionally assists his son, Dwight, who took over the family plumbing and heating business when they moved to Romania in 1997.

Johnny likes to hear from his readers and can be emailed at johnny@emypeople.net or written in care of Christian Aid Ministries, P.O. Box 360, Berlin, Ohio, 44610.

CHRISTIAN AID MINISTRIES

Christian Aid Ministries (CAM) was founded in 1981 as a nonprofit, tax-exempt, 501(c)(3) organization. Our primary purpose is to provide a trustworthy, efficient channel for Amish, Mennonite, and other conservative Anabaptist groups and individuals to minister to physical and spiritual needs around the world.

Annually, CAM distributes approximately fifteen million pounds of food, clothing, medicines, seeds, Bibles, Bible story books, and other Christian literature. Most of the aid goes to needy children, orphans, and Christian families. The main purposes of giving material aid are to help and encourage God's people and to bring the Gospel to a lost and dying world.

CAM's home office is in Berlin, Ohio. In Ephrata, Pennsylvania, CAM has a 55,000 square feet distribution center where food parcels are packed and other relief shipments organized. Next to the distribution center is our meat canning facility. CAM is also associated with seven clothing centers—located in Indiana, Iowa, Illinois, Maryland, Pennsylvania, West Virginia, and Ontario, Canada—where clothing, footwear, comforters, and fabric are received, sorted, and prepared for shipment overseas.

CAM has staff, bases, and distribution networks in Romania, Moldova, Ukraine, Haiti, Nicaragua, Liberia, and Israel. Through our International Crisis (IC) program we also help victims of famine, war, and natural disasters throughout the world. In the USA, volunteers organized under our Disaster Response Services (DRS) program help rebuild in low-income communities devastated by natural disasters such as floods, tornados, and hurricanes. We operate medical clinics in Haiti and Nicaragua.

CAM is controlled by a ten-member board of directors and operated by a five-member executive committee. The organizational structure includes an audit review committee, executive council, ministerial committee, several support committees, and department managers.

CAM is largely a volunteer organization aside from management, supervisory personnel, and bookkeeping operations. Each year, volunteers at our warehouses, field bases, and on Disaster Response Services and International Crisis projects donate more than 200,000 hours.

CAM issues an annual, audited financial statement to its entire mailing list (statements are also available upon request). Fundraising and non-aid administrative expenses are kept as low as possible. Usually these expenses are about one percent of income, which includes cash and donated items in kind.

CAM's ultimate goal is to glorify God and enlarge His kingdom. ". . . whatsoever ye do, do all to the glory of God." (1 Corinthians 10:31)

For more information or to sign up for CAM's monthly newsletter, please write or call:

Christian Aid Ministries
P.O. Box 360
Berlin, OH 44610
Phone: 330.893.2428
Fax: 330.893.2305

ADDITIONAL BOOKS
PUBLISHED BY CHRISTIAN AID MINISTRIES

God Knows My Size! / *by Harvey Yoder*
How God answered Silvia Tarniceriu's specific prayer
251 pages $10.99

They Would Not Be Silent / *by Harvey Yoder*
Testimonies of persecuted Christians in Eastern Europe
231 pages $10.99

They Would Not Be Moved / *by Harvey Yoder*
More testimonies of Christians who stood strong under communism
208 pages $10.99

Elena—Strengthened Through Trials / *by Harvey Yoder*
A young Romanian girl strengthened through hardships
240 pages $10.99

Where Little Ones Cry / *by Harvey Yoder*
The sad trails of abandoned children in Liberia during civil war
168 pages plus 16-page picture section $10.99

Wang Ping's Sacrifice / *by Harvey Yoder*
Vividly portrays the house church in China
191 pages $10.99

A Small Price to Pay / *by Harvey Yoder*
Mikhail Khorev's story of suffering under communism
247 pages $10.99

Tsunami!—*from a few that survived* / *by Harvey Yoder*
From a few who survived the tsunami in Indonesia
168 pages $11.99

Tears of the Rain / *by Ruth Ann Stelfox*
Poignantly honest account of a missionary family in war-torn Liberia
479 pages *$13.99*

A Greater Call / *by Harvey Yoder*
What will it cost Wei to spread the Gospel in China
195 pages *$11.99*

Angels in the Night / *by Pablo Yoder*
Pablo Yoder family's experiences in Waslala, Nicaragua
356 pages *$12.99*

The Happening / *by Harvey Yoder*
Nickel Mines school shooting—healing and forgiveness
173 pages *$11.99*

In Search of Home / *by Harvey Yoder*
The true story of a Muslim family's miraculous conversion
240 pages *$11.99*

HeartBridge / *by Johnny Miller*
Joys and sorrows at the Nathaniel Christian Orphanage
272 pages *$12.99*

The Long Road Home / *by Pablo Yoder*
Will prayers and the Spirit's promptings bring young Pablo "home"?
456 pages *$12.99*

Miss Nancy / *by Harvey Yoder*
The fascinating story of God's work through the life of an Amish missionary
in Belize   *273 pages* *$11.99*

Into Their Hands at any cost / *by Harvey Yoder*
Bible smugglers find ingenious ways to transport Bibles into Romania and
the former Soviet Union   *194 pages* *$11.99*

STEPS TO SALVATION

The Bible says that we all have "sinned and come short of the glory of God" (Romans 3:23). We sin because of our sinful nature inherited by Adam's sin in the garden, and this sinful condition separates us from God.

God provided the way back to Himself by His only Son, Jesus Christ, who became the spotless Lamb who was "slain from the foundation of the world." "For God so loved the world, that he gave his only begotten Son, that whosoever believeth in him should not perish, but have everlasting life" (John 3:16).

To be reconciled to God and experience life rather than death, and heaven rather than hell (Deuteronomy 30:19), we must repent and believe in the Son of God, the Lord Jesus Christ (Romans 6:23; 6:16).

When we sincerely repent of our sins (Acts 2:38; 3:19; 17:30) and accept Jesus Christ as our Saviour, God saves us by His grace and we are "born again." "That if thou shalt confess with thy mouth the Lord Jesus, and shalt believe in thy heart that God hath raised him from the dead, thou shalt be saved" (Romans 10:9). "For by grace are ye saved through faith; and that not of yourselves: it is the gift of God" (Ephesians 2:8).

When we have become born again in Jesus Christ, we must be baptized and then be careful that we do not go back to our sins, since we are new creatures (2 Corinthians 5:17). "He that hath my commandments, and keepeth them, he it is that loveth me: and he that loveth me shall be loved of my Father, and I will love him, and will manifest myself to him" (John 14:21). It is important to fellowship with a faithful group of believers to strengthen and enhance one's Christian walk (1 John 1:7). Enjoy new life in Christ and be faithful and grow in Him (1 John 2:3; Romans 6:13; Revelation 2:10b).